Linux® For Dummies, 5th Edition

Cheat Sheet

Getting Help

Command	Description
apropos [keyword]	Search a database for commands that involve the keyword.
info [command]	Display a file's help information in an alternate format.
man [command]	Display a file's help information.
whatis [command]	Display a short blurb about the command.

Common Commands

Command	Description
cat [filename]	Display file's contents to the standard output device (usually your monitor).
cd /directorypath	Change to directory.
chmod [options] mode filename	Change a file's permissions.
chown [options] filename	Change who owns a file.
cp [options] source destination	Copy files and directories.
date [options]	Display or set the system date and time.
df [options]	Display used and available disk space.
du [options]	Show much space each file takes up.
file [options] filename	Determine what type of data is within a file.
find [pathname] [expression]	Search for files matching a provided pattern.
grep [options] pattern [filename]	Search files or output for a particular pattern.
kill [options] pid	Stop a process. If the process refuses to stop, use kill -9 pid.
less [options] [filename]	View the contents of a file one page at a time.
ln [options] source [destination]	Create a shortcut.
lpr [options]	Send a print job.
ls [options]	List directory contents.
mkdir [options] directory	Create a new directory.
mv [options] source destination	Rename or move file(s) or directories.
passwd [name [password]]	Change the password or allow (for the system administrator) to change any password.
ps [options]	Display a snapshot of the currently running processes.
pwd	Display the pathname for the current directory.
rm [options] directory	Remove (delete) file(s) and/or directories.
rmdir [options] directory	Delete empty directories
su [options] [user [arguments]]	Switch to another user
tail [options] [filename]	Display the last n lines
tar [options] filename	Store and extract files f (.tar.gz or .tgz).
who [options]	Display who is logged o

For Dummies: Bestselling Book Series for Beginners

Linux® For Dummies, 5th Edition

Accessing and Removing CDs

Distribution		Commands/Actions
Red Hat and Mandrake	Accessing	If you're in the GUI, Red Hat should see the CD automatically as it's inserted.
		If you're at a command prompt, issue `mount /mnt/cdrom`.
	Removing	If you're in the GUI, right click on the CD icon on your desktop, and select Eject.
		If you're at the command line, utilize `umount /mnt/cdrom` to remove the CD from your filesystem, and then manually eject it.
SuSe	Accessing	You might have to try a few things to figure out what exactly to use in SuSE: On the command line, start by trying `mount /media/cdrom`. If this doesn't work, then the simplest method is to try `mount -t iso9660 /dev/device /media/cdrom`, where `device` is hda, hdb, hdc, and so on until it works — make a note of the results so you can use this again later. If you get up to hdg and it's not working, then something else is wrong.
	Removing	If you're not in the GUI, type `umount /media/cdrom` before you can eject the CD.

The vi Editor

Keystroke(s)	Initial Cursor Position	Result
A	One space before the place you want to add text	`vi` enters Insert mode directly after the cursor's position.
#cc	Anywhere within the (first) line you want to cut	`vi` cuts the entire selected line(s).
#dl	Directly on top of the (first) character you want to delete	`vi` deletes the specified characters.
#dd	Anywhere within the (first) line you want to delete	`vi` deletes the entire selected line(s).
P	Directly where you want the text to appear	`vi` copies the buffered text into the document.
u	Anywhere in the file	`vi` undoes what you last did.
#x	Directly on top of the (first) character you want to cut	`vi` deletes the specified characters into the buffer.
#yy	Anywhere within the (first) line you want to copy	`vi` copies the specified line(s) into the buffer.

For Dummies: Bestselling Book Series for Beginners

Linux®

FOR

DUMMIES®

5TH EDITION

Linux® FOR DUMMIES®

5TH EDITION

by Dee-Ann LeBlanc

WILEY

Wiley Publishing, Inc.

Linux® For Dummies®, 5th Edition

Published by
Wiley Publishing, Inc.
111 River Street
Hoboken, NJ 07030-5774

About the Author

Dee-Ann LeBlanc, RHCE (Red Hat Certified Engineer), RHCI (Red Hat Certified Instructor), and RHCX (Red Hat Certified eXaminer), is a writer, course developer, instructor, and trainer who specializes in Linux. She is the gaming industry editor for *LinuxWorld* magazine, and the author of numerous books on Linux and other computer topics, including an upcoming title from O'Reilly & Associates. Dee-Ann is also a regular contributor to *Computer Power User* magazine and a founding member of the AnswerSquad (www.answersquad.com), an online computer help service. When Dee-Ann isn't teaching classes for Red Hat and others, developing course materials, writing technical non-fiction or fantasy fiction, chatting about Linux online or at conferences, or trying in one way or another to save the world, she hikes with her dogs and experiments on her husband Rob with new recipes. See the latest that Dee-Ann's up to at www.Dee-AnnLeBlanc.com. (Contact Dee-Ann at dee@renaissoft.com.)

Author's Acknowledgments

Dee-Ann, as usual, has lots of people she'd like to thank. First off, thanks to John "maddog" Hall for giving her the opportunity to take over this book's evolution. He was too busy leading Compaq's UNIX Software Group, acting as Executive Director for Linux International, and sitting on the board of advisors for Sair Linux/GNU certification to take on the fifth edition.

Second, thanks to the folks at LANWrights for all of their hard work on the two previous editions. Third, thanks to Melanie Hoag, and Evan Blomquist for their strong efforts on the last two editions as well. Finally, of course, to the editors and staff at Wiley Publishing, Inc. Without them and their guidance, this book would not exist or continue to improve over time.

Most of all, I'd like to thank the readers who contacted me with their questions, suggestions, and concerns. I apologize to anyone who got lost in the great deluges of e-mail and didn't get an answer; but please trust that, at the very least, when I dug your e-mail out from the pile three months later, I filed it away as one more thing to consider in the next edition. It's reader participation that keeps books like this improving over the years, and it's my goal to continue refining *Linux For Dummies* to keep it the best desktop Linux book available.

— Dee-Ann LeBlanc

Publisher's Acknowledgments

We're proud of this book; please send us your comments through our online registration form located at `www.dummies.com/register/`.

Some of the people who helped bring this book to market include the following:

Acquisitions, Editorial, and Media Development

Project Editor:

Christopher Morris

(Previous Edition: Kala Schrager)

Acquisitions Editor:

Theresa Varveris

Copy Editor: Rebecca Whitney

Technical Editor: Dave Taylor

Editorial Manager: Kevin Kirschner

Permissions Editor: Laura Moss

Media Development Specialist: Travis Silvers

Media Development Manager:
Laura VanWinkle

Media Development Supervisor:
Richard Graves

Editorial Assistant: Amanda Foxworth

Cartoons: Rich Tennant
(`www.the5thwave.com`)

Production

Project Coordinator: Courtney MacIntyre

Layout and Graphics: Michael Kruzil, Lynsey Osborn, Heather Ryan, Jacque Schneider, Shae Lynn Wilson

Proofreaders: Laura Albert, Andy Hollandbeck, Carl Pierce, TECHBOOKS Production Services

Indexer: TECHBOOKS Production Services

Special Help
Andrea Dahl

Publishing and Editorial for Technology Dummies

Richard Swadley, Vice President and Executive Group Publisher

Andy Cummings, Vice President and Publisher

Mary C. Corder, Editorial Director

Publishing for Consumer Dummies

Diane Graves Steele, Vice President and Publisher

Joyce Pepple, Acquisitions Director

Composition Services

Gerry Fahey, Vice President of Production Services

Debbie Stailey, Director of Composition Services

Contents at a Glance

Table of Contents

Introduction

*W*elcome to the fascinating world of open source software that is Linux. In this book, I introduce you to the wonders of the Linux operating system, originally created as a labor of love by Linus Torvalds in the early 1990s. My goal is to initiate you into the rapidly growing gang of Linux users and enthusiasts busily rewriting the rules for the operating system marketplace.

If you have contemplated switching to Linux but find the prospect too forbidding, you can relax. If you can boil water or set your alarm clock, you too can become a Linux user. (No kidding!)

When this book appeared in its first edition, Linux was an emerging phenomenon that was neither terribly well known nor understood. In this edition — for a new generation of Linux users — so much is available that I have steered this particular title toward what Linux is and how you can make the best use of it on your desktop. To that end, these pages contain various online resources, tips, and tricks — as well as more general instruction.

I keep the amount of technobabble to a minimum and stick with plain English as much as possible. Besides plain talk about Linux installation, boot-up, configuration, and tuning, I include lots of examples, plus lots of detailed instructions to help you build and manage your very own Linux machine with a minimum of stress or confusion.

I also include with this book a peachy DVD-ROM that contains Fedora Core 1.

About This Book

Note: At press time, Red Hat renamed its consumer-level Linux product to *the Fedora Project*. Throughout the course of this book, I have tried my best to refer to the consumer-level product as Fedora Core, and the commercial versions you have to buy as Red Hat Enterprise Linux. You'll probably see the product referred to as the Fedora Project in the news, on the Web, and elsewhere, but you can rest assured that the different terms, as used in this book, are referring to the same product.

Think of this book as a friendly, approachable guide to tackling terminology and the Linux retinue of tools, utilities, and widgets. Although Linux isn't terribly hard to figure out, it does pack a boatload of details, parameters, and administrivia (administrative trivia, in Unixspeak). You need to wrestle those details into shape while you install, configure, manage, and troubleshoot a Linux-based computer. Some sample topics you find in this book include the following:

- ✓ Understanding where Linux comes from and what it can do for you
- ✓ Installing the Linux operating system
- ✓ Working with a Linux system to manage files and add software
- ✓ Setting up Internet access and surfing the Web
- ✓ Customizing your Linux system
- ✓ Managing Linux system security and resources

Although it may seem, at first glance, that working with Linux requires years of hands-on experience, tons of trial and error, advanced computer science training, and intense dedication, take heart! It's not true! If you can tell somebody how to find your office, you can certainly build a Linux system that does what you want. The purpose of this book isn't to turn you into a full-blown Linux geek (that is the ultimate state of Linux enlightenment, of course); it's to show you the ins and outs you need to master in order to build a smoothly functioning Linux system and to give you the know-how and confidence to use it.

How to Use This Book

This book tells you how to install, configure, and customize a Linux system. Although you can do most things in Linux these days by pointing and clicking, you still may want to try using Linux at the command prompt — where you type detailed instructions to load or configure software, access files, and do other tasks. In this book, input appears in monospace type like this:

```
rmdir /etc/bin/devone
```

When you type Linux commands or other related information, be sure to copy the information exactly as you see it in the book, including upper- and lowercase letters, because that's part of the magic that makes Linux behave properly.

A failure to follow instructions exactly can have all kinds of unfortunate, unseemly, or unexpected side effects. If you don't know exactly what you're doing at the command prompt, don't experiment for the sake of exploration — you may come to regret your carefree departure from my instructions!

The margins of a book don't give you the same amount of room as your computer screen; therefore, in this book some URLs and lengthy commands at the command prompt may appear wrapped to the next line. Remember that your computer sees these wrapped lines as a *single set of instructions,* or as a single URL — so if you're typing a hunk of text, keep it on a single line. Don't insert a hard return if you see one of these wrapped lines. I clue you in that it's supposed to be all one line by breaking the line at a slash mark (to imply "Wait — there's more!") and slightly indenting the overage, as in the following silly example:

```
www.infocadabra.transylvania.com/nexus/plexus/lexus/
        praxis/okay/this/is/a/make-
        believe/URL/but/some/real/ones/
        are/SERIOUSLY/long.html
```

Note that as you dig your way into and through this book — and other sources of Linux wit, wisdom, and inspiration that you're likely to encounter — you may find some terms used interchangeably. For example, you may see the same piece of software called a *program*, a *command,* a *utility,* a *script,* an *application,* or a *tool,* depending on the source, the context, and the author of the information you're consulting. To a large extent, you can treat these terms as interchangeable, and when an important distinction needs to be to be made among them, I'm sure to point it out. Similarly, when you're working with various commands or configuration controls, you may also encounter terms such as *flag, switch, option,* or *parameter* used more or less interchangeably. In this case, all these terms refer to ways in which you can control, refine, or modify basic commands or programs to make them do what you want. Again, wherever distinctions and clarifications may be needed, I provide them!

Three Presumptuous Assumptions

They say that making assumptions makes a fool of the person who makes them and of the person about whom those assumptions are made. (And just who are *they,* anyway? I *assume* that I know, but — never mind.) Even so, practicality demands that I make a few assumptions about you, gentle reader:

- ✔ You can turn your computer on and off.
- ✔ You know how to use a mouse and a keyboard.
- ✔ You want to install, configure, and use a Linux system because you're curious or interested or it's your job to do so.

You don't need to be a master logician or a wizard in the arcane art of programming to use this book, nor do you need a Ph.D. in computer science. You don't even need a complete or perfect understanding of what's going on in your computer's innards.

If you can boot a PC or install an application on your machine, you can install, configure, and manage a basic Linux system. If you have an active imagination and the ability to solve rudimentary problems, that's even better — you have already mastered the key ingredients necessary to making Linux work for you. The rest is mere details, and I help you with those!

How This Book Is Organized

This book contains six major parts, arranged in an order to take you from Linux installation and configuration through keeping a Linux system up and running, if not purring like a cat in the sun! Most parts contain three or more chapters or appendixes, and each chapter or appendix contains modular sections. Whenever you need help or information, pick up this book and start anywhere you like, or use the Table of Contents and the index to locate specific topics or key words.

Following is a breakdown of the book's six parts and what you find in each one.

Part 1: Getting Your Feet Wet

This part sets the stage and includes an overview of and introduction to the terms, techniques, and software components that make Linux the raging software tiger that's so ready, willing, and able do its thing. To be a little more specific, I start out with a Linux overview that explains what Linux is, where it came from, and how it works. Next, I tackle the various tasks and activities involved in preparing for and installing Linux on a PC. If you're not a diehard Fedora Core 1 fan, I also cover what's involved in installing Mandrake and SuSE, but in a little less detail. After that, I tell you how to give Linux the boot — not to get rid of it by any means, but rather, to fire up your brand-new system to reach the heights of computing ecstasy (at least, I hope it's as good for you as it usually is for me)! Finally, I help you explore standard Linux tools and interfaces, work with accounts, and get the skinny on various aspects of distribution-related Linux tools.

Part 11: Internet NOW

In this part, you explore the issues involved in connecting a Linux system to the Internet, including configuring a modem, managing a dial-up connection to an Internet Service Provider (or ISP), and configuring the various Internet protocols involved to make your Internet connection work. You also go through the details involved in configuring and using a Web browser and setting up and using an e-mail client and newsreader.

Part III: Getting Up to Speed with Linux

Linux includes a great many facilities and capabilities, so after you get past the initial installation and configuration, you probably want to use your system to *do* something. Here's where the doing begins! In this part of the book, you can read about the Linux file system and how to work with files, directories, and related access rights — called *permissions* in Linuxspeak. You discover how to move in, out, and around GNOME and KDE, the two major graphical interfaces (GUIs) in Linux. In addition, I include an in-depth exploration of the Linux command-prompt environments, also known as *shells*. Part III concludes with an overview of text editors available in Linux, office software such as word processors and spreadsheet programs, and how to get your computer humming with Linux multimedia tools.

Part IV: Sinking Your Teeth into Linux

In this part of the book, you delve into the Linux file system, meeting the root (/) directory and its subdirectories, and I show you how to keep them all in order. You also find out how to use removable media on your system, painlessly. In addition, you find out about adding software to Linux, working with the Red Hat Package Manager (RPM), and finding new software for your system. Finally, security issues are important on any computer available to a network, and Linux is no exception to this rule; that's why you can also read about what's involved in keeping tabs on who's messing with your machine's files and resources and how to plug holes and fix potential leaks.

Part V: The Part of Tens

In the penultimate part of this book, I sum up and distill the essence of what you now know about Linux and its inner workings. Here, you have a chance to read answers to the most frequently asked questions about Linux, visit some key troubleshooting tips and tricks for Linux systems, and identify and locate some cool Linux information and resources, online and in print.

Part VI: Appendixes

This book ends with a set of appendixes designed to sum up and further expand on this book's contents. Appendix A delivers a comprehensive list of Linux commands, complete with syntax and explanations, arranged in groups according to their function. Appendix B lists details about what's on the *Linux For Dummies,* 5th Edition, DVD. As I note in this appendix, the materials on the DVD include the Fedora Core 1 distribution.

Icons Used in This Book

Within each chapter, I use icons to highlight particularly important or useful information. You find the following icons in this book:

The Tip icon flags useful information that makes living with your Linux system even less complicated than you feared that it might be.

I sometimes use this icon to point out information you just shouldn't pass by — don't overlook these gentle reminders. (The life, sanity, or page you save could be your own.)

Be cautious when you see this icon — it warns you of things you shouldn't do. The bomb is meant to emphasize that the consequences of ignoring these bits of wisdom can be severe.

This icon signals technical details that are informative and interesting, but not critical to understanding and using Linux. Skip these if you want (but please come back and read them later).

Where to Go from Here

This is where you pick a direction and hit the road! *Linux For Dummies,* 5th Edition, is much like *1001 Nights* because it almost doesn't matter where you start out. You look at lots of different scenes and stories as you prepare yourself to build your own Linux system. Although each story has its own distinctive characters and plot, the whole is surely something to marvel at. Don't worry — you can handle it. Who cares whether anybody else thinks that you're just goofing around? I know that you're getting ready to have the time of your life.

Enjoy!

Part I
Getting Your Feet Wet

In this part . . .

This part includes an introduction to the history, development, and capabilities of the Linux operating system. I also cover the terms and tools that make Linux what it is, along with detailed step-by-step instructions about what it takes to prepare your computer for Linux and to install Linux on your very own PC. For those interested in Linux distributions other than Red Hat Linux 10, which is included with this book, I also cover what's involved in installing two other popular distributions — namely, Mandrake and SuSE. I even explain how to configure this marvelous operating system to do what you want it to do and how to boot your brand-spanking-new system into a powerful and productive computing colossus. After that, you find out what's involved in working with standard Linux tools and interfaces, working with accounts, and various aspects of distribution-related Linux tools.

Chapter 1

Getting Acquainted with Linux

Ford, you're turning into a penguin. Stop it!

—Arthur Dent

*W*elcome to the world of Linux, the operating system developed by thousands of people around the world!

Understanding Linux requires a radical shift of thought regarding the way that you acquire and use computer software. (***Note:*** By *radical,* I mean getting to the root of the matter rather than growing your body hair and camping out in the administration building.) Your first step toward shifting your mind-set is to alter your general connotation of the word *free* to represent *freedom,* rather than *free lunch.* That's right, you can sell "free" software for a fee . . . and you're encouraged to do so, as long as you relay the same freedom to each recipient of the software.

Don't scratch your head too hard; these concepts are tough to grasp initially, especially when you consider the conditioning you've received from the marketing departments of the commercial software industry. Perhaps you don't know that when you purchase most proprietary, shrink-wrapped software, you don't actually *own* the software; rather, you're granted permission to use the software within the bounds dictated by the licensor.

Linux also has a license, but the motives and purpose of the license are much different than those of most commercial software. Rather than use the license to protect ownership of the software, the GNU General Public License (GPL) that Linux is licensed under ensures that the software will always be open to anyone. No company can ever own or dictate the way in which you use or modify Linux — though they can have their own individual copyrights and trademarks on their various brands of it, like Red Hat. In essence, you already own Linux, and you can use it for anything you like, as long as you propagate the GPL freedoms to any further recipients of the software.

Linux: Revolution or Just Another Operating System?

> *Contrary to popular belief, penguins are not the salvation of modern technology. Neither do they throw parties for the urban proletariat.*
>
> —*Anonymous*

Author note: *Cute quote . . . obviously Anonymous has never been to a Linux convention!*

Before going any further, I need to get some terminology out of the way.

Tux is the formal name of the mascot penguin that represents Linux. Rumor has it that Linux's creator, Linus Torvalds, is rather fond of these well-dressed inhabitants of the Antarctic.

An *operating system* is the software that runs your computer, handling all of the interactions between you and the hardware. Whether you're writing a letter, calculating a budget, or managing your recipes on your computer, the operating system provides the essential air that your computer breathes. Furthermore, an operating system isn't just one program; it consists of hundreds of smaller programs and utilities that allow us humans to use a computer to do something useful. You then run other programs on top of the operating system, like a word processor, to get everything done.

In recent technological history, Linux has evolved from water cooler techie chatter to a rock-solid solution for the business enterprise. The same software that was once dismissed as rogue is now being adopted and promoted by industry leaders such as IBM, Hewlett-Packard, Motorola, and Intel. Each of these computer manufacturers has, in some way, determined that Linux provides value for their customers (as well as for their own operations). The only viable company that has publicly denounced Linux is Microsoft. Note that one doesn't have to look very far to conclude that Microsoft is merely running scared from the threat that Linux poses to its personal computer operating system monopoly.

So, where did Linux come from?

To understand Linux, you need to take a peek at its rich heritage. Although programming of the Linux core started in 1991, the design concepts were based on the time-tested Unix operating system.

Unix was developed at Bell Telephone Laboratories in the early 1970s. The original architects of Unix created it back when there were few operating systems, with the desire to have one that shared data, programs, and resources both efficiently and securely — something that wasn't available at this time. From there, Unix evolved into many different versions, and its current family tree is so complicated it looks like a kudzu infestation!

In 1991, Linus Torvalds was a computer science student at the University of Helsinki in Finland. He wanted an operating system that was like the Unix system that he'd grown fond of at the university, but both Unix and the hardware it ran on were prohibitively expensive. A Unix version called Minix was available for free, but it didn't quite meet his needs. So, as a computer science student, Torvalds studied Minix and then set out to write a new version himself. In his own words (recorded for posterity on the Internet), this project was, "just a hobby, won't be big and professional like gnu."

Writing an operating system is no small task. Even after six months of hard work, Torvalds had made very little progress toward the general utility of the system. He posted what he had to the Internet, and found that many people shared his interest and curiosity. Before long, some of the brightest minds around the world were contributing to Linus's project by adding enhancements or fixing *bugs* (errors in the code).

Linux has been accused of being "just another operating system." On the surface, it may appear so, but if you look deeper, you can see that this isn't so. The Linux project is a flagship leading the current trend toward open source and free (as in freedom, not free beer) software within the computing industry. A rock-solid operating system because of the model under which it was (and continues to be) developed, Linux represents much that is good and pure in software development.

Two fundamental distinctions separate Linux from the rest of the operating system pack:

- Linux is licensed under the unique and ingenuous *GNU General Public License,* which you can read about in the next section.

- Linux is developed and maintained by a worldwide team of volunteer programmers, working together over the Internet.

Linux is great for many reasons, including the fact that the folks who built it from the ground up wanted it to be

- **Multiuser:** More than one user can be logged in to a single computer at one time.

- **Multiprocess:** True *pre-emptive multitasking* enables the operating system core to efficiently juggle several programs running at once. This is important for providing multiple services on one computer.

- **Multiplatform:** Linux currently runs on 24 *platforms* (hardware types), including Intel-based PCs, Digital/Compaq Alpha, PowerPC-based Apple Macintosh, Sun SPARC, Amiga, and StrongARM-based computers.

- **Interoperable:** Linux plays nice with most network protocols (languages) and operating systems, allowing you to interact with users and computers running Microsoft Windows, Unix, Novell, both Mac OS 9 and OS X, and other, more niche groups.

- **Scalable:** As your computing needs grow, you can rely on Linux to grow with you. The same Linux operating system can run on a desktop computer or a very large, industrial strength server system.

- **Portable:** Linux is mostly written in the C programming language. *C* is a language created specifically for writing operating system-level software and can be readily *ported* (translated) to run on new computer hardware.

- **Flexible:** You can configure the Linux operating system as a network host, router, graphical workstation, office productivity PC, home entertainment computer, file server, Web server, cluster, or just about any other computing appliance that you can think of.

- **Stable:** The Linux *kernel* (the operating system itself) has achieved a level of maturity that makes most software developers envious. It's not uncommon to hear reports of Linux servers running for years without crashing.

- **Efficient:** The modular design of Linux enables you to include only those components that you need to run your desired services. Even older Pentium computers can utilize Linux and become useful again.

- *Free!:* To most people, the most intriguing aspect of Linux is the fact that it's often free. How (the capitalists murmur) can anyone build a better mousetrap with no incentive of direct monetary return?

In this chapter, I intend to answer that last question for you. I also hope to paint a picture of the open source software development model that created Linux.

Anatomy of an Open Source Software Project

Linux isn't a product. Linux is an organic part of a software ecosystem.

—*Michael Robinson,* Netrinsics

To the casual observer (and some corporate IT decision-makers), Linux appears to be a freak mutation — a rogue creature randomly generated by anarchy. How, after all, can something so complex and discipline-dependent as a computer operating system be developed by a loosely knit band of volunteer computer geeks from around the world?

Just as science is constantly attempting to classify and explain everything in existence, technology commentators are still trying to understand how this open source model can create superior software. Often, the reasons have much to do with the usual human desire to fill a need with a solution. When a programmer in the Linux world wants a tool, the programmer simply writes one or bands together with other people who want a similar package to write it together.

GNU who?

Imagine — software created out of need rather than projected profit. Even though Unix ultimately became expensive proprietary software, the ideas and motives for its creation were originally based on need. What people usually refer to in the singular as the *Linux operating system* is actually a collection of software tools that were created with the express purpose of solving specific computing problems.

Linux also wouldn't be possible without the vision of a man whom Steven Levy (author of the book *Hackers*) refers to as The Last of the Great MIT AI-LAB Hackers. This pioneer and advocate of *freedom* software is Richard Stallman.

The Massachusetts Institute of Technology (MIT) has long held a reputation for nurturing the greatest minds in the technological disciplines. In 1984, Stallman, a gifted student and brilliant programmer at MIT, was faced with a dilemma — sell his talent to a company for a tidy sum of money or donate his gifts to the world. He did what we'd all do . . . right?

Stallman set out on a journey to create a completely free operating system that he would donate to the world. He understands and continues to live the original hacker ethic, which declares that "information wants to be free." This wasn't a new concept in his time. In the early days of the computing industry, many advancements were made by freely sharing ideas and programming code. Manufacturer-sponsored user groups brought the best minds together to solve complicated problems. This ethic, Stallman felt, was lost when companies began to hoard software as their own intellectual property with the single purpose of profit.

As you may or may not have gathered by this point, widespread and accessible source code is paramount to successful software development. *Source code* is the term for the human-readable text (as opposed to the unreadable ones and zeros of binary code or an "executable") that a programmer types to communicate instructions to the computer.

Writing computer programs in binary is an extremely arduous task. Modern computer software is usually written in a human-friendly language and then *compiled,* or translated, into the computer's native instruction set. To make changes to this software, a programmer needs access to a program's source code. Most proprietary software comes only as precompiled, and the software developer keeps the source code for those programs under lock and key.

After determining that his operating system would be built around the conceptual framework of Unix, Stallman wanted the project name to distinguish his system from Unix. So, he chose the recursive acronym *GNU* (pronounced ga-*new*), which means GNU's Not Unix.

To finance the GNU project, Stallman organized the Free Software Foundation (FSF), which sold free software to help feed the programmers who worked on its continuing development. (Remember, we're talking free as in free speech, not free beer.) Although this organization and goal of creating a complete operating system was necessary and important, a much more important piece of the puzzle had to be put into place to protect this new software from big business pirates — a concern still all too relevant today as a former Linux company tries to hijack ownership of decades of volunteer work from thousands of people around the world.

The *GNU General Public License* (GPL) is a unique and creative software license that uses copyright law to protect the freedom of the software user, which is usually the opposite of how a copyright works. Generally, a copyright is an enforceable designation of ownership and restriction from duplication by anyone but the copyright holder. When software is licensed under the GPL, recipients are bound by copyright law to respect the freedom of anyone else to use the software in any way they choose. Software licensed with the GPL is also known as copy*left* software. Another way to remember the GPL is through its ultimate result: Guaranteed Public for Life.

Who's in charge of Linux anyway?

As an open source project evolves, various people emerge as leaders. This leader is often known as the project's *benevolent dictator.* A person who becomes benevolent dictator has probably spent more time than anyone else on a particular problem and often has some unique insight. Normally, the words *democratic* and *dictator* are never paired in the same sentence, but the open source model is a very democratic process that endorses the reign of a benevolent dictator.

Linus Torvalds is still considered the benevolent dictator of the Linux *kernel* (the operating system's core). He ultimately determines what features are added to the kernel and what features aren't. The community trusts his vision and discretion. In the event that he loses interest in the project, or the community decides that he has gone senile, a new leader will emerge from amongst the very competent people working with him.

Einstein was a volunteer

Someone who is a volunteer or donates their time to a project isn't necessarily providing a second-rate effort or only working on weekends and holidays. In fact, any human resource expert will tell you that people who choose to do a job of their own free will produce the highest quality products.

The volunteers who contribute to open source projects are often leaders in their field who depend on community collaboration to get useful work done. The open source concept is no stranger to the scientific community. The impartial peer-review process that open source projects foster is critical in validating something as being technically correct.

Those who paint the open source community as copyright violators and thieves often misunderstand or outright ignore these vital issues. Open source programmers are very proud of their work and are also very concerned about their own copyrights, not wanting their work to be stolen by others — hence licenses such as the GPL. This concern creates an atmosphere with the greatest respect for copyright. Those who claim that they are just being "open source" when they steal other people's hard work are grossly misusing the term to soothe their own consciences.

Many have also pointed out that if copyright is violated in open source, it is easy to tell. Watch the news and notice how often large software corporations are convicted of stealing other people's code and incorporating it into their own work. Tracking down such copyright violations is incredibly difficult in a closed source scheme.

Packaging Linux: The Distribution

What people call a *Linux distribution* is actually the culmination of the GNU project's tools, the Linux kernel, and any number of other open source (and closed source) software projects that sprang up along the way.

Robert Young, cofounder and current chairman of Red Hat, has coined an analogy comparing Linux to ketchup. Essentially, the operating system called Linux, with the GNU tools, Linux kernel, and other software, is a freely available commodity that, like ketchup, different distributors can package and label in different containers. Anyone is encouraged to package and market the stuff, even though the ingredients are fundamentally the same.

Linux is a complex, malleable operating system, and thus it can take on many appearances. The greatest Linux advancement in recent years has been making it easier to install. After all, the tools that today enable the casual PC user to install Linux originally weren't available. Companies such as Red Hat saw this as an opportunity to add value to an existing product, and the concept took off like gangbusters.

To draw again on the ketchup analogy, various distributions of Linux have a slightly different flavor or texture; your distribution preference may be spicy, mild, thick and gooey, or runny. However, you can rest assured that any of the following distributions have the same Linux and GNU heart and soul. Each short description includes a Web address where you can find more information about each project:

- **Debian GNU/Linux:** This distribution is one of the oldest and is a recognized favorite among advanced technical circles. Historically, it's relatively difficult to install. The Debian team works closely with the GNU project and is considered the most "open" of the Linux distributions. An easier to install (and use) distribution with Debian underneath is Xandros.

  ```
  www.debian.org
  www.xandros.com
  ```

- **Mandrake:** This distribution demonstrates the power of the GPL by allowing this competing company to stand on the shoulders of giants. Mandrake was originally based on Red Hat Linux, something that simply could not happen in a closed source environment, but has since become an excellent solution in its own right.

  ```
  www.mandrakelinux.com
  ```

- **Red Hat and Fedora:** Red Hat claims the prize for successfully mass marketing the Linux operating system. Red Hat has validated Linux by packaging the GNU and Linux tools in a familiar method of distribution (shrink-wrapped) and has included value-added features to its product, such as telephone support, training, and consulting services.

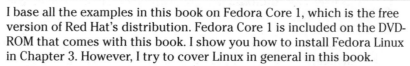

```
www.redhat.com
http://fedora.redhat.com/
```

I base all the examples in this book on Fedora Core 1, which is the free version of Red Hat's distribution. Fedora Core 1 is included on the DVD-ROM that comes with this book. I show you how to install Fedora Linux in Chapter 3. However, I try to cover Linux in general in this book.

✔ **Slackware:** Of all the more recognized surviving Linux distributions, Slackware has been around the longest. In fact, until about a year ago, the installation interface remained unchanged. Slackware has a very loyal following, but isn't well known. Like Debian in terms of spirit, the Slackware crowd is respected in Linux circles as the weathered old-timers who share stories of carrying around a shoebox full of diskettes.

```
www.slackware.com
```

✔ **SuSE:** (Pronounced *soo*-za) This distribution hails from Germany, where it has a very loyal following. SuSE works closely with the XFree86 project (the free X graphical server component of all Linux distributions). Consequently, SuSE has a terrific graphical configuration tool called SaX.

```
www.suse.com
```

As you can see, many paths (in the form of distributions) lead to Linux. It's important to note that, regardless of which distribution you choose, you're using the same basic ingredients: the GNU tools and the Linux kernel. The major differences that you'll encounter among distributions are

✔ **Installation programs:** Each distribution has developed its own installation program to help you achieve a running system. Some installation programs are designed for the casual computer user (hiding the technical details), whereas others are designed with the seasoned system administrator in mind. Some of the simpler ones offer an "expert mode" for those who want to have more control right from the beginning.

✔ **Software versions:** Different distributions may use different versions of the kernel (the core of the operating system) and other supporting software packages. Open source projects are dynamic and release new versions regularly, as opposed to the often sluggish development cycle of traditional commercial software.

✔ **Package managers:** Even though one Linux program should be able to run on any distribution, tools called *package managers* keep track of the software on your system and ensure that you have all the required supporting software as well. Distributions are usually dependent on one particular package manager. Chapter 15 provides more information about package managers.

It would be impossible to account for every possible installation of every Linux distribution. Okay, maybe not impossible, but you would need a forklift to bring your *Linux For Dummies* book home from the bookstore if I did. Consequently, I try to summarize the concepts needed to install any Linux distribution into this one book without detailing each. As you can imagine, this is a bit of a challenge!

I chose Fedora Core 1 as the sample distribution because Red Hat has become a recognized Linux standard, and its Fedora Core project is specifically aimed at home and small business users who cannot afford or have no need to purchase higher-level products. Even better, if you do use Red Hat Enterprise Linux (RHEL) in your office or organization, Fedora Core is a proving ground for the technologies that will make their way into RHEL.

In addition to Red Hat coverage, I also include information about two other popular distributions: in particular, Mandrake and SuSE. I certainly don't wish to discount Slackware and Debian because these are very powerful distributions. I just feel that they are more advanced than the others and best left for your post-*Linux For Dummies* endeavors.

Chapter 2

Prepping Your Computer for Linux

● ●

In This Chapter

▶ Taking basic preinstallation steps

▶ Using Linux and Windows on the same computer

▶ Customizing disk partitions before installation

▶ Knowing (and finding) your hardware information

▶ Preparing for CD or floppy disk installation

● ●

*M*ost current Linux distributions automatically detect your hardware and guide you through the installation process. In fact, some people just dive right in and start installing. However, if you're setting up a machine that will run both Windows and Linux (although not at the same time), don't leap in without at least reading the section "Preparing to Use Linux and Microsoft Windows Together," later in this chapter. You need to make sure that you have the space to install Linux and that you don't accidentally wipe out your Windows installation.

Other people like to start with a bit more caution. You can save yourself potential headaches — or make it easier to troubleshoot technical problems — by becoming familiar with your computer's hardware.

You should watch out for several issues when preparing to install Linux. In this chapter, I address the tasks that prepare you for the Linux installation process, such as setting up your system to install Linux directly from the DVD or CD, or with an installation floppy disk, if you end up needing one.

Installation Considerations

> *You got to be careful if you don't know where you are going, because you might not get there.*
>
> —*Yogi Berra*

If you have a spare machine that's only going to run Linux and nothing else, you're in luck! You can skip all of the "Preparing to Use Linux and Microsoft Windows Together" section. In fact, if you're feeling brave, you might want to skip right to Chapter 3 and start your installation. There's troubleshooting information in Chapter 19, as well.

If you plan to run both Linux and Microsoft Windows on the same computer — a scenario called *dual booting* — *DO NOT PROCEED TO CHAPTER 3* without reading the section, "Preparing to Use Linux and Microsoft Windows Together." Sorry for yelling, but you can wipe out your whole Windows installation if you don't take some precautions!

Preparing to Use Linux and Microsoft Windows Together

If you're planning to run Linux and Microsoft Windows on the same machine, the odds are that you've already got Windows installed and have been using it for some time. Because I hate to hear screams of anguish all the way up here in western Canada, take a moment to assess what you have and what you need to do.

On the off chance that you actually don't have Windows installed yet, you'll want to install it before you install Linux. Otherwise, during installation, Windows will overwrite the part of your hard drive that Linux uses to store its boot menu. This can create a bit of a mess later when you want to boot back into Linux! Those who are installing Windows should skip down to the section "Working with Disk Partitions," to learn how to set up your Windows installation so that it causes the least amount of fuss when it's time to add Linux.

The majority of you, however, want to dual boot because you've got one machine and it's already running Windows. If you have a brand new hard drive to work from that has nothing on it already, skip down to the section I just mentioned ("Working with Disk Partitions"). You won't need to do anything funny with the hard drive that Windows is using. However, if you need Linux and Windows to share the same hard drive and already have Windows installed, you have a bit of extra work to do. The rest of this section focuses on getting you through both of these processes.

Removable hard drives

One way to handle multiple operating systems is the *removable rack hard drive.* The installation entails placing a special carriage into one of your computer's hard drive bays. This setup can be installed in most computers by an experienced individual or a qualified technician.

After this component is installed, you can place individual hard drives into the carriage, plugging them in and pulling them out as you might do with a CD-ROM — although you wouldn't want to just yank one out in the middle of doing something on your machine! Using a removable rack hard drive setup allows you to have a separate Windows drive and Linux drive. When you're using Windows and want to switch to Linux, you shut down Windows and pull the drive out. Then you replace it with the Linux drive and boot as though the Linux drive were always there.

If you're nervous about managing multiple operating systems and don't have room for a second hard drive in the machine, this is a great alternative. You'll need to make sure that your existing hard drive can fit in the rack, as well as the new one, and it's wise to buy more than one loading chassis (used to slide the drive into the rack) so you can just leave your drives in the chassis when they're not in the machine.

For more information, see *PC Hardware in a Nutshell* from O'Reilly & Associates.

If you're new to computer hardware, I strongly recommend that you seek assistance or have a technician install an additional hard drive or removable rack setup for you. Improper handling of computer components can damage your computer. In addition, you must keep safety in mind when working with electrical components.

Peeking at your disk space in Windows 2000 and Windows XP

If you need Windows and Linux to share the same hard drive, you and I need to take a look at your disk space before we can continue. Windows 2000 and XP operating systems use accounts to control and secure the files and folders. To get information about the computer's disk space usage, you need to be logged on to the system as the Administrator or with an account that has administrative permissions. In Windows 2000/XP, you use the Computer Management application in the Administrative Tools collection to find the details of the computer's hard drive usage. Follow these steps:

1. **Open the Control Panel by choosing Start⇨Settings⇨Control Panel.**

2. **Open the Administrative Tools folder and double-click the Computer Management icon.**

3. In the left pane of the Computer Management application, click the Disk Management folder icon.

Within a few seconds, the right pane displays the current status of the storage devices on your computer, such as the hard drive(s), CD drives, DVD/CD drives, and so on. Figure 2-1 is an example of the Windows XP Disk Management display, and Figure 2-2 shows the Windows 2000 Disk Management interface.

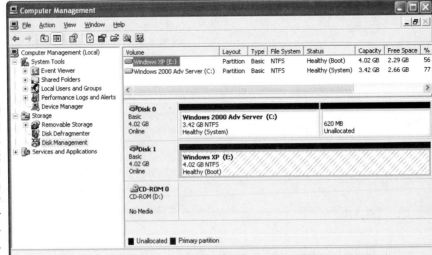

Figure 2-1: Disk Management information within the Windows XP Computer Management tool.

Figure 2-2: Disk Management information within the Windows 2000 Computer Management tool.

Figure 2-2 reflects a computer that has one hard drive and one DVD/CD drive. The hard drive is divided, or *partitioned,* into four pieces. Of these four pieces, three are in use, and one portion is free. In the Disk Management tool, partitions labeled Primary or Extended are sections of the drive that have already been assigned to an operating system, such as Windows. In Figure 2-2, the section identified as Unallocated is not assigned to any operating system and is free. This Unallocated portion could be used to install Linux since this portion is more than 3GB (you want plenty of room for programs and files, right?) and not assigned to another operating system.

Make a note of which partition is marked as Unallocated. You'll need this information later. Also, if you see NTFS (NT FileSystem) listed as a partition type, make note of this as well.

Checking your disk space in Windows 98

If you need Windows and Linux to share the same hard drive, I need you to do some detective work before I move on. Windows 98 does not provide a graphical tool like Computer Management. Instead it uses FDISK, which is a command-line tool that indicates the partitions on your hard drive. To find out the details about computer's hard drive in Windows 98, follow these steps:

1. **Open an MS-DOS prompt window by choosing Start➪Programs➪ MS-DOS Prompt.**

2. **Enter** FDISK **and press Enter.**

   In Windows you can enter FDISK in uppercase, lowercase, or any mixed case you like as long as you spell FDISK correctly!

   Depending on the size of your hard drive, you may be prompted to display large disk information. If you don't see the prompt, the FDISK menu options appear similar to the ones shown in Figure 2-3.

3. **If you see the large disk prompt, choose Y at this prompt and then press Enter.**

   The FDISK menu options appear.

4. **Display the current drive partition information.**

   If you have more than one hard drive in your computer, FDISK displays a fifth menu choice to change between disks. To change to another disk, type 5 and press Enter. The FDISK screen displays all the hard drives in your system. Type the number of the disk you want and press Enter. The top of the FDISK menu screen displays the number of the drive that FDISK is working with.

Figure 2-3:
FDISK
menu
options.

5. **To display partition information for the disk number displayed, type** 4 **and press Enter.**

   Figure 2-4 shows an example of the Display Partition Information screen within FDISK.

   The disk information shown in Figure 2-4 indicates that no free, unallocated disk space is on the drive. If the disk had unpartitioned space, FDISK would display the amount of space available.

   However, in Figure 2-4, you see that a portion of the disk space is configured as an *extended partition* EXT DOS. Extended partitions can contain what's called *logical partitions,* so it's possible that there might be free space available *inside* the extended partition that you could use to install another operating system, like Linux, or even another type of Windows.

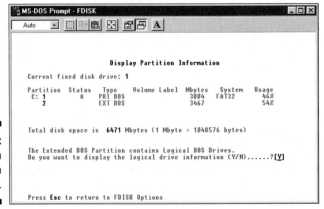

Figure 2-4:
Partition
information
in FDISK.

Think of primary partitions as empty boxes that you put data into. Extended partitions are those annoying boxes that have a collection of smaller boxes stacked next to each other inside. You only put data into the smaller boxes with an extended partition. These smaller boxes are the logical partitions.

Unfortunately, FDISK doesn't tell us anything about what's inside this extended partition. You'll have to dig deeper.

6. **To view the logical partitions within the extended partition, select the** EXT **DOS entry and press Enter.**

Figure 2-5 is an example of a logical partition setup. In this case, all space within the extended partition is currently assigned. If free space were available, FDISK would list how much. If it's 3GB or more, then installing Linux in there will be a breeze.

Figure 2-5:
Logical drive
information
in FDISK.

If you have free space available, make note of the names of all of your partitions. You'll need this information later. Also, if you see NTFS (NT FileSystem) listed as a partition type, make note of this as well.

If all the hard drive space is assigned to Windows and no unallocated space is available, you've got a problem. Fortunately, it's not impossible to solve!

Take a look in your Windows installation to see how much of your drive space you're really using. You can actually buy tools that can resize (decrease) the size of your Windows partition, and then open up a free partition to install Linux or another operating system within. Tools such as Partition Magic provide an easy way to resize and work with the partitions on your hard drives. You can find information about Partition Magic from the company's Web site at www.powerquest.com. You can read more about partitions — including the free alternative to Partition Magic — in the next section, "Working with Disk Partitions."

Working with Disk Partitions

In the section "Preparing to Use Linux and Microsoft Windows Together," at the beginning of this chapter, I discuss setting aside disk space for Linux on a computer already running Windows. The techniques I cover here assume that your system's hard drive contains space that is not already assigned to Windows or that there's enough free space to reorganize things and give it to Linux.

Choosing a partitioning tool

If you already have an existing operating system, such as Windows, on your drive(s), and you want to keep them, you will need to *resize* those before you install Linux. (Those who have plenty of unallocated space or a separate, empty hard drive can skip to the section "Assessing Your Computer" later in this chapter.)

As I said earlier, long as you either have 3GB of disk space or more available, or your existing Windows installation can give up about 3GB of disk space, you've got it made. If not, seriously consider a cheap hard drive for your Linux installation.

This is unfortunately the tricky part. If Windows has all of your hard drive space, you'll need to resize that existing Windows installation so you can have some of your space back. Before going any further, make a backup of anything you don't want to lose off your Windows installation! Things can go wrong during the various steps of this process, even when using Windows tools on Windows.

Perhaps the easiest and safest way to adjust your existing partitions is through the use of commercial programs, such as Partition Magic. Partition Magic enables you to view the partition information for your hard drive or drives. The utility also includes the ability to resize, move, and add partitions.

You can also use a free utility that comes with this book, on the included DVD: FIPS. See the section "Resizing partitions safely with FIPS" later in this chapter for more.

If you create an open partition using Partition Magic, after resizing your Windows partition, make a note of the name of that partition. You'll need it later.

Partitioning from scratch for a dual boot

If you plan to take a fresh hard drive and install both Windows and Linux on it, be sure to install Windows first. While you're going through the installation, you will be asked to partition your drives. Your hard drive can have three primary partitions and one extended partition. Inside that extended partition, you can have up to 12 logical partitions.

Make sure that you leave either a whole extended partition of at least 3GB available for Linux, or at least part of an extended partition with a minimum of two logical partitions available inside, for a total size of at least 3GB.

Make a note of the partition you leave open. You'll need this information later.

Resizing partitions safely with FIPS

Probably the most common free disk partition modification program out there is FIPS (First nondestructive Interactive Partition Splitting program). Most Linux installation media contains this program, and your DVD is no exception.

On the Fedora Core 1 DVD — or the first CD — that comes with this book, FIPS is in the /dosutils directory. In that directory, you find two subdirectories for FIPS — /fips15c and /fips20. The /fips20 directory contains the most recent version of FIPS and its documentation.

As the name implies, FIPS enables you to modify your disk partitions without destroying existing data or operating systems. Again, be sure to make a backup of your existing files and important data before using FIPS!

Also, I *highly* recommend that you read through the documentation on the DVD — or first CD — before attempting to use FIPS. You'll find it in the /dosutils/fipsdocs/fips.faq file.

FIPS does not work on NTFS partitions. If you've used NTFS, you will need to purchase Partition Magic to resize those partitions, or a separate hard drive you can start from scratch on with Linux.

If possible, have the FIPS documentation in front of you before proceeding. To set up and use FIPS, follow these steps:

1. **Insert a DOS bootable floppy disk into the disk drive.**

2. **On a system running DOS or in a MS-DOS/Command window in Windows 98, type** `format a: /s` **at the command prompt and press Enter. On a Windows 2000/XP system, skip the** `format` **command and copy the files** `boot.ini`, `ntldr`, **and** `ntdetect.com` **from the root folder (for example,** `C:\`) **to the floppy disk. In addition, if you see the files** `bootsect.dos` **or** `ntbootdd.sys` **on the Windows 2000/XP system, copy those files to the floppy disk.**

   In the `FORMAT` command, the `a:` refers to the drive letter of your floppy drive — insert the appropriate drive letter on your system if yours isn't `a:`. The `/s` copies the necessary files to the floppy to make it bootable.

3. **Copy the following files from the** `/fips20` **directory to the floppy disk:**

   - `restorrb.exe`
   - `fips.exe`
   - `errors.txt`

   If you're using Windows, you can use Windows Explorer to copy the files to the floppy disk. For DOS or in a MS-DOS/Command window under Windows, you can use the `XCOPY` or `COPY` command.

4. **Defragment your hard drive.**

   Before using `FIPS`, you must defragment your hard drive. Windows includes a defragmentation utility, so let's use that. The defragmentation utility shuffles around your files so that they occupy the beginning of a partition's storage area. This frees up unused space at the end of the partition so that you can shrink it. If you don't defragment your hard drive, shrinking the partition will destroy the data on it.

   Perform the following steps to defragment your partitions:

   a. **Choose Start⇨Run.**

   b. **Type** `defrag` **in the Open field and click OK.**

      The utility dialog box opens.

   c. **Select your drive or drives and click OK.**

      Depending on the size of your hard drive, the number of files, and how much the drive is already fragmented, defragmentation may take a *long time.* A long time may translate to hours. I recommend that you start this task in the evening and allow defragmentation to occur overnight.

5. **Reboot your machine with the bootable** `FIPS` **disk you created in Steps 1 through 3.**

   Make sure you reboot and run from the floppy. Do *not* use `FIPS` within an MS-DOS/Command window in Windows.

6. **After the system reboots to DOS, type** FIPS **at the command prompt and press Enter.**

   The initial screen that you see contains information about some FIPS cautions. After reading the information, press any key to continue.

   If your system has more than one drive, the utility presents the drives and asks you to select one.

7. **Type the number that corresponds to the drive whose partitions you want to modify.**

   The screen displays the partition table for the drive that you selected, and FIPS asks for a partition number, as shown in Figure 2-6.

8. **At the bottom of the screen, type the number that corresponds to the partition that you want to split.**

   The screen displays information about the partition you've selected. At the bottom of the screen, the application asks whether you want to make a backup copy of your root and boot sectors before proceeding. If you choose to make a backup, you can go back and undo the partition split. Having this backup also enables you to restore your partition architecture if you have a problem using FIPS.

9. **Insert a blank formatted disk into the disk drive and type** Y.

10. **Use the arrow keys on the keyboard to adjust the size of the two partitions to the values that you want and press Enter.**

    FIPS asks if you want to continue or edit the partition table.

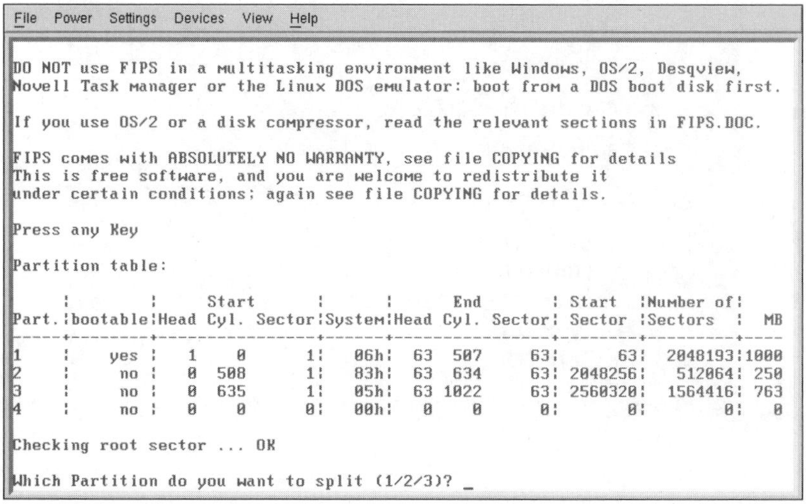

Figure 2-6: Example of the FIPS utility.

```
File  Power  Settings  Devices  View  Help

DO NOT use FIPS in a multitasking environment like Windows, OS/2, Desqview,
Novell Task manager or the Linux DOS emulator: boot from a DOS boot disk first.

If you use OS/2 or a disk compressor, read the relevant sections in FIPS.DOC.

FIPS comes with ABSOLUTELY NO WARRANTY, see file COPYING for details
This is free software, and you are welcome to redistribute it
under certain conditions; again see file COPYING for details.

Press any Key

Partition table:

        :        :     Start       :     :     End     : Start  :Number of:
Part.:bootable:Head Cyl. Sector:System:Head Cyl. Sector: Sector :Sectors  :  MB
-----+--------+-----------------+------+---------------+--------+---------+----
1    :  yes  :  1   0     1:  06h:  63  507    63:      63: 2048193:1000
2    :  no   :  0  508     1:  83h:  63  634    63: 2048256:  512064: 250
3    :  no   :  0  635     1:  05h:  63 1022    63: 2560320: 1564416: 763
4    :  no   :  0    0     0:  00h:   0    0     0:       0:       0:   0

Checking root sector ... OK

Which Partition do you want to split (1/2/3)? _
```

11. **If you're satisfied with your changes, type** C.

    At the bottom of the screen, the application asks if you want to write the new partition information to disk.

12. **To apply the changes and exit the application, type** Y; **to ignore the changes and exit the application, type** N.

Make a note of the particular partition you create. You'll need this information later.

Running Windows and Linux together

When you install Linux on a system that has Windows already installed, you can run only one operating system at a time. In other words, if you're using Windows and you want to run Linux, you need to shut down Windows, allow the computer to reboot, and then start Linux. Figure 2-7 shows the startup environment for a system that has Linux and Windows installed.

However, with the use of additional software, you can run Linux on a Windows system at the same time Windows is running. You can also run Windows software within Linux itself! See Chapter 15 for more information.

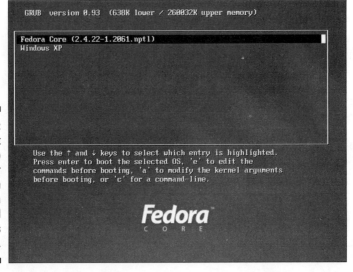

Figure 2-7:
Dual-boot startup screen for a system with Fedora Core 1 and Windows XP installed.

Assessing Your Computer

Most hardware these days works just fine with Linux. Sometimes, if you have the very latest whiz-bang video card or some other fancy new type of electronics, there might be some trouble, so if you're an early-adopter sort of person, you'll want to go to your distribution's hardware compatibility list and make sure you're covered. Fedora Core's list is available at `http://hardware.redhat.com/hcl/`. Hardware does not need to be listed as *Certified. Supported* will do just fine.

If you're new to computers or aren't that familiar with hardware definitions and details, you can find a lot of information on the Internet. (One good Web site is `www.tomshardware.com`.)

If your hardware isn't listed, don't panic. You might not be able to use the very latest features of your latest-generation video card, but you will be able to use it as a generic SVGA at the very least. All is not lost. In fact, sometimes older hardware is left off the lists but is still supported. Often you're better off with slightly older hardware than with the latest and greatest. If you can't find your hardware listed, do a Web search on the make and model of the hardware, plus the word *linux*.

Sometimes you'll find that drivers have been released for your hardware after this particular version of Linux came out. Make sure that you've obtained these drivers *before* installing Linux, whether you download them and save them onto a floppy disk, or they come on a floppy or CD with the hardware itself.

Also, try to have your computer manuals (especially the ones for your video card and monitor) handy, just in case you need them in order to answer a question asked by the installer — most people won't have to deal with this at all, but some will. At the very least, make sure that you know exactly what video card you have in your machine. You might find this information on your receipt, or you can track much of this information down by making smart use of your existing Windows installation. I'll show you how in a moment.

If you don't want to deal with this right now, skip to the section "Finally, Preparing for Your Installation" later in this chapter. Then, if the installer needs additional information from you later, you can either find what you need on the Internet or boot back into Windows and do your detective work before re-starting the installation.

If you can't find the information about what's in your computer that easily, you have the following options:

- ✔ **Use an existing operating system to document your hardware.** If your computer is already running Windows, you can collect a lot of information from the Windows environment. Use one of the following methods, depending on your system:

  - In Windows 98, select Start⇨Settings⇨Control Panel⇨System⇨ Device Manager to access the dialog box shown in Figure 2-8.

  - In Windows 2000, select Start⇨Control Panel⇨System⇨Hardware⇨ Device Manager to access the list of hardware installed on your machine, as shown in Figure 2-9.

  - In Windows XP, select Start⇨Control Panel⇨Printers and Other Hardware. Here, you can select one of the items from the dialog box under "or Pick a Control Panel Icon," or you can look to the "See Also" section and select System. If you choose System, from there it's Hardware⇨Device Manager (Figure 2-10).

If you don't want to deal with this right now, skip to the section "Finally, preparing for your installation" later in this chapter. Then, if the installer needs additional information from you later, you can either find what you need on the Internet or boot back into Windows and do your detective work before re-starting the installation.

Each of the items within the Device Manager can be double-clicked to display the corresponding details.

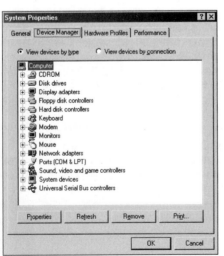

Figure 2-8:
In Windows 98, the Device Manager gives you information on what hardware you have installed.

Figure 2-9:
The
Windows
2000 Device
Manager.

✓ **Download PC hardware detect tools.** If you don't have any diagnostic tools and you have a relatively current version of DOS, you can download various PC hardware detect tools, such as PC-CONFIG, from the Internet. The PC-CONFIG tool contains several screens of information and menus to choose hardware areas and options. This tool is shareware, and the usage and fee information is available from the Holin Datentechnik Web site (www.holin.com).

✓ **Gather information by reading the screen when the computer starts.** If your system doesn't contain any operating systems and you don't have any of your system's documentation, you can resort to reading the screen as your computer starts. On some systems, the video information is displayed as the computer boots. You may have to reboot several times to read the information if it goes by too fast. Also, some systems display the PCI components and their settings as the system is starting up. Again, you may need to reboot several times to gather all the information.

✓ **Access the Basic Input/Output System (BIOS) information.** Stored in a small area of memory and retained by a battery, this is sometimes referred to as (Complementary Metal-Oxide Semiconductor) CMOS, which indicates the type of computer chip that can store and retain information. The amount of information stored in the BIOS can be very little to quite a lot. Some newer systems may display several screens of information about the computer's hardware.

To access the BIOS, you need to do so before any operating systems load. Most manufacturers indicate the keyboard key or key sequence to get into the BIOS, or Setup, on the screen when the system is starting up — for example, `Press Del to enter Setup`. If you can't find the keyboard sequence, check the manufacturer's Web site. After you've entered the BIOS, you typically navigate around with the arrow keys, Tab key, or Enter key. In some BIOS environments, the function keys are also used. Look for a list of function key options on the top or bottom of the screen.

You especially need to be cautious of labels on hardware boxes and Web sites that include the term *Win* (as in Windows). These components, such as *WinModem,* don't contain all the configuration and software in the hardware — even worse, there might be nothing on the packaging that suggests this limitation. These components are designed to use the Windows operating system to handle some of the load. Only a very slight chance exists that you can find a Linux driver for *Win* hardware. If you do find one, copy it to a floppy *before* installing Linux. If you can't find a driver and you need to use a modem, put down a little cash and get a modem that is supported properly. For more information about WinModems, see Chapter 7.

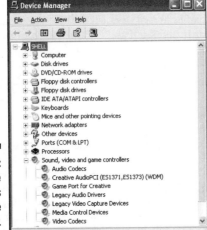

Figure 2-10: The Windows XP Device Manager.

Finally, Preparing for Your Installation

Yes, this is a lot of prep work, but it's worth it. Now you can finally look at the actual pre-installation routines. The first thing you need to do is figure out which method you're going to use to install Linux. This isn't actually as hard as it sounds. You have three choices:

✔ **DVD or CD:** If your computer can boot from a DVD or CD, and your Linux distribution installation CD or DVD is bootable, you can start the installation directly from the CD or DVD. Most current Linux distributions come on bootable CDs or DVDs, and most current computers are capable of booting from CD and DVD. *The distribution included with this book comes on a bootable DVD, and if you use the coupon to get the CDs, the first CD is also bootable.*

✔ **Floppy:** You can also start the installation from a floppy disk if you cannot boot from the DVD or CD. After booting from a floppy disk, the installer program then uses the DVD or CD to continue the installation.

✔ **Network Source:** This method enables you to install Linux over a network. In this procedure, you start your computer, establish a network connection to where the Linux installation files reside, and then complete the installation by accessing the files across the network.

This chapter concentrates on preparing to install Linux from the DVD (with notes for the CD users as well) or with an installation floppy disk. Once you have decided which one of these you want to use, the second large decision you need to make is where on your target hard drive you want Linux to reside. If you have a brand new, empty hard drive, that's your best choice. Make a note of which drive it is before proceeding. As I covered earlier in this chapter, you can also install within disk partitions on a drive you're already using for Windows. Be sure to have your notes handy on which partition(s) you'll be giving to Linux before proceeding to Chapter 3.

Laptop considerations

The current distributions of Linux do very well on relatively new notebooks and laptops (see www.linux-laptop.net for an excellent research site for how Linux gets along with various makes and models). If your laptop is a common brand, you shouldn't encounter any problems installing Linux. However, laptops often contain WinModems (as mentioned elsewhere in this chapter, hardware labeled with the Win prefix is for Windows, not Linux).

If you plan on purchasing a laptop for Linux, check out the modem and other hardware, such as network cards, to make sure they're not Win branded. If the built-in or default hardware for the laptop is Win labeled or you discover while researching the machine that it contains a Win product even if it isn't properly labeled, you might be able to switch the offending hardware for a PC (or PCMCIA) card. Most current laptops contain at least one PC Card slot so that you can slip in a PC card modem, network card, or combo modem-network card. As long as you stick with a common brand of PC card, it should be able to work well with Linux.

Now, before you go any further, there's one more thing I want you to do: locate your Linux distribution's documentation. These manuals can help you get past installation roadblocks and contain lots of useful information for after the install is finished.

Finding this documentation depends on how you got your distribution:

- ✔ Many boxed sets come with printed manuals.

- ✔ Downloaded materials (and the boxed sets) might come with the documentation on your distribution CDs or DVD. Unfortunately, this is not the case with the media included with this book.

You can also (usually) find both help files and the full manuals in Web form on the distribution's Web site, and you might even be able to purchase manuals separately if you'd like to have them in hardcopy.

What about situations where the documentation doesn't cover your problem? Check out one of the many Linux reference Web sites, especially:

- ✔ **General sites and publications:** www.linux.com, www.everything linux.org, www.linuxgazette.com, www.linuxjournal.com, www.linuxtoday.com, www.linuxworld.com, www.lwn.net, www.linuxcare.com, www.slashdot.org, www.freshmeat.net, and www.linuxdoc.org.

- ✔ **Security sites:** www.linuxsecurity.com, security.ucdavis.edu/sysadmin/linux.html, and www.portalux.com/system/security.

- ✔ **Kernel and software sites:** www.linuxhq.com and www.linuxapps.com.

Enabling Booting from a CD- or DVD-ROM

A really nice installation option is that you can install Linux from the CD- or DVD-ROM. Many systems these days come set up to boot from a CD or DVD if there's one in the drive, but yours may not already be configured for this. Just pop in the installation DVD (or CD) and try it! If booting from DVD (or CD) doesn't work when you try it:

1. **Determine if your Linux installation CD or DVD is bootable.**

    Almost all modern Linux distribution CDs and DVDs — including the DVD that comes with this book (and the first CD from the CD set you can order as a replacement using the included coupon) — can be used to boot into the installation routine.

However, if you've chosen a distribution not covered in this book, your DVD or CD may require a boot disk. The distribution's documentation will tell you whether this is possible or not. Follow the documentation's instructions on how to make a boot disk.

2. **Determine if your system is capable of booting from a DVD or CD.**

If you've ever booted your system from a CD or DVD, you'll have no problem booting from the Linux installation CD. You'll find this information in your BIOS, in the section that lets you tell the machine which *storage devices* (drives) to check at boot time. If CD-ROM or DVD-ROM isn't listed in the options, proceed to the section "Preparing to Boot from the Floppy Installation Disk."

If you have to make changes in your BIOS, make sure to save them when you exit! It's easy to forget and end up wondering why the machine isn't doing what you told it to do.

Preparing to Boot from the Floppy Installation Disk

If you're having trouble booting from the DVD or CD, you can start the installation from a floppy disk. When you purchase a boxed set, a floppy disk comes with it. Downloading the CDs or DVD   or getting them through a source such as this book   doesn't give you a physical floppy disk, but you can make your own anyway!

Usually, the Linux DVD or installation CD contains a directory of DOS utilities called dosutils. Within this directory is a program you can use to create an installation floppy, called rawrite.exe. You'll find the documentation for rawrite in the same location.

You can use Windows Explorer or the DOS dir command to investigate the contents of the /dosutils directory.

In addition, the DVD that comes with this book also contains *disk image* files, which contain a kind of snapshot of the installation boot disk. With Fedora Core 1, these image files are kept in the /images directory.

To make a boot disk on a Windows system using Fedora Core 1 and the DVD (or CD) that came with this book, follow these steps:

1. **Insert the DVD that comes with this book into the DVD drive, and make a note of the drive letter that corresponds to your DVD drive.**

If you are using the CD set, insert the first CD.

2. **Accessing a command prompt depends on your Windows version:**

   • In Windows 98, open an MS-DOS window by choosing Start⇨ Programs⇨MS-DOS Prompt.

   • In Windows 2000 and XP, open a command prompt window by choosing Start⇨Programs⇨Accessories⇨Command Prompt.

3. **Change to the drive that corresponds to your DVD or CD drive by typing the drive letter followed by a colon at the command prompt and pressing Enter.**

   The prompt in the MS-DOS/Command window changes to reflect the CD's or DVD's drive letter.

4. **To change to the /dosutils directory, type** cd dosutils **at the command prompt and press Enter.**

5. **To create a boot disk in floppy drive A:, type**

```
rawrite -f ..\images\bootdisk.img -d a
```

   The -f parameter specifies the location and name of the image file. The -d option indicates the floppy drive letter.

   The following instruction phrase is echoed in the MS-DOS window:

```
Please insert a formatted diskette into drive A and press -ENTER- :
```

6. **Insert a blank, formatted, 1.44MB floppy disk into the floppy drive and press Enter.**

   When the process is complete, the MS-DOS command prompt returns to reflect the /dosutils directory, and the flashing underscore cursor appears.

After you've created the installation boot disk, you need to configure, or verify, that your computer is set to boot from the floppy drive. The easiest way to do this is to insert a floppy disk into your main floppy drive, make sure no other drives have media in them (such as a DVD in your DVD-ROM drive), and then reboot your computer. If your computer boots from the floppy, you're set.

If for some reason your machine seems to be ignoring the floppy drive as it boots, check in your system's BIOS as we discussed earlier in this chapter. Make sure that the floppy is listed first. Then, save your changes before exiting the BIOS; otherwise, the items you set don't take effect.

Chapter 3

Installing Fedora Core

· ·

In This Chapter

▶ Checking out some neat features and installation improvements

▶ Installing Linux as a personal desktop by using the graphical interface

· ·

Do, or do not. There is no "try."

—*Yoda,* The Empire Strikes Back

*L*inux has clawed its way out of the geek-only realm and into the average-user light. No longer are arcane glyphs and complex sorcerer's spells required to install Linux. For this reason, the graphical installation of Linux is now quite easy to perform and will be familiar to users coming from another graphical operating system, such as Microsoft Windows. This chapter provides the details.

If you're installing SuSE or Mandrake Linux, proceed to Chapter 4. There's plenty for you to learn in this chapter, but you can start by looking at the specifics for your particular distribution first.

Things to Consider before You Begin Installation

You can install Fedora Core by

✔ Booting with the Fedora Core DVD-ROM.

✔ Booting with the Fedora Core installation CD, which is CD number 1 if you ordered the CD set.

✔ Booting with an installation floppy disk and having the remainder of the installation files read from the DVD-ROM or CD.

To begin the installation from the DVD-ROM or CD-ROM, you must first change your system to start, or *boot,* from a DVD-ROM or CD-ROM. In Chapter 2, I cover how to configure a computer to boot from these devices.

If you want or need to make the installation floppy disk and have access to a Windows system, perform the steps to create the installation floppy covered in Chapter 2. If for some reason the installation floppy (or the CD- or DVD-ROM's installation routine) won't work on your system, you may need to download a new version of just the installation portion.

You can get the updated install images from the "Security & Errata" page (http://www.redhat.com/apps/support/errata/). Click through the link for Fedora Core 1 and search through for the words "boot," "image," and "anaconda." If there's a new boot disk image, that's how you'll find it. The site explains what you need to do from there.

What's this "image" thing? An image is a file that has to be precisely placed into storage media (like a floppy disk or a writable CD- or DVD-ROM). You can't just copy it. I cover the RAWRITE utility in Chapter 2.

The instructions in this chapter tell you how to follow the installation for Fedora Core 1. I concentrate on Fedora Core 1 and its installation for two main reasons:

- Fedora Core 1 is included on the DVD with this book, and the CDs you can order with your coupon.
- Covering the installation of every Linux distribution in existence would make this book into a set of encyclopedias.

I cover the Personal Desktop installation because it requires little or no hard drive preparation and doesn't use umpteen partitions like other installations do. In addition, the Personal Desktop installation option installs the X Window System (graphical interface) and applications that are commonly used on desktop and laptop systems. Server or service-type applications, such as the Apache Web server and FTP server, aren't installed with the Personal Desktop option. However, you can add these to your Personal Desktop package selection before actually beginning your installation.

Please note that if you're installing Red Hat Enterprise Linux, a different version of Fedora Core, or a different distribution of Linux, your screens *will* look different from what is shown in this book. Each Linux distribution installation covers the same basic tasks, but each action may be presented in a different order. For example, one distribution may present account creation before net-working configuration, and another may have these two topics reversed.

Up until you reach the About to Install (GUI install) screen, you can back out of the installation without changing anything on your system. None of the configuration options you make before the About to Install screen are saved to your disks. After you continue beyond the About to Install screen, data is written to disk, and your system is changed.

If you have really new hardware and an older version of Linux, the installation software and process may not be "happy" with the newer hardware. If you have installation troubles and suspect that this may be the cause, I recommend checking out the Linux distribution's Web site for newer installation floppy disk images. The Linux community is usually very quick to address new hardware for the different distributions and versions of Linux. However, if you are attempting to install a version of Linux that is more than a couple of years old on new hardware, you may be out of luck finding updated installation floppy disk images.

The Installation Process

In this chapter, I follow the graphical installation. If you can't use the graphical installation for some reason (if Linux doesn't support your video card, for example), follow the text-based installation instead. The steps are the same, it's just not as pretty. You can find more detailed coverage of the text install in Red Hat's manuals, which are available on their Web site, and I will include the occasional image of the text installer as well.

Dealing with damaged CDs

If your media check fails, what you do next depends on where you got the DVD or CDs. If the DVD came with this book, contact Wiley Customer Care at 800-762-2974 to get them replaced. Do not contact Red Hat's technical support to have the DVD replaced in this case.

On the other hand, if you burned your own CDs or DVD, there may be one of two different problems. Try burning the media again at a slower speed. If these media also fail the media check, download the images again. Or, they may have been corrupted during the file transfer, though it's unlikely.

To install Fedora Core 1, follow these steps:

1. **If you want to boot and install from the Red Hat DVD-ROM, place the DVD that comes with this book in your DVD-ROM drive and reboot your system.**

   Otherwise, place the installation floppy disk (see Chapter 2 for details) in your floppy drive, put the DVD in your DVD-ROM drive, and reboot your system.

   If you are using the CDs, boot with the first CD in the CD-ROM drive.

   Whether you start the installation from the floppy disk, CD-ROM, or the DVD-ROM, the first installation screen appears. The screen contains several options, as shown in Figure 3-1, which are each described in the following list:

   • **Install or upgrade in graphical mode.** The first option in the graphical interface is for installing Fedora Core for the first time or for upgrading an existing version of Linux. This installation probes to detect your system's hardware. The graphical interface is designed to work with a mouse to select options. If you don't have a mouse, you can use the keyboard to navigate around the screens. In most places, the Tab key or the arrow keys advance you to the next option; the space bar toggles options off and on; and the Enter key accepts the choices and moves to the next screen. In most screens, if you want to change a previous setting, a Back button is available to navigate to earlier selection screens. The graphical installation screens also include help in the left panel. The content changes to reflect information about the current configuration screen.

   • **Install or upgrade in text mode.** The second option enables you to install or upgrade Fedora Core using a text menu interface. This interface presents the options in text menus, and you use the arrow keys or Tab key to move the selection area. In some areas, the spacebar is used to turn options off and on. To install by using the text interface, type `linux text` at the `boot:` prompt and press Enter.

   • **Use the function keys.** The last item listed points out the function keys displayed at the bottom of the initial installation screen.

     The F1 function key presents the initial installation screen, which allows you to install or upgrade via graphical mode, install or upgrade via text mode, or use the function keys labeled F2 through F5.

The F2 function key includes options for disabling hardware detection during installation (you must know the details of your hardware before proceeding); testing the installation media before proceeding (good option to use if you downloaded the Fedora Core distribution from Red Hat's Fedora Project Web site (http://fedora.redhat.com) and burned the software to CDs or a DVD); enabling rescue mode (this is also the function of the F5 key); using a driver disk, CD, or DVD that isn't included with the Linux installation media; and updating your existing Linux installation.

The F3 function key allows you to set the video options. If you have experienced problems installing Fedora Core 1 with the graphical interface, you may want to try a lower resolution. Type linux lowres at the boot: prompt to use a lower graphic resolution to install Linux. The linux lowres nofb command allows you to turn off frame buffering, which can cause problems with some video cards.

The F4 function key, labeled Kernel, enables you to enter parameters when you install Linux. For example, some help files will tell you to do something like "turn off autoprobing for your PCI hardware bus." Here's where you find out what you need to type.

The F5 function key enables you to boot into rescue mode when the Linux system doesn't start properly. Rescue mode includes many useful utilities to restore your system to a functional state. To start rescue mode, type linux rescue at the boot: prompt and press Enter.

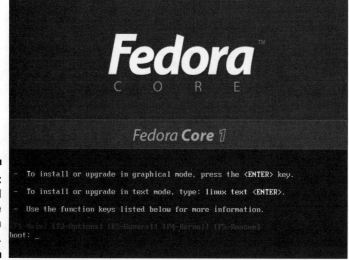

Figure 3-1:
The initial
Fedora Core
installation
screen.

If you don't choose any options and just press Enter, the graphical installation process starts. The default installation mode for Red Hat Linux is graphical. Other Linux distributions, such as SuSE and Mandrake, also have graphical installation options. Even though the installation screens in other distributions are different from Fedora Core, they all follow the same basic steps.

2. **Press Enter to start the graphical installation.**

Many lines of information scroll past as the installation begins. During this time, a *mini* version of Linux is loading. If you downloaded the full version of Fedora Core and burned it onto CDs or a DVD yourself, the CD Found (mediacheck) screen appears. This allows you to check the integrity of the media that you are using to install Linux. If this is the case, I recommend taking the time to perform this test on all of the CDs or the DVD. It's best to know now if one of them is damaged or incomplete.

The DVD that accompanies this book is a full edition of Fedora Core 1, so it's the same one that you can purchase or download. Just as with the boxed sets, the media check for this edition is not run by default. You can perform the same function by pressing F2 in the initial installation screen and typing `linux mediacheck` at the prompt.

3. **What you do here depends on whether or not you want to test your media:**

   • If you see the CD Found window or manually start the media check, press the Tab key until the OK button is enabled. Test each of the CDs or the DVD in turn. If any of them receives a Fail notice, see the "Dealing with damaged CDs" sidebar. After you're finished testing, tab to the Continue button and press Enter to proceed to the next installation step.

   • If you do not want to check your DVD or CDs, press the Tab key until the Skip button is enabled. Press the Enter key to advance to the next installation step.

In either case, after you're ready to move on, the CD Found image disappears and additional text scrolls across the screen. The last few lines load the graphic engine, a gray screen with a small X in the middle appears, and then a screen with a large Red Hat logo appears.

After a moment, the Welcome to Fedora Core screen appears, indicating where you can read or obtain the Red Hat manuals. The information recommends that you read the installation documentation before you install Linux for the first time, and so do I!

4. **After you've finished with the material on the Welcome to Red Hat Linux screen, click Next.**

The Welcome screen automatically disappears and is replaced by the Language Selection screen, as shown in Figure 3-2. Linux supports many different languages.

Figure 3-2:
The
Language
Selection
screen.

5. **Use the mouse or the ↑ or ↓ keys to select your language and click Next.**

The Keyboard Configuration screen appears, as shown in Figure 3-3.

Different languages arrange the keys differently on keyboards; you may want to choose the matching language for your keyboard (the default is U.S. English).

6. **Choose your keyboard configuration and click Next.**

The Mouse Configuration screen appears, as shown in Figure 3-4. Notice this screen also includes a Back button, which enables you to go back to the previous configuration installation screen if you need to make changes.

7. **Configure your mouse.**

By this stage of the installation, you're probably already using a mouse to make your selections. The Mouse Configuration screen enables you to choose the model and features of your mouse. If you're unfamiliar with mouse hardware, the important distinction to understand is between the serial, PS/2, and USB mice. A serial mouse has a wide rectangular connector with pins in the end that plugs into the computer. A PS/2 mouse has a round connector, and a USB mouse has a small rectangular connector, much smaller than the connector that hooks up your monitor to your computer.

If you're using a two-button mouse, you also have the option to emulate three buttons. If this feature is enabled, you can emulate the middle button by pressing both mouse buttons at the same time.

Figure 3-3:
The
Keyboard
Configura-
tion screen.

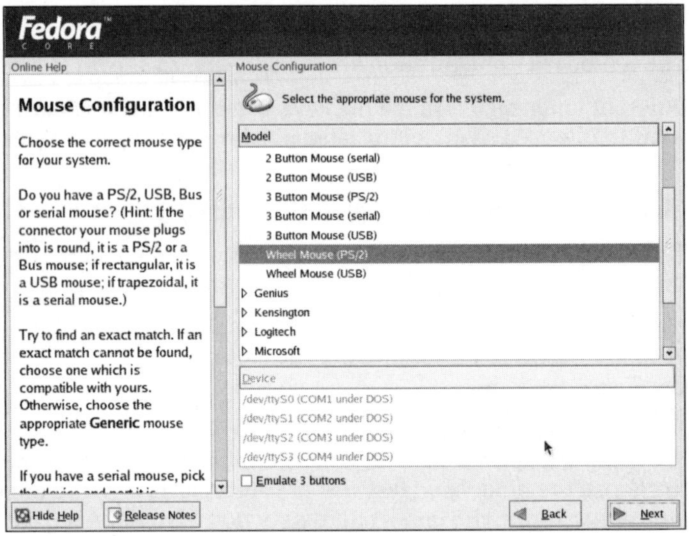

Figure 3-4:
The Mouse
Configura-
tion screen.

8. **After making any adjustments to your mouse settings, click Next.**

The Monitor Configuration screen appears, as shown in Figure 3-5, with your monitor type highlighted.

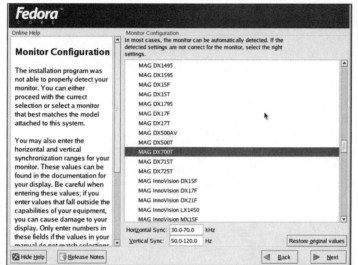

Figure 3-5:
The Monitor
Configura-
tion screen.

9. **If the monitor configuration information is correct for your hardware, click Next; if the information isn't correct, scroll through the list and click the triangle next to the vendor's name to expand and collapse the choices. In the expanded list, choose the brand and model of your monitor (or the one that matches your hardware), and then click Next.**

   If you can't find your monitor at all, you have three choices. You can simply choose Unprobed Monitor and keep your monitor's documentation handy to answer questions about the hardware. You can also choose either Generic LCD Display (for laptops) or Generic CRT Display (for desktop monitors), and then select the resolution the monitor is capable of. Again, it's best to have your monitor's documentation handy if at all possible. If you don't have the physical papers, you can usually find what you need on the manufacturer's Web site or by doing a Web search on the make and model.

   It is vital that you make sure not to push your video hardware harder than it's made to go. You can actually damage your hardware this way. If you're not sure, err on the side of a lower resolution or refresh rate.

10. **After making any adjustments to your monitor settings, click Next.**

    The Installation Type screen appears, as shown in Figure 3-6.

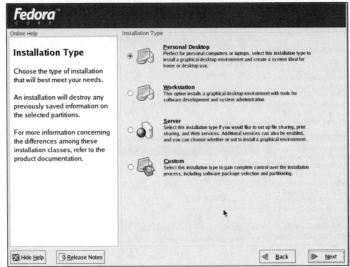

Figure 3-6:
The Installation Type screen.

Four options are available under Installation Type:

- **Personal Desktop:** This option performs an installation for personal desktop or laptop use and installs a graphical interface. If your system already contains a copy of Linux, the default for the Personal Desktop installation is to remove any existing Linux-related partitions and use all the remaining free, unpartitioned disk space. If you choose this default, any existing non-Linux partitions, such as DOS/Windows, remain untouched. After installation, you can boot to Linux and your other existing operating system or systems.

- **Workstation:** This option installs the graphical interface (X Window System) and the desktop manager(s) of your choice, much like the Personal Desktop installation, but also includes tools for software developers and system administrators.

- **Server:** This option is designed for a basic Linux-based server for file and print sharing and Web services. You can also enable other services and choose to install a graphical environment. When you select this option, the default disk-partitioning scheme is to remove *ALL* existing partitions on *ALL* your hard drives. This means that all partitions and operating systems of any type, Linux and others, are removed, and all drives are erased.

- **Custom:** This option enables the most flexibility to retain your existing operating systems and configuration options. This option enables you to choose the packages or applications/roles you want to install, the size of your disk partitions, and how you want the system to boot.

I cover the Personal Desktop installation in this book for demonstration purposes, but you may select any of the other options that pertain directly to your system. If you choose another option, keep in mind that the instructions I include here may vary from your installation experience.

11. Click the Personal Desktop installation option to select it; then click Next.

The Disk Partitioning Setup screen appears, as shown in Figure 3-7. You're given the option to accept an automatic partitioning strategy, or you can define your own partition(s) manually. Your hard drive must contain at least one Linux partition to continue with the installation. I choose to cover automatic partitioning in this book. If you really, really want to partition manually, see the nearby sidebar "Defining partitions manually."

12. Choose Automatically Partition; then click Next.

The Automatic Partitioning screen appears, as shown in Figure 3-8. You can choose to remove all Linux partitions on your system, remove *all* partitions on your system, or keep all existing partitions and use free space. You also have the option of marking a particular hard drive to work with. As suggested in Chapter 2, be sure you know which hard drive you want to work with! As a hint, the first hard drive in your computer is hda, the second is hdb, and the third is hdc. If you have SCSI drives, you will see sda, sdb, and sdc instead.

If you're really nervous, check the Review check box so you can double-check the partition assignments before the installer changes anything.

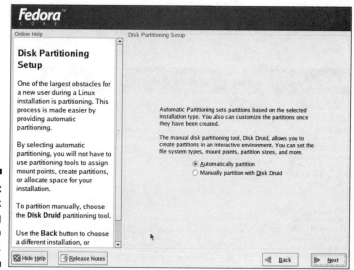

Figure 3-7: The Disk Partitioning Setup screen.

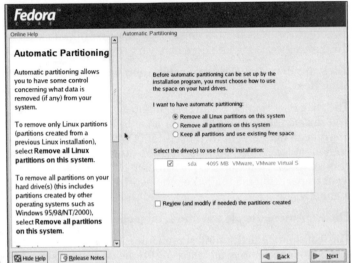

Figure 3-8:
The
Automatic
Partitioning
screen.

Be careful — you lose *all* data in existing partitions when you choose to remove partitions.

13. Choose the Remove All Linux Partitions on This System option; then click Next.

A Warning dialog box appears asking if you want to remove the partition(s). Click Yes. The Boot Loader Configuration installation screen appears, as shown in Figure 3-9.

The first option allows you to change the boot loader from the default of GRUB to LILO, or choose no boot loader. Keep the default.

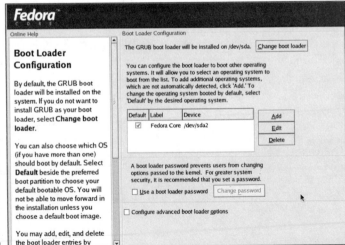

Figure 3-9:
The Boot
Loader
Configura-
tion screen.

The second option allows you to boot to other operating systems than Linux. If you have other operating systems installed on non-Linux partitions, such as Windows, you can choose to boot to them.

The third option enables you to configure a boot loader password for added security.

The last option allows you to select advanced boot loader options.

14. **After making any selections to the boot loader configuration settings, click Next.**

The Network Configuration screen appears, as shown in Figure 3-10.

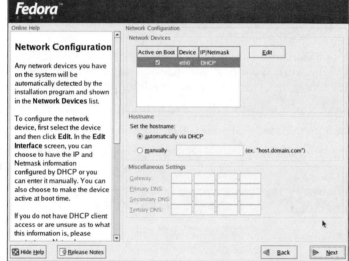

Figure 3-10: The Network Configuration screen.

15. **If you're using Dynamic Host Configuration Protocol (DHCP) on your network to set the computer's hostname, choose the Automatically Via DHCP option. If you aren't using DHCP to define the hostname, choose the Manually option and enter a hostname.**

First, make sure the eth0 checkbox is checked so your machine will activate its networking when it boots. Then, if you're using DHCP, this setup allows another service or system to set all the networking parameters for your computer so it can communicate properly on a network or on the Internet. If you're connected to a high-speed Internet service, such as DSL, your computer is probably configured to use DHCP for all the settings except the hostname, which gives an identity to your machine. If your computer is part of a company network, the DHCP services may provide the hostname in addition to the rest of the parameters. Check with the network administrator or IT department for the appropriate information for your network.

To set the hostname of your Linux system, make sure the Automatically via DHCP option is not selected and then configure the following:

- Type a name for your machine in the field to the right of the Manually label. I recommend that you use only alphanumeric characters for the name of your machine. Sometimes, using other characters may interfere with an application and make it difficult to access your machine from a network.

- If you're not using DHCP for the other network settings, click on the Edit button to the right of the Network Devices list. In the Edit Interface eth0 window, remove the check next to Configure using DHCP. Enter values for the IP Address and netmask settings and click OK. After you enter these two values, the remaining fields under the Miscellaneous Settings label are enabled. If you don't know what your IP address or netmask are supposed to be, ask your administrator.

- Enter values in the Gateway and DNS fields that are valid for your network. If your network has more than one DNS server, you can enter up to three DNS server addresses.

I cover DHCP and other IP-related information in more detail in Chapter 7.

16. After you've made all your selections and entered your data, click Next.

The Firewall Configuration screen appears, as shown in Figure 3-11.

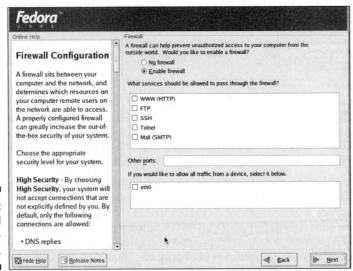

Figure 3-11: The Firewall Configuration screen.

Firewalls protect your system from unauthorized access and discovery. When you're connected to the Internet with a high-speed connection, your computer appears as one of the hundreds of thousands of other systems on the Internet. For starters, you may want to choose the Medium level. If you're on a corporate or private network, check with the network administrator or IT department for information on the appropriate firewall setting. (Your Internet connection hardware may include a firewall. Contact your Internet connection hardware provider for information about its firewall features.)

17. **After you've made all your selections and entered your data, click Next.**

    The Additional Language Support screen appears, as shown in Figure 3-12. Your Linux system can support multiple languages at the same time. If you add languages, be sure to set which you want for your default.

18. **Select the languages for your Linux installation and click the Next button to continue.**

    The Time Zone Selection screen appears, as shown in Figure 3-13. If you don't find the exact name of the city you're in, choose another city in your same time zone that supports the same options, such as daylight savings time. You can also click the UTC (Universal Time, Coordinated) Offset tab at the top of the screen and select your offset from UTC time and whether you use daylight savings time. If your computer uses UTC, you can also choose this option.

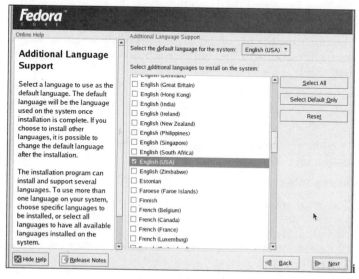

Figure 3-12:
The
Additional
Language
Support
screen.

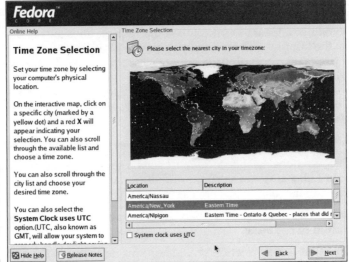

Figure 3-13:
The Time
Zone
Selection
screen.

19. **Choose the time zone in which your Linux system resides and click Next.**

    The Set Root Password screen appears, as shown in Figure 3-14.

20. **In the Root Password screen, type the root account password into the Root Password field and then type the same password in the Confirm field.**

    You don't see the password when you type it — just an asterisk for each character. This prevents unauthorized individuals from seeing the password.

    After the values in the two fields agree, the phrase `Root Passwords Do Not Match`, which appears below the Confirm field, is replaced with the message `Root Password Accepted`.

    Don't forget your root password! You'll need it to do to do any administration task on your Linux box.

21. **After you've entered your root password twice, click Next.**

    The installation system pauses and displays a progress dialog box for a few seconds while it reads in the package (software programs) options. When this is complete, the Package Defaults screen appears. You can choose to install the current default list of packages or choose to customize the set of packages (as shown in Figure 3-15).

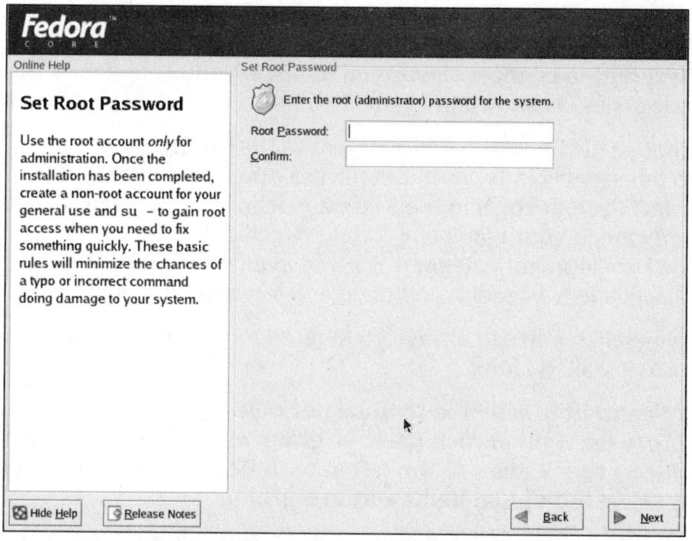

Figure 3-14:
The
Set Root
Password
screen.

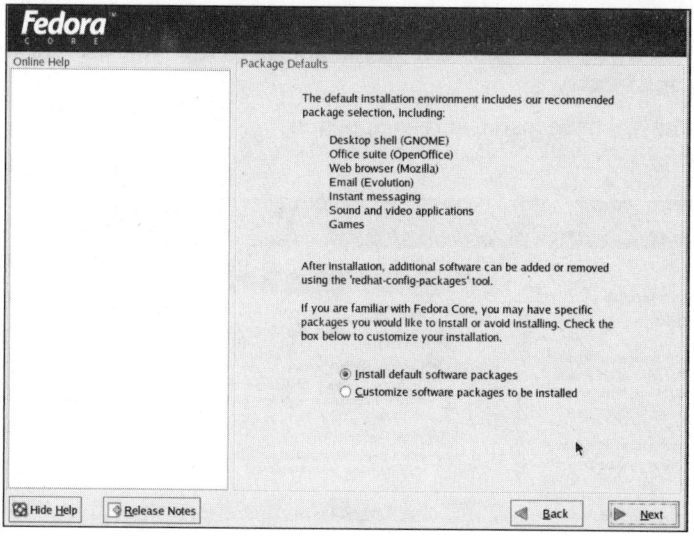

Figure 3-15:
The
Package
Defaults
screen.

22. **Choose the Install Default Software Packages option or the Customize Software Packages to Be Installed option.**

In this example, I want to install the KDE desktop in addition to the default GNOME desktop. Choosing the Customize option and then clicking the Next button changes the screen to display the contents of the package categories, as shown in Figure 3-16.

Choose KDE Desktop Environment in the Desktops category. If you plan to have your Linux computer access other computers on your network, select System Tools in the System category. If you plan on developing software in your Linux environment, select the appropriate options in the Development category. You can even scroll to the bottom to the Miscellaneous section and choose Everything if you want!

Remember, you can always go back and add other packages after you have installed Linux.

23. **If you want to select individual packages in a group, click the Details link to the right of each package group name. In the Details for window, place a check mark to the left of each item in the package group name to select individual items within a group.**

Don't feel obligated to do this. This is probably a task you want to save for when you're feeling more comfortable with Linux. When you have completed any selections you decide to make, click the OK button.

24. **When you have selected all the packages that you want to install, click Next.**

The About to Install screen appears.

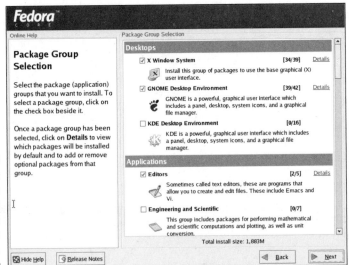

Figure 3-16:
The
Package
Group
Selection
screen.

25. **When you're ready to commit to the installation, click Next in the About to Install screen.**

    The Required Install Media dialog box appears, as shown in Figure 3-17.

Figure 3-17:
One version
of the
Required
Install
Media
dialog box.

If you want to stop your installation of Linux, this is the *last* place where you can stop without changing anything on your hard drive(s). To stop the installation, press Ctrl+Alt+Del, and your system reboots.

26. **After you read this and ready the media — not much of a chore if you're installing from one DVD! — click Continue.**

    The Installing Packages screen appears. As the system is installing, you see progress bars for each individual package being installed and total installation progress.

    After the packages and software are installed, the Boot Diskette Creation screen appears. This enables you to create a disk that you can use to start your system for troubleshooting booting problems. These days, almost all modern Linux distributions allow you to use the installation DVD as a rescue disk, so boot disks aren't as important as they once were. Still, the phrase "better safe than sorry" is a cliché for a reason. If it makes you more comfortable, make a boot disk.

27. **If you started the Linux installation from the floppy installation disk, remove the floppy disk from the drive, insert a blank 1.44MB floppy disk into your drive, and click Next in the Boot Diskette Creation screen to create the boot disk. If you *don't* want to create a boot disk, select the No, I Do Not Want to Create a Boot Disk option and click Next.**

    After a boot disk is created, you reach the final installation screen. Congratulations, you've made it through the first Linux gauntlet! Give yourself a good pat on the back, remove the DVD from the DVD tray, and click Exit to reboot your machine. Then, proceed directly to the next section, "Your First Boot."

Defining partitions manually

If you choose to define partitions manually, you'll be using Red Hat's Disk Druid.

Disk Druid enables you to delete existing partitions and add new partitions. If you don't know how to use Disk Druid, I recommend that you *not* proceed any further. Click Back to return to the Automatic Partitioning screen and choose to review the automatic setup Disk Druid suggests instead of starting from scratch.

If you choose to Review, there's some things you'll want to know. For example, the *mount point*, or starting point in the Linux directory hierarchy, for this example is /boot. For Linux native partitions, you need to define the mount point, size, and hard drive. For a Linux swap partition,

you need to define the size and hard drive. An ext3, or Linux native, partition is used for the operating system and user files. The swap partition may come into play when you are running Linux and getting low on free memory. When you install Linux, you have to have at least one swap partition and one native partition. After you've finished making all your changes, click Next to continue the installation.

If you're installing Linux by using the text interface, the Disk Druid text interface is similar to the graphical interface, except that you use the Tab key and arrow keys to navigate to various portions of the screen. To find out more about Disk Druid, consult the Fedora Core documentation.

Your First Boot

The first time your Fedora Core system boots, you'll have the first chance to see the boot menu. Select the Linux entry and press Enter. Your machine should start to boot. If you run into trouble, see Chapter 5, "Booting and Stopping Linux." This first boot is special so I cover it separately here.

After your machine boots up, you see the first boot Welcome screen, as shown in Figure 3-18.

1. **Click Next to proceed to the setup routine.**

   The Date and Time screen appears, as shown in Figure 3-19.

2. **Verify that the date and time are accurate. If they are not, adjust them now.**

   If you're on a computer network that is currently connected to the Internet, you might want to check the Enable Network Time Protocol check box to let your system use the Internet to make sure it has the right time. After you've checked this box (sometimes this can take a while to set itself up, but after that you're fine), choose one of the servers from the Server drop-down list box.

Figure 3-18:
The Fedora
Core
Firstboot
Welcome
screen.

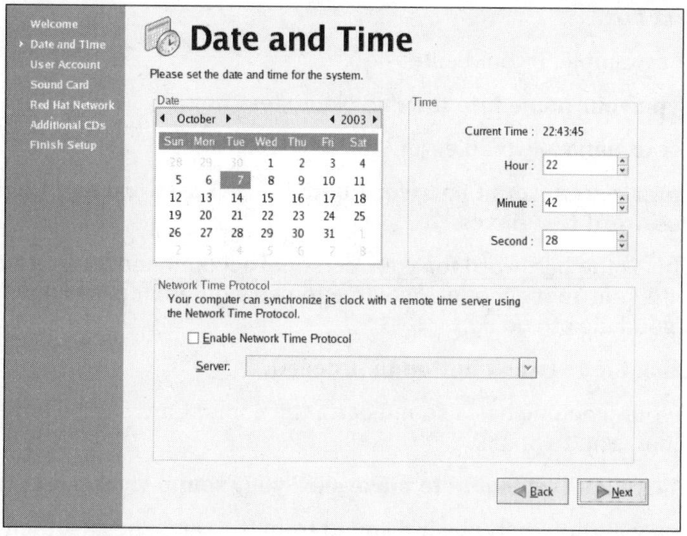

Figure 3-19:
The Fedora
Core
Firstboot
Date and
Time screen.

3. After you've finished adjusting the date, click Next to proceed.

The User Account screen appears, as shown in Figure 3-20.

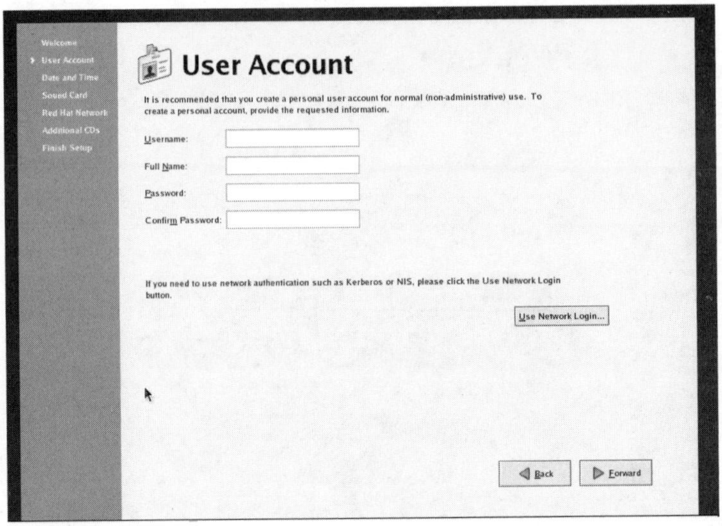

Figure 3-20:
The User
Account
first boot
screen.

4. Type the name you want for your personal account into the Username text box.

For example, I would enter `dee`.

5. Type your name into the Full Name text box.

For example, I would enter `Dee-Ann LeBlanc`.

6. Enter your account password both in the Password and Confirm Password text boxes.

This is the password for your personal account and has nothing to do with your root account. Feel free to use a different password. In fact, it's a good idea to do so.

7. Click the Forward button to proceed.

If your machine has a sound card, the Sound Card screen appears. If not, skip to Step 9.

8. Click Play Test Sound to make sure your sound card is set up properly.

You will (hopefully) hear a sound from the right speaker, then the left, and then both. After the sound plays, a dialog opens asking if you heard the sound properly. If you heard nothing, click No, and you'll be informed that the card could not be autodetected. This is something to fix later. If you heard the sound, click Yes. If the sound doesn't work, refer to http://www.tldp.org/HOWTO/Sound-HOWTO/ for assistance.

9. **Click Forward to proceed.**

   The Additional CDs screen appears. If you have any of these CDs that it lists and want to add software from them, feel free to do so now. If you don't have them but you want them, you could download them and burn them onto a CD later if you have the proper hardware. See Chapter 15 for more on multimedia.

10. **When you're finished with the additional CDs, click Forward to continue.**

    That's it! Click Finish Setup. You've just survived the second Linux gauntlet! Your machine now brings you to a graphical login prompt. Skip to Chapter 5 for instructions on how to proceed.

Chapter 4

Installing Other Distributions

. . . .

. . . .

*T*he *Linux distribution* refers to the "packaging" that wraps up the free operating system everyone has come to know as Linux. At the core of all distributions are the same general components: the Linux *kernel* and the GNU utilities. Just as many other commodity products are packaged and delivered differently to accommodate various recipients and applications, Linux is also packaged differently to provide for a variety of target uses.

After our earlier discussions, you should understand that Linux is more than just some newfangled computer program. Linux is a fully equipped workshop of software tools and building materials that can be used to construct any of a wide spectrum of computing solutions. Developing the killer Linux distribution has been the Holy Grail of the Linux community. This ultimate Linux distribution would provide all the support and capability that the preschooler, the rocket scientist, the housewife, and the crotchety old computer science professor would need to harness the power available with GNU/Linux. Although the competition to create the perfect distribution continues, you don't need to do much research to determine which distribution is right for your needs.

In this chapter, I survey two more of the most popular and easiest-to-install distributions. Although I don't have the space to cover every installation in detail, I hope to point out some of the shiny chrome — or notable, characteristics that these distributions have to offer.

Distribution Geography

More than 200 different Linux distributions are now available. Furthermore, a dozen or so new distributions are created each year and rapidly fade, either from a lack of publicity or perhaps because the innovative features they provide simply aren't popular enough to draw a loyal following.

Although all distributions provide the same software and can ultimately produce the same configurations, seeing how various countries tend to gravitate toward one distribution over another is interesting. For example, SuSE is from Germany and has a large contingent of supporters in Europe; TurboLinux is popular in Japan; Red Flag Linux is a favorite in China; Conectiva goes over well in Spanish-speaking countries; and Red Hat, with its new Fedora Core, maintains a high profile in the United States.

Regardless of your choice and curiosity, most Linux distributions have matured to the point where you can be confident that your installation will be successful.

Finding various distributions

Every major distribution has its own Web site. After you're there, hunt around for a download link. Of course, most companies that distribute Linux would rather have you purchase a boxed set of their products.

Pay for free software, you say? Preposterous! Buying free software is not such a bad deal, though, when you think about it. When you purchase a distribution's boxed set (when one is available, you can't do this with Fedora Core), you receive a tremendous value. You not only get some nicely bound books to scribble in and dog-ear (as well as some telephone or online support), but you also help support companies to develop better service and support for your free software.

Okay, okay! Both purchasing your Linux distribution and downloading it for free (in most cases) are legitimate options, both ethically and legally. How often does life come that easily these days? But if you don't have the bandwidth to do all of this downloading, or just get queasy at the thought of burning your own CDs and DVDs, there are some places you can turn in order to pick up the media on the on the cheap without giving yourself a headache.

The site `www.linuxiso.org` offers a ton of distributions for downloading, for example. Armed with your DVD-ROM or CD-ROM burner and a high-speed Internet connection, you can download and burn your own CD Linux distributions all day long, for both yourself and for sharing with friends (again, legally).

However, I want to emphasize that a high-speed Internet connection is necessary because a CD image is typically in the 650MB range. So just imagine how large a DVD image would be! *A DVD contains around seven CDs' worth of information!*

However, if you haven't tangled with broadband yet, don't despair. You can still get your evaluation distribution on CD or DVD, and you can even purchase CDs and DVDs on the cheap off of eBay (and legally too). Just ask a Linux geek: Linux geeks are plentiful these days and can usually hook you up with a CD or two — they're just happy that another computer user has seen the light.

If you don't know any Linux geeks, you may want to look up a local Linux Users Group (LUG). You can find a list of LUGs worldwide, listed by geographic region, on the GLUE (Groups of Linux Users Everywhere) Web site: www.ssc. com:8080/glue/groups. These folks are always happy to help the technologically challenged. These user groups also regularly sponsor events, called *demo days* or *install-fests,* where you can bring your computer and get all the help you need. These events are usually lots of fun for computer enthusiasts — hot and cold running caffeine and enough know-how to do just about anything with a computer.

Putting Linux distributions in perspective

Just so you know that I'm not using any special smoke and mirrors, here's a description of the system I used to evaluate these distributions:

- ✔ Intel Pentium III 450MHz processor (not exactly a fighter jet these days — not even a passenger jet)
- ✔ 258MB RAM
- ✔ 6GB IDE hard drive
- ✔ ATI 128RT video adapter
- ✔ PS2 mouse and keyboard

In both systems I surveyed (Mandrake and SuSE), I elected to use the entire hard disk setup and chose to install the recommended software rather than get fancy with software selections. Essentially, I was after the fewest possible keystrokes, mouse clicks, and brain cycles to get Linux up and running on my system.

Both Linux distributions proved exceedingly simple to install. In the past, Linux installation was fraught with partition pains and cryptic decisions, but those days appear to be gone.

Mandrake

- **Tagline:** Easy for everyone
- **Web site:** www.mandrakelinux.com
- **Version surveyed:** Mandrake 9.2

The Mandrake distribution pioneered the art of easy installation. With Mandrake, you finally get a distribution that can resize your existing Windows partition for dual booting without any effort on your part. That's right! You no longer need to do any of those preinstallation partition-resizing stunts; Mandrake does all of it for you automagically.

Mandrake, created in 1998 with the goal of creating an easy and intuitive installation for everyone, specializes in ease of use for both server and home/office installations. To accomplish this objective, the creators of Mandrake focused on the goal of making an easy transition from your Microsoft Windows or Mac skills to Linux. Having a system that resembles what you're used to working with greatly shortens your Linux learning curve.

If you like strong user communities, Mandrake has many dedicated supporters. Check out the Mandrake User's Club (www.mandrakelinux.com/en/club). For a minimal fee, you can have access to all kinds of cool extras and opportunities.

Installing Mandrake

The installation screen lets you know the status of your installation at all times (see Figure 4-1 for an example). You're shown which tasks have been successfully completed and which tasks are yet to be performed via a progress list on the left side of the screen.

The time it takes to perform the installation depends on the number of packages you choose to install. You have three options for partitioning:

- Use existing partition.
- Erase entire disk.
- Use custom disk partitioning.

I chose the Erase Entire Disk option. I then used the package selection defaults and added the rest of the Workstation options, including all the fun packages: games and multimedia stuff. The package installation ran for about 20 minutes, and the total installation took about half an hour. Just don't forget to go through the various items offered in the Summary page before finishing your install! Otherwise, half of your system won't be configured. Also take the opportunity to test your X configuration before completing the install.

As with most current popular distributions, during the installation you're kept amused by advertising for support services, helpful Web sites, and tips and tricks for making the most of your Linux computer. You're asked to accept a license agreement, essentially just reiterating the terms of the GPL, and you see a reminder to be aware of the license variations that may apply to other software included with the distribution.

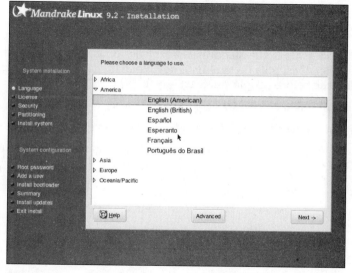

Figure 4-1:
The
Mandrake
installation
screen.

Recognizing some special Mandrake features

One unique option (after Mandrake has asked you for the root password and other user information) is whether you want the computer to log on automatically to one specific user when it boots. If you're the only person who uses this computer and you have no need to provide user authorization, this feature is handy — though not necessarily a good idea since it would let anyone access all of your personal information. Note that even though you don't have to supply a username or password to see your desktop, you're still bound by the security settings in your user profile. The program's not bypassing any type of security; it's simply automating the login process for you.

The last item on the installation checklist is handy, as long as you have a decent Internet connection. The installer connects, if you choose to let it, to an authorized Mandrake download mirror site and fetches all appropriate updates to your existing version of Mandrake. Considering the time lag in any publishing event between the time the product is packaged and the time you install it, this feature can be quite important to maintaining a secure system with the latest software updates.

The first time you boot, you're prompted to register your contact information, which may be automatically passed to Mandrake so the company can keep you up to date with security information, and more. The first login also takes a few moments to establish the initial settings of your desktop, so please be patient.

Here are some random notes about Mandrake:

- ✔ Membership in the Mandrake club gives you access to more than 50,000 applications, plus the ability to download the latest version of Mandrake for free before people can even buy it.
- ✔ The shrink-wrapped sets cost $39 and more.
- ✔ MandrakeUpdate provides easy updates through the Internet.
- ✔ Versions exist for computers that are based on these architectures: Pentium (i586 and higher), Alpha AXP, IA64, PPC, and Sparc.

SuSE

- ✔ **Tagline:** The Linux Experts
- ✔ **Web site:** www.suse.com
- ✔ **Version surveyed:** 8.2 Live Evaluation

The SuSE ("SOO-za") company and Linux distribution were founded in 1992. The distribution is named after a German acronym for *Software und Systementwicklung* (Software and System Development). One SuSE claim to fame is its international support (most major distributions provide a level of support for users around the globe, but some have better language integration for particular groups than others; SuSE understandably excels in the German and otherwise European space), including distributions in these seven languages:

- ✔ Brazilian Portuguese

- ✔ Dutch

- ✔ English

- ✔ French

- ✔ German

- ✔ Italian

- ✔ Portuguese

- ✔ Spanish

As with other widely used distributions, SuSE has service and support offices and staff members around the world to help businesses and industries support their Linux solutions.

Installing SuSE

Of all the latest and greatest distributions claiming to be better than all the rest, SuSE has made the most dramatic leap in providing a truly simple Linux evaluation system. You can download the live evaluation version from the Web site (`www.suse.com/us/private/download/suse_linux`) and burn it to a CD. After you boot from this CD, you're prompted with the typical installation questions: which types of keyboard and mouse you have and which type of video hardware, for example.

Notice that one important and necessary setup step is omitted: how you want to partition and format your hard disk. Omitting such an important step seems goofy, don't you think? Well, the folks at SuSE didn't forget to include this step; rather, it comes in an ingenious feature to keep you from nuking your existing operating system while trying to see what this Linux thing is all about. Intrigued?

If you pay close attention when the CD is initially loading into memory, you may see a message regarding file system detection. Here's the scoop: The CD isn't really installing Linux to your hard drive. If you recall, the title of this distribution states *Evaluation* in its wording. SuSE has drastically reduced the time gap between wanting to use Linux and being able to interact with a usable system, by booting a virtual system that utilizes your computer's memory, any available existing file system volumes, and the directories and files already on the CD.

Another distribution designed to change nothing on your hard drive is Knoppix (www.knoppix.org).

Using the SuSE evaluation version

If you have an operating system on your computer, the SuSE evaluation version detects what your file system is and borrows some space to write several files of its own. The information kept in these files includes usernames, passwords, and hardware information about your computer. By establishing a virtual system, you don't have to make any critical decisions about partitioning and disk formatting that could ultimately trash your existing system.

After you perform this virtual installation, you can simply drop the SuSE 8.2 Evaluation CD in the caddy and boot from it whenever you want to run Linux. Note that you wouldn't want to use this evaluation CD for any serious work with Linux. You would instead want to make a full and permanent installation to your hard drive. You notice quickly that your SuSE Linux evaluation tends to run slowly because accessing a CD-ROM drive takes much longer than accessing the average hard drive. Mouse clicks and keystrokes tend to be sluggish. Just remember that it's intended for only evaluation purposes. The upside is that the distribution is a remarkable one and likely provides the quickest way to see a full Linux graphical workstation in action with the least amount of computer knowledge required.

SuSE has created a powerful, central tool for installation and configuration: *called YaSTst2* (a descendant of YaST, which is an acronym for Yet Another Setup Tool). Following a few prompts and mouse clicks, the SuSE evaluation CD installs in fewer than 15 minutes (see Figure 4-2).

After the evaluation system is booted and running, you see several menu options, including the SuSE tour, a browser link to the SuSE home page, a link to free installation support, and a couple other links that provide additional information for the curious.

Without creating its own file system to store information, SuSE needs a place to store your settings and user accounts. It creates the following four files on the existing file system to maintain the variable information you change in your SuSE evaluation:

- suselive.800: Data for the SuSE Version 8.2 evaluation CD
- suselive.swp: Swap file
- suselive.usr: Users' home directories
- suselive.txt: Descriptions of these files

To remove SuSE from your system, you simply need to delete these files from the root of your current file system. For Windows, they're in your C:\ directory, and for an existing Linux installation, they're at the root mount point (/). These files take up about 120MB of disk space, not exactly small potatoes.

Here are some additional notes about SuSE:

✔ You can still do a permanent SuSE installation to your hard drive, but you need to visit the SuSE Web site (www.suse.com) or a mirror to download the appropriate files and instructions for making a complete installation. The partitioning options are similar to those available with Red Hat Linux.

✔ Several boxed sets are available from SuSE and the company's retail vendors. Prices for these sets start at $39.95 (U.S.).

About SuSE 9.0 Professional

If you want to stick with the defaults, the initial SuSE 9.0 Professional installation is a very simple operation. You answer a few quick questions, glance over a summary screen to make sure that everything will be set as you would like it, and then start the install. Then, after most of the packages are placed on your computer, you fine-tune it all.

This two-part practice is more and more common in modern Linux distributions because it means that first installation segment has a better chance of working without any problems, making it easier for experienced users to then go in and repair if the second portion of the installation and setup process fails.

Not only does this version have a simple installation process, but with SuSE 9.0 Professional, you receive more than 2,000 applications on both CD and DVD, saving you from having to spend an inordinate time tracking down and downloading additional programs.

Chapter 5

Booting and Stopping Linux

● ●

In This Chapter

▶ Understanding what happens when you turn on your Linux machine

▶ Identifying and isolating boot problems

▶ Shutting down safely

● ●

I like work; it fascinates me. I can sit back and look at it for hours.

—Jerome K. Jerome

*I*f you came here from Chapter 3 or 4, you likely just survived the first gauntlet of the Linux world: installing the operating system. I hope that booting for the first time worked well. If it did and you decide that most of this chapter isn't for you, at least skip to the last section in this chapter, "Don't Just Turn Off the Machine!" Otherwise, if you're interested in learning about what your machine does as it boots, read on.

If your Linux installation didn't boot properly, don't panic. Much of this chapter is designed to help you deal with any problems you ran into. Before you curse Linux, remember that installing an operating system is no small task and that, because many technical variables are associated with such an installation, many computer manufacturers insist on performing the task at the factory.

In this chapter, I unravel the mystery of booting a Linux system by taking you through the boot process step-by-step. Although you may encounter all sorts of potential problems during the boot, identifying the culprit is often the most important component of the solution. Seeking an answer to the source of a boot error is much like solving a crime. Discovering the first of many clues always led Mr. Holmes to an *elementary* solution.

So grab your giant magnifying glass and turn your hat around so that you can start sleuthing.

Giving Linux the Boot

Let's face it: As enjoyable as the experience of staring at a dormant computer is, the real fun starts when you turn the computer on. As with any electronic device, opening the electron floodgate is the first step to fun. A computer, however, has much more stuff to do than your toaster oven, for example. Rather than act as a simple heating element, your computer has to check all those gizmos that you (or the manufacturer) plugged into your computer's motherboard. After the initial power-up, the computer performs some simple hardware tests to determine whether those various components are working properly.

Checking all your hardware is just the beginning. Between the time you turn the computer on and the moment the glowing phosphor on your monitor prompts you for a login name, the computer is building itself an empire. If you listen and watch carefully, your computer and monitor show signs of the boot process through bleeps, buzzes, whirring motors, clicks, messages on the monitor, and blinking lights. In this section, I help you identify each stage in the boot process.

Although you have heard the cliché "Rome wasn't built in a day," the boot process goes fairly quickly. This is pretty amazing, considering that the architecture of an operating system makes Rome's look like a stack of cardboard boxes and that each time you power up your computer, it must build its whole operating system in memory. (Remember that an *operating system* is software that resides between your programs and the computer hardware.) Electrons move at the speed of light, of course, which gives the computer an advantage over the Romans — but that's enough jibber-jabber.

Making certain that this operating-system software is installed and running correctly is the purpose of the boot process. This process can be broken into four main steps, which I discuss in the following sections.

Step 1: Power-On Self-Test (POST)

The POST process really has nothing to do with the operating system. Your computer performs this step whether you're running Linux or another operating system. Inside your computer is a chip containing a program that carries out the POST process. The program

- ✔ Checks your computer to ensure that fundamental components are functioning properly.

- ✔ Counts and tests memory.

- ✔ Verifies that no resource conflicts exist for the current adapters and settings, kind of like a traffic cop.

- ✔ Performs certain basic tests to verify whether each system component is working properly. (The set of rules that determine how these components communicate is called the BIOS, or Basic Input-Output System.)

Some symptoms of a failed POST include

- ✔ An unusual series of long and short beeps.

- ✔ Nothing displayed on the monitor.

- ✔ No apparent activity other than the fan on the power supply.

- ✔ A puff of smoke or the pungent smell of burning electrical components seeping out the vent of your computer case.

- ✔ An error message, displayed on the monitor, indicating a hardware failure.

If you encounter any of these problems, you have hardware problems that need to be resolved before you can proceed. Chances are, if your computer was running properly before you began your Linux installation, your computer should be getting through the POST just fine. If not, it's time to question your nephew Mortimer, who was last seen lurking around your computer with a screwdriver.

Step 2: The BIOS passes the baton to the boot loader

After the BIOS gives the okey-dokey with a successful POST, the BIOS locates the first hard drive in your system and reads the first sector of that disk. On that first chunk of disk is a small program called a *boot loader*. The boot loader doesn't know much about anything, except how to load your operating system.

Two boot loader programs understand how to load a Linux operating system: LILO (LInux LOader) and GRUB (GRand Unified Boot loader). LILO has been a tried-and-true boot loader for as long as Linux has been a gleam in a geek's eyeball. GRUB is a newer and much more sophisticated boot loader program than LILO. The current version of Fedora Core allows you to choose your boot loader, but uses GRUB by default.

I recommend that you stick with whatever your chosen distribution uses by default. This boot loader has the best support with the distribution's built-in software.

One common symptom of a missing or corrupt boot loader is a message saying that the operating system could not be found. To get the boot loader working again, reinstall the boot loader to the master boot record of your first drive. I explain later in this chapter how to reload and install the boot loader. You may also see this message if the disk geometry has changed in the BIOS from the time you installed the operating system. If, for some reason, you change the heads, tracks, and sectors setting, the BIOS may not be able to find the first sector on the first drive.

Step 3: The boot loader (GRUB or LILO) loads the system kernel into memory

A *boot loader* is a program that understands how to load a system kernel into memory. A *kernel* is the software at the heart of any operating system and communicates directly with the hardware. For example, when you choose to save a file in your word processor application, your word processor is making a request to the kernel to perform the saving of the file to disk. The loaded kernel acts as the maestro, orchestrating all the components of your computer and delegating resources in a logical and cooperative manner. The boot loader is the red carpet on which the maestro enters.

This list shows some symptoms of a missing, incorrect, or corrupt system kernel:

- The system freezes after the boot loader continues.
- A few dots appear across the top of the monitor and then the system freezes.
- A few messages appear on the screen, and the final message reads `kernel panic`.
- The system reboots automatically after the kernel starts loading.

You know when the kernel is loading because several screens full of kernel messages scroll up your monitor. Note that a kernel error results in a wide variety of symptoms because the loading of the kernel is the first introduction of Linux to your hardware. With a seemingly infinite combination of computer components, making certain that they're compatible can be a challenge — especially with really old or really new hardware. Kernel support for this type of hardware may be minimal or nonexistent.

The remedy for an apparent missing kernel is to correctly tell the boot loader where to find the kernel. Although this task can be relatively easy to do with GRUB, it requires a crowbar and a rescue disk with LILO. Although a description of this task is beyond the scope of this book, you can check out Chapter 2 for other sources of Linux information.

One key step in installing Linux on your computer is the configuration of a boot loader. If your installation is successful, you never need to give another thought to this component. It just runs silently each time you turn on your machine. However, some situations require that you interact with the boot loader program. You may want to start Linux in a mode other than the default, for example, or perhaps you need to pass special information regarding a new adapter you just installed.

The way you invoke the boot loader depends on your Linux distribution. The text displayed on your monitor following the power-on typically provides you with instructions. If you loaded the GRUB boot loader, you can get to an interactive prompt by pressing A.

The GRUB manual is available online at `www.gnu.org/manual/grub-0.92/ grub.html`.

Step 4: Control is handed over to init

Up to this point in the boot process, only the components that run behind the scenes have been loaded. A program named `init` is the common ancestor to all other programs that run while the system is operating. The `init` program is responsible for starting all services and programs. You can see these processes starting as they scroll up the screen with `[OK]` or `[FAILED]` on the right side of the monitor. If you see these lines, you know that your kernel has loaded.

The only problems you may encounter with `init` are services that fail to load, as is indicated by the `[FAILED]` status. Many of these services don't keep you from logging in and using your system. Services usually fail because of misconfigurations or unsupported hardware drivers.

Troubleshooting the Boot

The emergency boot disk you create for your system and a rescue disk are subtly different. A boot disk still requires the capability to access your Linux installation on your hard disk, whereas the rescue disk does not. The rescue boot simulates your hard disk in what is called a *RAM disk,* holding the files entirely in memory. The benefit of this disk is that you can perform necessary system surgery without requiring utilities that are part of the installed system; everything you need is part of the rescue disk.

The DVD — or the first CD — in your Fedora Core distribution doubles as a rescue disk. To enter rescue mode:

1. **When the disk first loads, type** linux rescue **at the boot prompt prompt.**

   This action begins booting the system into maintenance mode.

2. **Select your language and press Enter.**

3. **Select your keyboard type and press Enter.**

   The rescue system does its thing for a while, perhaps a minute or two on a slow system.

4. **When asked if you want to start the network interfaces, answer No unless you know there is something you need to download.**

5. **At the Rescue screen, select one of the three options offered, and "then press Enter.**

   Your three options are

   • Continue: The rescue interface will track down your installed Fedora Core system for you. Make a note of where it says it will *mount* the files so you know which directory contains them.

   • Read-Only: The same as Continue, but you will not be able to make any changes to your hard drive installation.

   • Skip: Don't bother trying to locate the filesystem, just give me a prompt!

   I will assume that you chose Continue.

6. **In the next screen, make a note of the command that the rescue interface gives you to help your file navigation easier, and then press Enter.**

   You now have access to the rescue interface. This is a command-line setup, so if you haven't delved into Linux at the command line yet, it's time to do so! Appendix A has a handy reference of commands you can use for a variety of purposes if you want a good starting place.

If you're having problems with your boot loader, the GRUB configuration file is /etc/grub.conf. Remember, the GRUB manual is available online at www.gnu. org/manual/grub-0.92/grub.html.

Does the process above sound a bit too painful? As useful as rescue mode is, it doesn't take away your need for a boot disk. With a boot disk, if your boot loader gets messed up, you can boot with the special floppy instead. How handy is that?

You had the opportunity to create one during installation. If you have already created a custom boot disk, you're set. Label it clearly and keep it somewhere convenient in case you have problems with the machine. If you're the conservative type, you may also want to keep another version off-site, maybe at home.

If you haven't already created a boot disk, many distributions have special programs or tools available to make custom boot disks for you! The Red Hat tool — and hence, the Fedora Core tool — is mkbootdisk. See your documentation for details.

You shouldn't limit the boot disks you keep on hand to Linux — things can go wrong with Windows and other operating systems too. Each operating system has a method of creating boot disks. Be sure to make one and keep it handy, especially if you start dual- or triple-booting.

In fact, you have the opportunity to create a custom boot disk when you perform the installation. If you've already created a custom boot disk, you're set. Label it clearly and keep it somewhere convenient in case you have problems with the machine. If you're the really conservative type, you may also want to keep another version off-site, maybe at home.

Many distributions have special programs or tools available to make custom boot disks for you! Fedora Core has mkbootdisk, Mandrake has mkbootdisk and drakfloppy (graphical), and SuSE has yast.

Also, a lot of modern Linux distributions allow you to boot with the CD-ROM and choose rescue as your boot option without necessarily needing a custom disk. If you haven't yet made a custom boot disk, refer to Chapter 2 for instructions.

The emergency boot disk that you create for your system and a rescue disk are subtly different. A boot diskette still requires the capability to access your Linux installation on your hard disk whereas the rescue disk does not. The rescue boot simulates a root file system in what is called a RAM disk or entirely in RAM memory. The benefit of this is that you can perform necessary system surgery without requiring shared libraries or utilities that are part of the installed system; everything that you need is part of the rescue disk.

"My system never booted properly"

If you have just installed your system and it isn't booting properly, I suggest that you try reinstalling Linux from your DVD or CDs. If that doesn't work, try booting from the special boot floppy you created during installation. Your computer's hard drives may be misconfigured, a common problem with hand-me-down computers that have obviously been *Frankensteined,* or pieced together. (Symptoms include unnatural bolts jutting from the side of the case or entrails dangling from empty drive bays.). If your computer still doesn't work, you have a hardware incompatibility or configuration issue, and helping you debug it is beyond the scope of this book. I recommend that you find a friend or neighbor who understands PC hardware and can help you diagnose your hardware's health. Another valuable resource is your local Linux Users Group. In most cities, active groups often gather for install-fests, where you can take your computer for some friendly and expert advice.

"I could swear I saw an error while it was booting"

Some boot problems appear as the kernel initializes the system. Lots of information scrolls by as the Linux computer boots, which makes it hard for you to catch specific pieces (especially if your machine is really fast). Fortunately, most Linux distributions keep a log in the form of a text file. This log contains a record of what happened during the boot process. Table 5-1 lists where you can find this information in several popular Linux distributions.

Table 5-1	Log File Locations in Linux Distributions
Distribution	**Log File Locations**
Mandrake	/var/log/boot.log, /var/log/dmesg, /var/log/messages
Fedora Core	/var/log/boot.log, /var/log/dmesg, /var/log/messages
SuSE	/var/log/boot.msg, /var/log/messages

Type **dmesg** at a command prompt and press Enter to get your boot information to come back up at any time. You can also use **dmesg | less** to ensure that it doesn't just scroll past you again. (Note that this command is two commands in one.) If you run dmesg by itself, it scrolls through the initialization messages, probably off the screen. The less command is another command that displays one screen full of messages at a time. The vertical bar that glues these commands together is a *pipe*. See Chapter 11 for more information.

Don't Just Turn Off the Machine!

Even when you're not tapping anything into the keyboard or clicking any buttons, Linux is still running along in the background and doing lots of housekeeping chores. Some of these chores may involve swapping cache and memory data to and from the fixed disk. When you deprive your computer of its power, it may not be able to complete its transaction.

You may need to recondition yourself from the bad habits of older versions of Windows (for example, shutting down the computer when you're done). A Linux computer doesn't need to be turned off after use; rather, you just log out and perhaps turn off your monitor. The next time you want to use the computer, you simply log in rather than go through the arduous boot process.

At times, however, you may want to turn off your Linux machine. Perhaps you need to add new hardware, the power company is turning off the power to your house, or you're going on vacation for a few weeks and just want to save on your electric bill. Regardless of the reason, you must shut down Linux in an orderly manner.

You can use one of these methods to shut down Linux properly:

✔ If you're in the GUI, log out of your account using the main menu's Log Out option, and then click the display manager option that says, strangely enough, Shut Down.

✔ If you have a command prompt open, enter the `halt` command at the shell prompt (#) followed by the root password, and Linux shuts itself down and tells you when it's all right to turn off the machine.

✔ If you have a command prompt open, enter the `reboot` command, and Linux goes through the motions of shutting itself down and then immediately reboots the machine.

✔ If you have a command prompt open, entering `shutdown -r now` is the most traditionally accepted method. The `shutdown` command optionally allows you to send messages to logged-in users and determine how long until the shutdown takes place. Another method is the `poweroff` command, which is just an alias to the previously mentioned `halt` command.

If you do accidentally cut the power to your Linux box, take heart; all is not lost. Chances are that you can reboot your computer and pick up where you left off. However, you may have to pay for your error by waiting during a quick file system check while the machine makes sure that nothing was damaged. This process is similar to the one in Windows, where, if you power off incorrectly, the operating system performs a Scandisk operation.

Chapter 6

Dip in Those Toes

· ·

· ·

A bus station is where a bus stops.

A train station is where a train stops.

On my desk, I have a workstation. . . .

—*Steven Wright*

*O*ne of the great things about Linux is that you can customize the environ-ment to fit your needs and your style. You can choose to use a "standard, out-of-the-box" look, or you can be unique. Whichever way you decide to go, you can always go back to the original settings or choose a different look.

A base, or typical, Linux installation provides you with an elegant and capable system that can certainly give you all the necessary elements you need for work or for fun. However, you may want to explore the various configuration options and tools to mold Linux to your personal preferences and needs.

In this chapter, I provide an overview of common configuration options — from system-level configuration to customizing individual user environments. Modular design, one of the great strengths of Linux, enables you to customize your system in any way you want and for any computing need. Along the way, I point into the dark corners of the file system, where the configuration files lurk. I also introduce you to helpful configuration tools so that you don't have to get your hands dirty with these often cryptic files.

Before I delve into the innards of Linux configuration, I take a brief tour of the various Linux interfaces. Whatever Linux configuration you choose or whatever other applications you use, you find that you can do almost anything, no matter what Linux "looks like." After I have spent some time discussing the faces of Linux, I cover user accounts and the root account a bit. You see why you should create a user account for yourself and for others who use your Linux system.

The Interfaces

Linux has two interface types: the command-line interface and the graphical user interface (GUI). If you use other computer systems, such as Windows or the Macintosh, you're already familiar with a GUI interface. Most Linux distributions include different versions of the GUI, and you can configure all aspects of the graphical interface.

If you have been using computers for many years, you may also be familiar with a command-line interface. The initial release and early development of Linux was all command-line-oriented; GUI interfaces only recently became popular and powerful on Linux. One important deciding factor when choosing between a command-line interface and a GUI is speed. If you plan to compile programs or perform other processor-intensive tasks that tend to slow down your machine, running the GUI will add to the speed problem, especially if you don't have a fast computer. However, if you have a new computer with a gigahertz or two of power, tons of memory, and a nice, big hard drive, speed won't be a problem.

Remember that even with gobs of power and speed, the more applications or services you run at the same time, the more the overall speed of any one of the running applications is reduced.

Readability can also be a big issue when choosing between the GUI and the command prompt. If you have a hard time reading text in those small command-prompt windows from within the GUI, you can make the windows and the font bigger, or you can work directly with the command prompt outside the GUI. In this case, you may or may not want to close the GUI.

The two biggest GUI contenders for Linux are GNOME and KDE. Because Fedora Core 1 comes with this book and this distribution is backed by Red Hat — which has its own versions of GNOME and KDE, called Bluecurve — I cover these versions. Every Linux distribution customizes the interface to some degree. I'm as explicit as possible in pointing out when you're looking at something that's specific to Red Hat (Bluecurve GNOME) and when it's not (just GNOME).

The command line

The Linux command-line interface provides a quick and fast way of entering commands and executing actions. Even if you are mostly a "GUI person," after you get the hang of using the command line, you discover that it's faster to perform some tasks at the command line than with a mouse in the GUI environment. However, if you prefer to use a GUI interface as your working environment, you can easily open a *terminal window,* which is a command-prompt window, to perform your command-driven tasks.

When you installed Fedora Core 1, it gave you a graphical login by default. Other versions may give you the option of choosing a graphical or command-line login. If you don't have a graphical login, when you start up, your screen is mostly black with a few lines of text displaying the Linux distribution, the name of your machine, and a blinking line. To log in to Linux at a command prompt, follow these steps:

1. **Type your account name and press Enter.**

   The system responds with a password prompt.

2. **Enter your password at the prompt and press Enter to send the password to the operating system.**

For security purposes, the password isn't displayed on the screen. After you have successfully logged in to Linux, the command prompt points to your default location, which is your home directory.

Most Linux distributions have quite a flexible command-line interface and allow you to use the arrow keys to move the cursor and the Backspace and Delete keys to remove text. One difference between the Linux command line and other interface command lines, such as in Windows, is that Linux commands are case sensitive. The Linux command line also has an autocompletion feature for commands. If you know the first few characters of a command, type part of the command and press Tab to complete the rest of the command automatically. If you hear a beep when you press Tab, more than one command is available that starts with the same sequence of characters. To see the list of matching commands, press Tab again. To autocomplete the command you want, type a few more characters and press Tab again.

The trick to using the Tab key for autocompletion is to type just enough of the command so that the typed characters are unique to the command.

Most Linux distributions also keep a running history of the most recently used commands. To access the history list, press the up-arrow key on your keyboard. As you continue to press the up-arrow key, you step through the most recently entered commands in reverse chronological order. If you have moved too far back in the command history, use the down-arrow key to reverse direction in the history list. When the command you want is displayed at the command prompt, press Enter to execute the command.

You can modify the Linux command prompt and the entire command-line interface. In Chapter 11, I cover some techniques for customizing the command interface and other aspects of the command-line environment.

GNOME basics

The Bluecurve GNOME interface, which is shown in Figure 6-1, is the GNU Network Object Model Environment. I know — the full name doesn't tell you much, does it? This is a full *desktop environment,* which means that it gives you everything you need for the GUI all-in-one package. You may find it odd to even talk about this subject if you're used to Windows or Macintosh systems because for them, it has always been that way. Things are different under Linux. You can stitch together a Frankensteinian mismatch of many different GUI pieces, if you want.

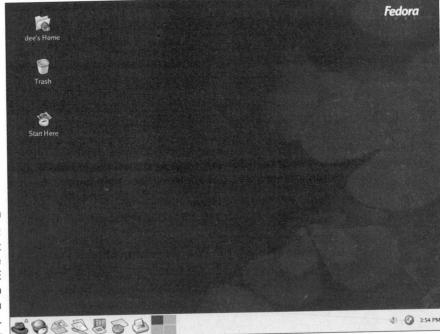

Figure 6-1:
The default
Bluecurve
GNOME
desktop
in Fedora
Core 1.

To find out more about GNOME, visit the main GNOME site, at `www.gnome.org`.

Many folks find that GNOME has an intuitive layout. Take a tour through the menus and see what's available in this environment. Keep in mind that the tools you have on the menus may depend on the type of installation you chose; if what you have is different from what you see in descriptions or the figures, don't panic.

The GNOME desktop environment is essentially broken into three separate parts:

- The menus
- The Panel at the bottom of the screen
- The icons along the top of the background on what's known as the desktop

The menus

The GNOME menus are normally accessible through the button that looks like a big footprint in the lower-left corner of the Panel, but Fedora Core uses a button with a red fedora (hat) in Bluecurve — this is the Red Hat symbol. Either way, this button is called the *Main Menu button*. The main menu that opens after you click the Main Menu button is shown in Figure 6-2.

Figure 6-2: The Bluecurve GNOME main menu in Fedora Core 1.

The contents of this and many of the submenus are slightly different, depending on exactly which programs you installed. Often, the submenus have their own submenus within that offer even more programs.

I describe in Table 6-1 the contents of the submenus on the main menu.

Table 6-1	Bluecurve GNOME Main Menu Contents, Listed in the Order That They Appear
Menu Choice	*What You Find*
Accessories	Small, specific-function GNOME and X programs. Contains a calculator, character map, dictionary, file roller, Pilot/Handspring tool, and text editor.
Games	A collection of games.
Graphics	A variety of graphics programs, including The GIMP.
Internet	A few Internet tools, such as Evolution (e-mail and calendar program), Gaim (instant messenger), and Mozilla (Web browser).
Office	The OpenOffice.org suite of applications (word processing, drawing, and more).
Preferences	Access to programs to control the look and feel of the GNOME and Linux graphical interface.
Programming	Applications and tools used in programming. This menu appears only when Linux is installed with one of the programming-related packages selected.
Sound & Video	Programs, such as a CD player and sound recorder, for working with your computer's multimedia hardware.
System Settings	Many tools for working with your computer's hardware, such as display settings and packages to view and configure the software packages installed on your system.
System Tools	Many tools for managing, monitoring, and updating your system, such as the Internet Configuration Wizard, Red Hat Network, and a System Logs viewer.
Help	The Help Browser, for exploring the electronic documentation included in the Linux distribution.
Home Folder	The Nautilus file manager, defaulting to your home folder's contents.
Run Application	The dialog box you can use to run a specific program without opening a virtual terminal.

Menu Choice	What You Find
Search for Files	The Search Tool window, for locating files in the file system.
Open Recent	A selection of the last files you opened from the file manager.
Lock Screen	The capability to set your machine so that no one can use your GNOME login without entering your password. This feature is a good one if you need to walk away from the computer for a while (but don't want to log out of your account) and other people are around.
Log Out	The capability to exit the GNOME session, shut down, or reboot the machine — if you know the password of the root account.

The Run Program tool

After you choose the Run Program option on the main menu, the Run Program dialog box appears, as shown in Figure 6-3. To run a program using this dialog box, select the application from the Known Applications list and click the Run button.

Figure 6-3:
The Run
Application
dialog box
with Show
List of
Known
Applications
selected.

The Lock Screen tool

If you're not the root user and you choose the Lock Screen option on the main menu, your screen fades to black or your screen saver appears. Then, if anyone moves the mouse or uses your keyboard, a dialog box appears with your login name in it and a password field. You can access this GUI session again by entering your password. Note that if you're logged in as the root user, the Lock Screen option doesn't work.

Notice that I say GUI *session* and not machine. Folks who know how to sidestep out of GNOME (something I discuss in Chapter 12) can start a virtual terminal session and do whatever they want. Don't think of this feature as something that completely secures your machine.

The Log Out tool

After you choose the Log Out option on the main menu, the screen darkens somewhat and the Are You Sure You Want to Log Out? dialog box opens. To use this box, follow these steps:

1. **If you want GNOME to remember which items you have open and return you to its current state after you log back in, make sure that you select the Save Current Setup check box.**

2. **Click Log Out, Shut Down, or Restart the Computer to set the appropriate action into motion, or click Cancel if you don't want to do any of them.**

   These options do the following:

   - **Log Out:** Closes GNOME and returns to the command prompt.

   - **Shut Down:** Shuts the machine down and then off. You must be able to enter the root password (the password for the root user) to use this option.

   - **Restart the Computer:** Shuts down the machine and then brings it back up. You can use this option only if you know the root password.

3. **Click OK to go through with your choice or Cancel if you change your mind.**

The Panel

Along the bottom of your GNOME desktop is a long bar with icons on it. It's *the Panel.* Because this bar is neatly divided into sections, take a look at what's in each section from left to right. On the far left side of the Panel is the GNOME Main Menu button (refer to Figure 6-1), which opens the appropriately named main menu.

As you continue your journey to the right, you run into the standard set of Bluecurve GNOME tools (refer to Figure 6-1). You can reach all these items through the main menu, but they're placed on the Panel so that you can find them quickly and easily:

- ✔ **Mozilla:** The Worldplanet-with-a-mouse icon. It launches the Mozilla Web browser if you're using Red Hat Linux; if not, it's a red dinosaur.

- ✔ **Evolution:** Just to the right of the Mozilla button; launches an e-mail and calendar program.

- ✔ **OpenOffice.org Writer:** Resembles two pieces of paper and opens the OpenOffice.org Writer word processing program.

- **OpenOffice.org Impress:** Opens the OpenOffice.org Impress presentation creation program.

- **OpenOffice.org Calc:** Opens the OpenOffice.org spreadsheet program.

- **Print Manager:** The next button opens the Print Manager, which allows you to check and see which documents are waiting to go to the printer.

- **Workspace Switcher applet:** Allows you to work in four different desktop environments during a single login session. Each desktop environment has the same menus, Panel, and background, but you can run different programs in each of the environments. It's an easy way to remain organized while you're working in multiple programs.

What you see in the segment to the right of the icons depends on the programs you have open. Every program you have open has a task box dedicated to it in this portion of the Panel, called the *status,* or *task,* section. For an example of what you may see, take a look at Figure 6-4.

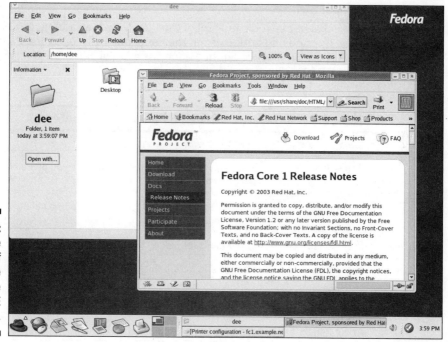

Figure 6-4:
A sample
collection of
tasks on the
Bluecurve
GNOME
Panel.

You can change a program's status in three different ways by using the boxes indicated in Figure 6-4:

✔ If the text in a task box is shaded so that it's harder to see than the others, the program is minimized. You can open the window by clicking the box.

✔ If the text in a task box isn't shaded, but the program's window is hidden by another program, you can click the box of the hidden program to bring this program to the front.

✔ If the text in a task box isn't shaded and the corresponding window is the program you're using, you can minimize the program by double-clicking the unshaded task box.

To the right of the task section is the area where applets show up. You can add small programs to the Panel for a variety of reasons, which I describe how to do in Chapter 12. Notice that the clock applet appears in the applets section by default.

The Panel menu

You can change the look and feel of the Panel, such as adding or deleting applets, by choosing options from the Panel menu. To open the Panel menu, right-click any free space on the Panel. For a list of what this menu's items offer, see Table 6-2.

Table 6-2	GNOME Panel Menu Contents
Menu Choice	*What You Find*
Add to Panel	The applets, menus, and other objects you can add to your main panel
Delete This Panel	The capability to delete a secondary panel but not the main icon panel
Properties	The options for setting this panel's behavior
New Panel	The options for creating new panels that sit on different parts of the screen
Help	The Help browser for GNOME
About Panels	A dialog box with some basic Panel information
About GNOME	A dialog box with some basic GNOME information

For detailed information about using the Panel menu items, see Chapter 12.

The Add to Panel menu

The Add to Panel menu is accessible from the Panel menu (right-click any free space on the Panel). I show you how to add and remove applets in Chapter 12. In Table 6-3, I describe the tiny wonders you may find on the Add to Panel menu.

Table 6-3	GNOME Add to Panel Menu Contents
Menu Choice	**What You Find**
Accessories	Items such as Clock and Weather Report
Actions	Items for various ways of logging out of your account
Amusements	Games and other fun stuff that can reside on the Panel
Internet	Both the Inbox Monitor and Modem Lights utilities
Multimedia	Simple sound utilities
Utility	Miscellaneous applets that don't fit easily on the other menus, such as Keyboard Layout Switcher and Window List
Launcher	A feature that enables you to create a shortcut to an application
Launcher from Menu	An option that enables you to create a shortcut to a menu
Main Menu	The ability to add the main Footprint (or Red Hat fedora) icon to the Panel
Menu Bar	The same as Main Menu but in a different format
Drawer	An extension to the Panel to provide growth in a different direction from the main menu

Playing with desktop icons

What you see on your *desktop* (the main GNOME screen) may be quite different from distribution to distribution. In the case of the Fedora Core 1 setup, a horizontal row of icons lines the top of the screen. The first icon (refer to Figure 6-1), the Home icon, opens the Nautilus browser with your home directory's contents displayed. The next icon is a GNOME shortcut that opens the Start Here window, whereas the Trash icon opens ~/.Trash. A trashcan is a welcome sight to users who accidentally delete files in Linux and need to recover them!

To use the trashcan, drag into it any files you want to delete. Later, if you're sure that you want to be rid of them, you can empty the trash in one of three ways:

✔ Open the trashcan by double-clicking the icon. Then choose to delete the entire contents of the trashcan by choosing File➪Empty Trash

✔ Open the trashcan by double-clicking the icon. Then items by right-clicking the item (or items), choosing Delete from Trash from the pop-up menu, and clicking the Delete button.

✔ Another way to remove items from the trashcan is to delete them manually from ~/.Trash.

KDE basics

KDE, the *K Desktop Environment* — in Bluecurve style — is shown in Figure 6-5. Notice that the main menu button for KDE (in the lower left corner) is a big K.

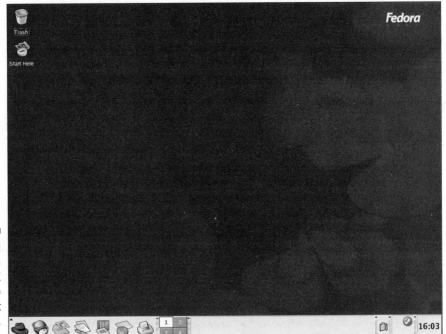

Figure 6-5:
The
Bluecurve K
Desktop
Environment
(KDE).

To find out more about KDE, visit the main KDE Web site, at www.kde.org.

The KDE appearance

As you can see from Figure 6-5, Bluecurve KDE looks pretty familiar, and that's by design. Red Hat is trying to make it easier on folks who swap from one GUI to another. However, if you're using the non-Bluecurve versions, they still look somewhat similar. An item that should be familiar is the Workplace Switcher's set of four boxes (numbered 1 through 4) on the Panel. Almost all Linux GUIs, including GNOME, allow you to have multiple GUI screens — even if the boxes look a bit different.

Suppose that you have lots of clutter on your desktop and want to open even more programs, or maybe you like to have just one item on the desktop at a time. You can have *more than one* desktop! The boxes for the additional screens are numbered 1 through 4 by default. The highlighted box is the one you're in. If you click 2, for example, you suddenly have a totally new desktop. If you have a bunch of programs in 1, they're still there after you go to 2. You just have the equivalent of four screens in one!

The KDE menus

The KDE menus are available through the *Main Menu button,* which looks like a big K (or, in Red Hat, a fedora) in the left corner of the Panel. The contents of the main menu are shown in Figure 6-6. Depending on what applications and options you choose when installing Linux, the contents of the main menu vary.

Because of the variety and number of icons, I briefly cover the contents of the submenus of the main menu in Table 6-4.

Figure 6-6:
The KDE
main menu.

Table 6-4	KDE Main Menu Contents
Menu Choice	*What You Find*
Accessories	A collection of typical desktop applications
Games	An assortment of text and graphical games
Graphics	Various applications for working with graphics
Internet	Web browsers and other Internet applications
Office	The OpenOffice.org collection of word processor, spreadsheet, and other office-oriented applications
Preferences	Tools for configuring the KDE environment
Programming	This menu contains applications and tools used in programming. This menu appears only when Linux is installed with one of the programming-related packages selected
Sound & Video	Programs, such as an audio player and sound recorder, for working with your computer's multimedia hardware
System Settings	Many tools for working with your computer's hardware, such as display settings and packages to view and configure the software packages installed on your system
System Tools	Applications for working with the Linux system
Control Center	A group of small applications to configure the Linux system
Find Files	A shortcut to a search-file application
Help	Access to the online Linux and KDE documentation
Home	A shortcut to the home directory of the account that's logged on when KDE started
Run Command	The ability to launch applications by selecting or typing the name of the application
Lock Screen	The ability to lock the KDE environment to prevent unauthorized access to the graphical environment
Logout	The ability to close the KDE session, shut down, or reboot the machine — if you know the root password

Accounts Great and Small

Linux is a *multiuser* operating system. It allows everyone to have his own account and allows more than one user to log on at the same time. Even if

you're the only person to use this system, you need an account of your own
that isn't the root user's. Multiple accounts are especially fun for experimenting with different user setups.

Avoiding root

The *root user,* also known as the *superuser* or just *root,* has access to anything
and everything on the machine. No matter how you set things up, you can't
keep the root account out of any area. The root user also has access to all
commands and devices. Many Linux beginners figure that they may as well
always use the root account because it's so convenient.

However, for good reasons, you shouldn't use the root account for
everyday use:

   ✔ You don't always need root-level access.

   ✔ Root-level access is as much a curse as it is a blessing. If you mess up as
     a user, you mess up only the stuff in your account. If you mess up as the
     root user, you can wipe out everything — *all the files on the entire Linux
     system!*

     Don't think that can happen to you? Many experienced Linux administra-
     tors tell horror stories about the day they made a fatal typo or weren't
     paying attention to what they were doing when they were logged in as root.

   ✔ If you send e-mail or news posts as root for anything other than serious
     administrative business, people think that you don't know what you're
     doing or are showing off.

   ✔ Root comes with too much temptation. The superuser can read other
     people's e-mail messages and files, which introduces a few tiny ethical
     issues. Many Linux distributions give you a nasty red background when
     you're in the root account so that you don't forget.

Creating user accounts

Fedora Core 1 and most other modern Linux distributions enable you to
create one or more user accounts during the installation and setup process,
so you may have already added some accounts. You can do this task at any
time, however, after your Linux machine is up and running.

The GUI way

Most Linux distributions include a graphical interface application for creating
and managing user accounts. As an example, I go to the main menu and choose
System Settings⇨Users and Groups. Because I'm on my regular user account,
I'm asked to enter the root password before I'm allowed in, which is good for

security, and then the Red Hat User Manager window opens, as shown in Figure 6-7. When the application opens, the user accounts already in your Linux system appear. Figure 6-7 shows an example of the initial Red Hat User Manager window contents for a Fedora Core 1 system.

Figure 6-7:
The opening window of the Red Hat User Manager application.

Most graphical Linux account-management programs work in this same manner.

To create a new user account, follow these steps:

1. Click the Add User button.

The Create New User dialog box opens, as shown in Figure 6-8.

2. Enter a name for your new user in the User Name field.

In Linux, the case of the user account is important, so note the case as you type the information.

The defaults for the fields, such as Login Shell and Home Directory, should work just fine for typical users. You may want to fill in the Full Name field to complete the account information.

New accounts need to have an initial password set. To assign the new account a password, follow these steps:

1. In the Password field, enter the password, and in the Confirm Password field, reenter the same password.

2. Click OK to close the Create New User window, and then click the X in the upper-right corner of the Red Hat User Manager window to close the application.

Passwords are case sensitive!

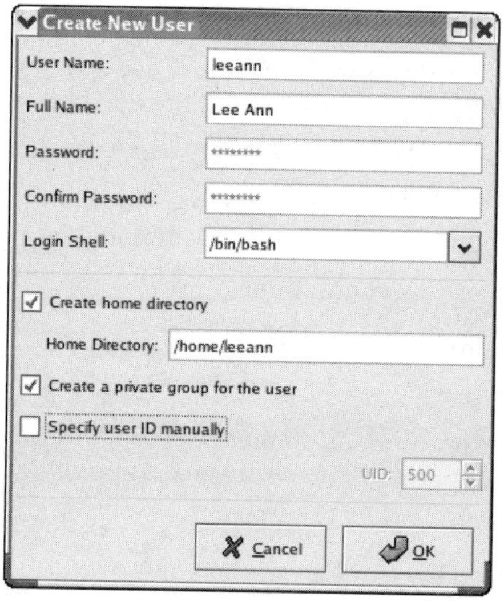

Figure 6-8:
The Create
New User
dialog box
in the Red
Hat User
Manager
application.

See the Mandrake and SuSE configuration sections later in this chapter for where to find things in these distributions.

To create a user account at the command line in any distribution, issue the useradd command. Although not all Linux distributions have the same useradd functionality, they all have the command. The generic version of useradd works very simply. Here are the steps:

1. **Type** su - root **and enter your password with prompted.**

   Doing this lets you temporarily access the root account.

2. **To create an account, type** useradd *accountname*, **where** accountname **is the name of the new account.**

   For example, to create an account for a user called named *test,* you type useradd test.

Now you need to create a password for this account; otherwise, you can't log in to it! Follow these steps:

1. **Type** passwd *accountname*, **where** accountname **is the name of the account that needs the new password.**

   To create a password for a user named *test,* for example, you type passwd test. You then see the following text:

   ```
   Changing password for user test
   New password:
   ```

2. **Type the password for this user.**

If this isn't one of your own accounts, you should use a set of random numbers and letters, such as 5A2g1AG, and tell the account user to change the password to something else when first logging in.

Good passwords consist of the following:

- A combination of numbers, letters, and even punctuation marks
- Uppercase and lowercase characters
- No dictionary words
- Six or more characters
- No family or pet names, friends' names, birthdays, anniversaries, or other items that someone can easily guess about you

3. **Press Enter.**

You see both the following lines or just the last one:

```
BAD PASSWORD: it is based on a dictionary word
Retype new password:
```

If you get warnings about the password, pay attention to them! A password is the first line of defense against people snooping around in your files or, even worse, messing with your machine.

4. **If you see only that last line, retype the password and press Enter, and you're done!**

When the password has been set properly, you see the following line on the screen:

```
passwd: all authentication tokens updated successfully.
```

You have to type the password twice for confirmation. If you mistype one instance, you see

```
Sorry, passwords do not match.
Enter new password:
```

Just try again until you get a working password, and the new user account is ready to go! While you're logged in as root, you can run the passwd *username* command again at any time, to change the password for this user's account later. A user can also change her own account by typing passwd at the command prompt.

5. **Type** exit **to leave the temporary root login.**

Printing

Printing is probably one of the most common tasks performed while working on a computer. Unless you live in a paperless environment, you most likely need to print something (such as a letter, a picture from your digital camera, or an invoice) from time to time. Therefore, you need to set up your Linux system to print. Because printing is such a common task, people often wonder why they have to set up printing. The reason is that many different makes and models of printers are available and many ways exist in which your computer can communicate with a printer. Fortunately, most Linux distributions include tools to step you through the printer configuration process. All you really need to know is the make and model of your printer and how it's connected.

In this section, I describe how to set up a printer with the Red Hat graphical tool. Follow these steps:

1. **To access the printing setup tool , open the Main Menu and then choose System Settings⇨Printing.**

   The Red Hat Printer Configuration window appears, as shown in Figure 6-9. If you're not logged in as root, you're prompted to enter the root password.

2. **To begin setting up your printer, click the New button.**

   The Add a New Print Queue window appears. Click the Forward button to advance to the next step.

3. **In the Queue Name window, type the name you want to assign to this particular printer.**

   If you have multiple printers, add something in the Short description text box to help you tell them apart later. When finished, click the Forward button to advance to the next step. The Queue Type window appears (as shown in Figure 6-10).

Figure 6-9:
The opening window of the Red Hat Printer Configuration tool.

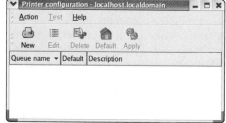

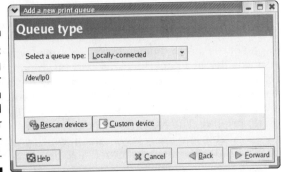

Figure 6-10:
Setting
printer
information
in the Red
Hat Printer
Configura-
tion tool.

4. **In the Queue Type window, select the type of queue you need.**

The queue type corresponds to how the printer is connected. If the printer is directly attached to your Linux system, choose the Local Printer option. If the printer is attached to another computer, select the appropriate operating system, such as Networked Windows (SMB). If the printer is directly connected to the network, choose Networked CUPS (IPP). Depending on what you select, you may have to fill in further information. For example, if you chose CUPS, like I did, you have to enter in the Server text box the IP address assigned to your networked printer.

5. **After you have entered the information, click the Forward button.**

The Printer Model dialog appears, as shown in Figure 6-11.

6. **In the next window (Printer Model), click the Generic (click to select manufacturer) button to choose your printer's manufacturer.**

The selection of models below changes, according to your manufacturer's list.

7. **Select your printer model and then click the Forward button.**

The Finish and Create New Print Queue dialog appears.

Choosing the correct make and model of your printer is important because Linux loads and associates a specific print driver that corresponds to the information you supplied. If the wrong printer make and model are specified, the wrong print *driver* (the software the operating system uses to talk to the printer) is used. The result of this mismatch is usually garbled characters and symbols when you attempt to print to your printer.

8. **In the Finish and Create the New Print Queue window, click Finish to enable your new printer.**

You're offered the opportunity to print a test page. Click Yes. If this page doesn't print properly, make sure that you set the proper make and model for your printer. Some manufacturers make the model numbers similar, and it's easy to get them confused.

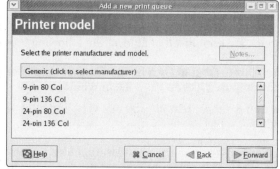

Figure 6-11:
Assigning
your printer
make and
model in the
Printer
Configura-
tion tool.

9. **If the test page comes out great, click Yes when you're asked whether it looks okay. If it doesn't come out at all or it looks garbled, click No.**

   If your answer was is No, you're shown a copy of all of the data that went to the log file when you tried to print. Scroll down to the last few lines to find hints to what your problem is. This situation happened to me once, and it turned out to be a problem with my networking, not a problem with my printer!

10. **The main Red Hat Printer Configuration window appears, and your new printer is listed in the tool.**

    Click the X in the upper-right corner to put away the printer tool. From now on, whenever you want to deal with your printer or print jobs, you can use the Print Manager icon on the panel.

See the configuration sections, "Mandrake tools" and "SuSE tools," later in this chapter, for where to find things in these distributions.

Zen and the Art of Linux Configuration

Anyone can use Linux, but to become a true Linux master requires an intimate knowledge of your system's internal mechanics. This task may seem daunting when you consider that Linux is the sum of many different software subsystems, each written by different programmers with different backgrounds and beliefs regarding problem solving. Fortunately, software developers try to comply with a few universal truths.

One of these truths is that mere mortals must be able to configure a program. You can define a *computer program* as a series of instructions that directs the computer to perform a specified task. You can't change any instructions that are hard-coded into the program (unless, of course, you make the required changes to the source code and recompile the program). As you can imagine, the slightest variance in program use requires the handiwork of a skilled programmer.

File types

Most Linux subsystems are composed of at least the following types of files:

- **Executable file:** This is most likely a binary file that speaks only the language of the computer, like an .exe file in Windows.
- **Configuration file:** A simple text file you can view and alter with your favorite text editor.

Executable files read directives from the configuration files to know how to behave. Because the executable must understand the directives in the configuration files, you must RTFM (Read The Fine Manual) before doing any heavy lifting in a configuration file.

Providing details on the configuration files themselves is beyond the scope of this book. Instead, I cover some handy tools that you probably prefer to use over a text editor any day.

Configuration tools

Linux comes with a number of configuration tools at both the command line and within the GUI environment. In the following sections, I take a look at what comes with the three major distributions covered in this book. If you want to know more, see your distribution's documentation.

Red Hat and Fedora Core tools

The Fedora Core distribution of Linux contains many configuration tools in the graphical and command-line environments. At the command line, Red Hat has made sure that all of their specialized tool names, for convenience, start with the text redhat-config. For example, redhat-config-network lets you work with your network settings (see Figure 6-12).

You can make use of the Red Hat package management program (rpm) to find which configuration tools you have installed by typing the following line at the command line:

```
rpm -qa | grep redhat-config
```

Not all these tools have a command-line component. Some try to open GUI windows after you type their names, and if they can't do so, they don't work.

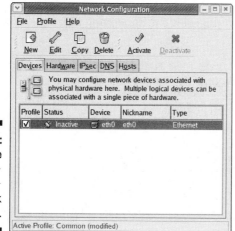

Figure 6-12:
The
redhat-
config-
network
tool.

In the graphical environment, you can find a good portion of the GUI configuration tools by going to Main Menu⇨System Settings. The graphical tools typically present the same options as the command-line tools but with a GUI interface. The rest are available by choosing Main Menu⇨System Tools.

For most configuration tools, both command line and GUI, you need to know the root password for security reasons.

You also find additional tools if you look through the menus. Lots of fun widgets are available in Linux. Explore!

Mandrake tools

Mandrake includes many tools (such as the Mandrake Control Center, HardDrake, and PrinterDrake) to help configure the hardware. HardDrake is used to set up the hard drives and partitions, and PrinterDrake is designed to configure the printing environment. To find these, choose Main Menu⇨ Configuration. You can open up either the entire Mandrake Control Center (as shown in Figure 6-13) or an individual tool by looking through the menus.

SuSE tools

YaST2 (Yet Another Setup Tool) is the name of the main configuration tool for SuSE Linux, as shown in Figure 6-14. YaST2 includes tools to configure and work with the mouse, keyboard, video card, monitor, and desktop. The *desktop,* in this case, refers to the look and feel of the graphical interface you have chosen to work with on SuSE Linux. SaX2 is another configuration tool found on SuSE systems, used for configuring the underlying GUI, such as for the number of colors to show.

To find either of these tools, select the SuSE Main Menu (to the right of the KDE or GNOME Main Menu icon). You can either select the entire YaST2 Control Center (or SaX) from here or choose the YaST2 Modules submenu to look for only one configuration component.

Figure 6-13: The Mandrake Control Center.

Figure 6-14: The SuSE YaST2 Control Center.

Part II
Internet NOW

The 5th Wave   By Rich Tennant

"SINCE WE GOT IT, HE HASN'T MOVED FROM THAT SPOT FOR ELEVEN STRAIGHT DAYS. ODDLY ENOUGH THEY CALL THIS 'GETTING UP AND RUNNING' ON THE INTERNET."

In this part . . .

In this part, you make the necessary mental and physical connections to hook up your Linux machine to the Internet, including configuring telephone dialup to an Internet Service Provider (ISP). You also learn how to work with the all-essential protocol that makes the Internet possible — namely, TCP/IP, otherwise known as the Transmission Control Protocol/Internet Protocol protocol suite. (Say THAT three times in a hurry!) Next, you set up your Web browser, e-mail client, and newsreader software so that you can surf the Web, send and receive e-mail, and access newsgroups. Armed with the facilities you install in this part, you enable yourself to extend and customize your Linux system to your heart's content. You also learn how to travel on the electronic highways and byways of the Internet to get things done!

Chapter 7

Connecting to the Internet

● ●

In This Chapter

▶ Understanding common Internet connection methods

▶ Setting up your Internet connection

▶ Connecting to your Internet Service Provider (ISP)

▶ Understanding enough TCP/IP to be dangerous

● ●

*Y*ou may already be connected to the Internet if you're on a machine that's connected to a LAN and configured the networking during installation. To test this, open up a Web browser and try to go to an outside Web site (like `www.redhat.com`). If it works, you're up! No need for this chapter. Otherwise, read on.

In this chapter, I slash a trail through the networking jungle and help you link your Linux machine to the rest of the world. However you choose to connect, configuring your Linux computer to connect to the Internet has never been easier. Red Hat provides you with a graphical tool to help you configure your Internet connection in a snap. In this chapter, I explain how to configure your modem, and after you're connected, I show you how to mingle with the Linux community by using a few cool tools.

But, first, a little background.

Internet Connectivity 101

Every Internet surfer is on a quest to find open lanes on the information super-highway. Telephone, cable, and satellite television companies are now jockey-ing for a strategic position to fill your future Internet-connection needs. In the following list, I briefly examine a few popular Linux-friendly options that may be available to you:

- **Cable modems:** Many cable television companies have expanded their product lines to include Internet access over their cable infrastructure. When you subscribe to a cable Internet service, the installation technician provides you with a special device, called a *cable modem*, along with a standard network adapter. The technician then installs the network adapter into your computer and connects the cable modem. If cable Internet connectivity is available in your area, it provides the best cost-to-bandwidth ratio now available. In other words, whereas the service is likely to cost you more than a dial-up connection, a cable connection can reach speeds 50 times faster than a 56 Kbps modem dial-up account and typically costs only about twice as much.

  You may have to configure your Linux machine to work with cable Internet service on your own. Most cable companies don't yet provide technical support for Linux. The following Web page provides a document that fills you in on all the details:

  ```
  www.linuxdoc.org/HOWTO/Cable-Modem/index.html
  ```

- **Integrated Services Digital Network (ISDN):** Not too long ago, ISDN was one of the only residential high-speed options. It appeared when 28 Kbps was about all that you could milk from the copper strands that connected your telephone to the telephone company. ISDN is still available and promises a steady 128 Kbps — as long as you're within 3.4 miles of the telephone company's central office. You need two special devices to use ISDN: a terminal adapter (an ISDN modem) and a network adapter. The Red Hat Network Configuration tool includes support for ISDN setups.

- **Digital Subscriber Line (DSL):** DSL works much like ISDN in that it carries data to your telephone jack in a digital format. DSL is popular because it provides a faster connection with lower installation and service costs than ISDN, and it utilizes the existing copper telephone wiring provided by your telephone company. (DSL costs about the same as a cable modem connection.) A DSL connection requires additional communication hardware, which your Internet Service Provider (ISP) should provide. The Red Hat Network Configuration tool includes support for DSL.

  Note that several variants of DSL exist:

  - IDSL (over an IDSN line)
  - Symmetric Digital Subscriber Line (SDSL)
  - Asymmetric Digital Subscriber Line (ADSL)
  - Generic DSL (XDSL)

Typical residential connection service ranges from 128 Kbps to 1.0 Mbps. For an overview of DSL, visit the following Web page:

```
www.linuxdoc.org/HOWTO/DSL-HOWTO/index.html
```

✔ **Dial-up modems:** The dial-up modem is still widely used. It translates the digital signal from the computer into an analog signal required for transmission from the wall jack to the telephone company. Because the modem utilizes existing voice telephone service, you don't need any special setup beyond subscribing to an ISP. Red Hat includes support for modem setup.

Because most people who aren't hooked up through a network are connected via either DSL or dial-up modems, I had to decide which one to cover. Throughout the rest of this chapter, I guide you step-by-step through setting up your Linux workstation to connect to the Internet by using a dial-up modem. Like any good guide through a deep, dark forest, I point out the slippery parts of the trail as I go. If you're using DSL, the process is similar.

Creating Your Internet-O-Matic

Sara, could you connect me with Goober down at the fillin' station?

—Andy Griffith

If only it were that simple. Fortunately, the good folks at Red Hat have provided a few tools that reduce the complexity of networking with Linux. It's not that networking has changed, but rather that many of its details have been abstracted so that you just have to click here and press a key there. Not long ago, configuring dial-up networking on a Linux machine was nothing short of debugging a defective Rube Goldberg contraption.

Then came broadband

Before I focus on dial-up modem configuration, a few words regarding the broadband options (DSL and cable) are in order. The word *broadband* has a technical definition, but I just use it to mean high-speed Internet access. Although a high-speed dial-up modem can typically transmit information at speeds only up to 56 kilobits (thousand bits) per second, broadband connections can reach 50 times that speed. Nowadays, the Web contains lots of images and multimedia elements, and enjoying these features through a dial-up line and a 56 kbps modem is similar to drinking a cold glass of water with an eyedropper when you're dying of thirst.

Beware of devices posing as modems

I try to save you from some frustration — and your computer from the rounded end of your ball-peen hammer. Many Linux newbies have become irritated by not being able to communicate with their internal modems. "After all," the newbie reasons, "the same hardware worked when I was running Microsoft Windows."

Well, here's the story: Several years ago, hardware manufacturers developed a device, called a *software modem,* in an effort to reduce hardware costs. The idea was to trim some responsibility from the modem and relegate these tasks to the CPU through the operating system. The result was an inexpensive interface card that routed signals to proprietary software that operated only under Microsoft Windows. In short, these so-called modems, also known as *WinModems,* aren't really modems, but, rather, are telephone cable interfaces to Windows.

The following list shows methods you can use to determine whether you have a software modem:

✔ The model number has a HCF-, HSP-, or HSF- in front of it.

✔ The packaging refers to the device as a WinModem or designates that it works with only Windows.

✔ Windows recognizes your modem, but Linux doesn't.

In short, if you determine that you have a software modem, Linux simply doesn't work with it. For the adventurous out there, the LinModem project (linmodems.org) has successfully written Linux drivers to work with a few of these software modems. I encourage you to become involved in this type of project, if you're so moved. These explorers drive the wonderful world of *freedom* software, which Linux is a prominent part of.

The bummer in all this is that, although you probably saved a few bucks by buying a machine with a software modem, you most likely need a real modem to use with Linux (unless you have a LinModem).

I strongly advise searching the Linux modem-compatibility list to determine whether your modem is a good buddy with Linux. You can use the money you ultimately save in headache medicine to buy a real modem.

Don't let high-speed providers discourage you from using Linux with their services. Just because they don't support Linux directly doesn't mean that the technology doesn't work with Linux. TCP/IP (the set of traffic rules for the Internet) was developed for the Unix operating system, from which Linux descends. The irony is that most broadband support provided by ISPs is for Windows, which was never intended for use on a network, much less TCP/IP. The protocol-to-network support for Windows was added to the software much later.

If you have the luxury of dual-booting to Windows, your ISP can help you install your broadband connection, and then you can tinker with getting Linux connected as you have the time and inclination. I point you to some sites that can help you configure your broadband connection in the section "Internet Connectivity 101," earlier in this chapter.

Connecting the hardware

Before you get too comfortable in your chair, you must physically check some items that may require you to do some low-level maneuvers (such as crawling under your desk):

- **External modem:** If you have an external modem (one that's independent of your computer case), you need to verify that

    - A cable is securely connected from the modem to the serial port on the computer.

    - The modem is powered on. (External modems have their own power supply.)

    - One end of a telephone cable is plugged into the wall jack and the opposite end is plugged into the modem.

- **Internal modem:** If you have an internal modem, you need to verify that

    - The modem is *not* a software modem. See the sidebar, "Beware of devices posing as modems," if you're not sure what a software modem is or whether you have one.

    - One end of a telephone cable is plugged into the wall jack and the opposite end is plugged into the phone plug on the back of your computer.

Okay, now you can climb back into your chair.

If you determine that your modem is, in fact, a software modem, I recommend that you get an external modem. You don't have to touch your existing internal modem (Linux conveniently ignores it); just plug the external modem into an available serial port and step through the external modem checklist in this section. If you're still unsure of the identity of your internal modem, go ahead with the configuration and cross your fingers. If it works, great! If not, no harm done, and you can start shopping for a good external modem.

Selecting an Internet Service Provider (ISP)

Because of the recent meteoric rise in the popularity of Linux, many ISPs are training their support staff in the ways of Linux. If you already have a dial-up service, give one of them a call to let them know of your Linux pursuits. Chances are, that person already has information pertinent to Linux subscribers and can provide you with that information. If you're shopping for a new ISP, read on for some practical selection advice.

Some ISPs provide their own proprietary software that you must install on your PC to connect to the Internet. The software they provide is likely to run only on Windows. Several free dial-up services don't work with Linux because of this fact. The proprietary software meddles with the operating system to ensure that banner advertising isn't hidden or that you stay dialed in for only a specified duration.

If you're shopping around for an ISP, consider these questions:

- **Can you get local dial-up numbers across the country and around the world?** If you travel often and need Internet access from different cities, this service is a handy money saver.

- **Does it provide technical support for Linux?** If you're planning on running Linux, this consideration is an important one.

- **Can you get a recommendation?** Ask a friend. An ISP's best friend is an endorsement from a satisfied customer.

- **Will you have trouble dialing in?** Although a subscriber-to-line ratio of 7-to-1 (an average of seven or fewer subscribers per line) or better isn't an entirely accurate measure, it should help you avoid frequent busy signals. Hey, it doesn't hurt to ask.

Information you need from your ISP

Most reputable ISPs provide you with a customer information sheet after you sign up for its services. This sheet should include the following information at the minimum:

- Local telephone dial-in numbers
- User login name
- User login password
- E-mail address
- E-mail outbound host or Simple Mail Transport Protocol (SMTP) server
- E-mail inbound host or Post Office Protocol (POP) server
- News host

With this information, you can establish an Internet connection by using your Linux system.

Configuring your dial-up service

If you haven't already done so, start your computer and log in to your GUI desktop. You shouldn't be logged in as the root user, but you *do* need to know the root password.

With your ISP information in hand and a glowing monitor in front of you, follow these steps to configure your dial-up connection to the Internet:

1. **From the GUI desktop, click the Main Menu button on the Panel and then choose System Settings⇨Network.**

   In default GNOME and KDE setups, the Main Menu button in the lower-left corner is a footprint in GNOME or a big K in KDE. If you installed Fedora Core 1, the Main Menu button is the Red Hat fedora icon in both GNOME and KDE.

2. **Enter your root password in the dialog box, if necessary.**

   If you're logged in as a regular user (not root), you're prompted to enter the root password.

   The Network Configuration dialog box should open (refer to Figure 6-12, in Chapter 6). The entries listed in the dialog box depend on whether you have an existing network adapter that was established during your installation. The remaining steps assume that you don't now show a modem entry.

3. **In the Network Configuration dialog box, click the New button.**

   The Select Device Type dialog box appears, as shown in Figure 7-1.

4. **Select Modem Connection from the Device Type list box and then click the Forward button.**

   Take a moment to make a mental note of the other options listed. This area is also where you perform your configuration for an ISDN, xDSL, or Ethernet network connection. Each network option requires distinct configuration parameters, which your ISP should supply.

   After you click Forward, the tool probes for your modem. If your modem could not be found, the Select Modem dialog may appear, as shown in Figure 7-2. If you do encounter this dialog, make your selections and then choose Forward again.

   If you know your modem is on COM1 or COM2 in Windows, translating this to Linux isn't hard: You just need to subtract 1. So, it's ttyS0 for COM1 and ttyS1 for COM2.

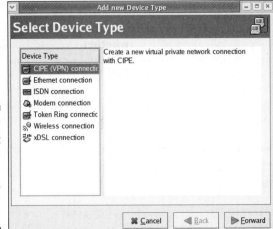

Figure 7-1:
The Select
Device Type
dialog box in
the Network
configura-
tion tool.

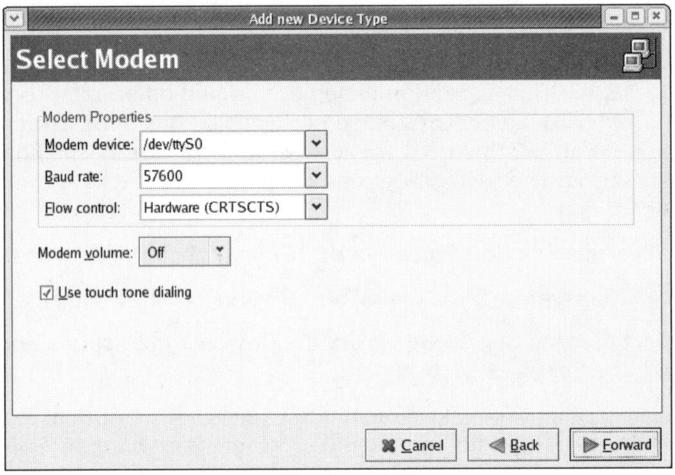

Figure 7-2:
The Select
Modem
dialog box in
the Network
configura-
tion tool.

5. Enter your ISP information and then click Forward.

In the Select Provider dialog, shown in Figure 7-3, the default list of countries that your ISP might be from is pretty limited. Unless you live in one
of these regions, you can safely ignore this list. When you select one of
these countries, the dialing entries are completed for you. If you don't
pick one of these countries, enter the information your ISP provides. Be
sure to add any dialing prefix you may require in order to obtain an outside line. (For example, if you have a PBX system with a 9 prefix, be sure
to enter the 9.) Click the Forward button when you're done.

After you click Forward, the IP Settings dialog box appears as shown in Figure 7-4.

6. **In the IP Settings dialog box, indicate whether your modem needs to obtain its IP addressing information from the ISP or whether you need to tell it what its IP data is, and then click Forward to continue.**

Your ISP should have given you which of these you require. If you have to enter the data manually, do so now. After you click Forward, the Create Dialup Connection dialog box appears.

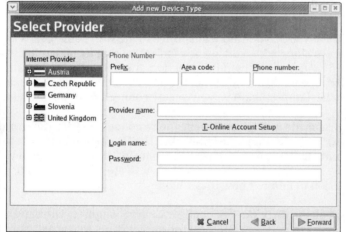

Figure 7-3:
The Select
Provider
dialog box in
the Network
configura-
tion tool.

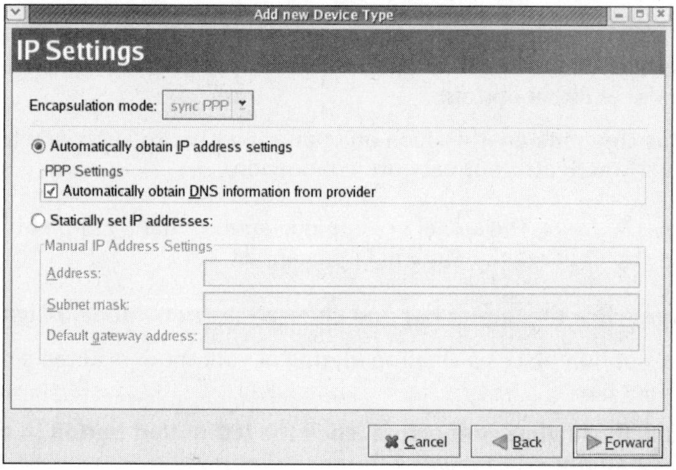

Figure 7-4:
The IP
Settings
dialog box in
the Network
configura-
tion tool.

7. **Click the Apply button to confirm your selection.**

   At this point, your modem and dial-up connection is complete. You probably received much more information from your ISP than what you just entered (username, password, and connection telephone number). Settings such as e-mail and news servers are applied in the various applications to which they pertain, such as Mozilla.

   Look at the Network Configuration dialog box again. It should now list a device named ppp0 (PPP stands for *Point-to-Point Protocol*) along with an Inactive status.

8. **To connect to the Internet, simply highlight the ppp0 entry you just created and click the Activate button.**

   With any luck, your modem springs to life with some beeps and then buzzes along with a dialog box indicating that a connection is being made. After a successful connection, the Network Configuration dialog box appears again; this time, the Status column of the ppp0 device reads Active. Congratulations; you're now connected to the Internet!

Whew, you made it. If all went well, you're connected with the worldwide Linux party! To disconnect, simply click the Deactivate button in the Network Configuration dialog box. Your settings remain; the next time you want to connect, just open this dialog box and click Activate. If all is not well, skip to the next section to find out how to get help.

Now that all the dirty work of configuration is complete, you can add a simple Dialer applet to your GNOME desktop applet panel to use as a shortcut:

1. **From the GUI desktop, click the Main Menu button and select System Settings.**

2. **Right-click the Network option and choose the Add This Launcher to Panel menu option.**

   This step puts another icon on your applet bar to allow you to conveniently activate your network connection.

As long as we're on the subject of applets, another handy applet to include on your applet bar is the Modem Lights applet:

1. **Right-click the applet bar and choose Internet⇨Modem Lights.**

   This option places a small rendering of your modem activity on the applet bar.

2. **To activate your connection, click the left dotted button in the Modem Light applet.**

   A dialog box appears, asking whether you want to connect.

3. Click the Yes button, and your modem springs to life.

The modem applet displays a green (rather than black) dot when you're connected, and send/receive statistics appear as you start surfing the Internet. When you're ready to disconnect, use the same button.

It's all fun and games until something doesn't work

In a perfect world, the dial-up configuration steps in the preceding section would work 100 percent of the time. Red Hat has truly hidden all the mystery that has traditionally surrounded dial-up networking. Unfortunately, in many situations (mostly related to modems and hardware), a simplified configuration doesn't work. If you cannot connect to the Internet after you have followed these steps, I recommend that you access a copy of the Modem-HOWTO from the Linux Documentation Project (`www.tldp.org`). This written treatment is updated often and includes a wealth of information and reference resources for configuring your modem on a Linux computer.

Turning to TCP/IP

It's a good thing.

—*Martha Stewart*

You can make it all the way to the Internet without one single mention of Internet Protocol (IP) numbers. This ease in configuration demonstrates the progress that renders Linux easier to use. However, TCP/IP is still humming away in the background, carrying digital information for you in all its complex and robust glory.

Transmission Control Protocol/Internet Protocol (TCP/IP) is a set of rules for moving information from one point in a network to another. These TCP/IP delivery rules are similar to the methods that a parcel service, such as UPS, uses to move packages. Each package contains a label with a destination, return address, and content that is important to the sender or receiver. Using this address, the package carrier can make a decision about how to route the package. Each routing decision shuttles the package closer to its intended destination until it arrives. The network component that provides this routing information is known as, strangely enough, a *router*.

Every computer on a TCP/IP network requires a distinct IP number. You can use one of two methods — static or dynamic — to assign this number to your computer:

- ✔ **Static:** You assign a static IP number when you configure the machine, and the number remains the same until you change it. Servers and other computers that are required to continually service the network usually have static IP numbers. (Seasoned networking professionals usually administer static IPs.)

- ✔ **Dynamic:** Typically, dial-up Internet users or workstations that aren't continuously logged in to the network use dynamic IP numbers. If your computer is configured to obtain an IP number dynamically, the computer requests an IP number from another network host computer configured as a *DHCP server.* The Dynamic Host Configuration Protocol (DHCP) server has authority for a range of IP numbers that it can assign as needed to trusted computers. The DHCP server also provides other handy services, such as dishing out DNS, gateway, and routing information that you're otherwise required to know and stitching all this information into those cryptic and sometimes elusive configuration files.

You can be thankful that the dial-up networking tools provided with your Red Hat distribution, along with services your ISP provides, perform these geeky functions for you transparently.

The IP number looks like this to your computer (remember that the computer stores information in the form of *ones* and *zeroes*):

```
11010001100101001111010101100100
```

Ouch — do your eyes hurt? Is this any better?

```
11010001.10010100.11110101.01100100
```

Hardly. What about this?

```
209.148.245.100
```

The last example is a decimal representation of the first binary number example. It's known as an IP number, and every computer on the Internet requires a unique one.

The *IP number* is the mailing address for your information packages. Granted, the casual cybestrian doesn't keep a list of friends' IP numbers. Instead, you use more familiar names. The Internet uses an ingenious method, called the *Domain Name System (DNS),* to resolve names into IP numbers.

A *domain registrar* is a company that provides the authority for the popular, top-level domains of `.com`, `.org`, and `.net`. By registering a unique domain with one of these designated organizations, you can become the authority for your own network domain. Linux also comes with a free software package, called BIND, that provides the tools you need to become part of the Domain Name System.

Putting IP to work on your network

The `ping` command is akin to a submarine using sonar to detect other objects in the ocean. Sonar sends out a `ping` signal, which reflects off a hard surface. By measuring the amount of time between sending the `ping` and the `ping`'s return, the submarine's engineer can determine whether an object is out there and how far from the submarine that object is.

The `ping` command in Linux provides information similar to what sonar provides. If you consider the Internet to be your ocean, you can determine, by pinging, what other network computers exist and also how long it takes for your `ping` to return.

Another fun command is `traceroute`, which allows you to see all the routing points your package touches on its way to a destination. Simply type the command **traceroute *hostname***. The hostname can be either a valid DNS name or IP address of a computer on the network. After a few moments, you receive a list of all computers between you and the designated hostname.

The `ping` and `traceroute` utilities determine whether your network connection is working. Whereas `ping` reveals whether another network host is now available, `traceroute` provides a trail to that host. For example, if your Web browser can't seem to find a particular site, you can jump out to a shell prompt and run a `traceroute` command to the site to determine where the hold-up is.

Latency, or the amount of time it takes for a signal to travel, on the Internet has little to do with physical distance. Rather, factors such as network traffic, bandwidth, and network hardware all contribute to a slow latency. These factors determine whether a `ping` to your neighbor's computer takes longer than pinging a host at the South Pole.

Checking whether an address exists with ping

To use the `ping` command in Linux, you must have an object in mind that you want to `ping`, which is usually another host computer that's connected to the network. You can `ping` an IP number of another host or a hostname if your DNS is working correctly.

For example, you can ping the Yahoo! site. Jump to a command prompt and type the following command:

```
ping www.yahoo.com
```

Press Ctrl+C to break the `ping`; otherwise, your machine continues to `ping` the target.

The `ping` line, as shown in Figure 7-5, provides information about what the `ping` is doing. If the host is unreachable, a message indicates so. If the host is located, you receive a line that provides some useful data — namely, the last item on the line: `time=`. This number is the time, in milliseconds (ms), that it takes for the signal from your computer to get to the destination computer and return. Lower numbers are better. For an Ethernet, a `ping` time of 1 ms to 3 ms is an acceptable response time from another machine on the same local net (that is, the gateway). For dial-up connections, expect somewhere around 150 ms. When you start seeing `ping` times climbing to 900 ms or higher, some serious network traffic likely sits between you and your target host.

The `ping` command lets you know immediately whether a network is between you and the host that manages the Yahoo! Web site. Although these widely varying times may indicate a network problem, `ping` doesn't provide much more information than that. To flush out more of the problem, you can use the `traceroute` command.

Tracking the path of your packets with traceroute

The `traceroute` utility enables you to map the route that your IP packets are taking from your computer to their intended destination. Just because you may not be able to visit your favorite Web site doesn't mean that the Web site is down. It may simply mean that a link along your route is down. A significant router or conduit *going down* (basically, crashing) is like traffic congestion on your morning commute because of a pile-up.

To use `traceroute`, you need to know of a destination. Try Yahoo.com! again. Open the main menu and then choose System Tools⇨Traceroute (see Figure 7-6). Type **yahoo.com** in the Hostname field and press Enter.

```
evan@localhost:~
File  Edit  View  Terminal  Go  Help
[evan@localhost evan]$ ping yahoo.com
PING yahoo.com (66.218.71.198) from 192.168.1.101 : 56(84) bytes of data.
64 bytes from w1.rc.vip.scd.yahoo.com (66.218.71.198): icmp_seq=1 ttl=247 time=60.2 ms
64 bytes from w1.rc.vip.scd.yahoo.com (66.218.71.198): icmp_seq=2 ttl=247 time=68.3 ms
64 bytes from w1.rc.vip.scd.yahoo.com (66.218.71.198): icmp_seq=3 ttl=247 time=103 ms
64 bytes from w1.rc.vip.scd.yahoo.com (66.218.71.198): icmp_seq=4 ttl=247 time=144 ms
64 bytes from w1.rc.vip.scd.yahoo.com (66.218.71.198): icmp_seq=5 ttl=247 time=123 ms
64 bytes from w1.rc.vip.scd.yahoo.com (66.218.71.198): icmp_seq=6 ttl=247 time=81.7 ms
64 bytes from w1.rc.vip.scd.yahoo.com (66.218.71.198): icmp_seq=7 ttl=247 time=225 ms
64 bytes from w1.rc.vip.scd.yahoo.com (66.218.71.198): icmp_seq=8 ttl=247 time=63.7 ms
64 bytes from w1.rc.vip.scd.yahoo.com (66.218.71.198): icmp_seq=9 ttl=247 time=165 ms
64 bytes from w1.rc.vip.scd.yahoo.com (66.218.71.198): icmp_seq=10 ttl=247 time=81.2 ms

--- yahoo.com ping statistics ---
10 packets transmitted, 10 received, 0% loss, time 9024ms
rtt min/avg/max/mdev = 60.291/111.797/225.992/50.873 ms
[evan@localhost evan]$
```

Figure 7-5: Sample results of the `ping` command.

```
My traceroute [v0.49]
Hostname  yahoo.com                              1.00   Pause  Restart  Quit
```

Hostname	Loss	Rcv	Snt	Last	Best	Avg	Worst
192.168.0.1	0%	11	11	1	1	1	2
10.36.0.1	0%	11	11	12	9	26	140
srp4-0.austtxc-rtr1.austin.rr.com	0%	11	11	11	8	16	39
srp0-0.austtxrdc-rtr2.austin.rr.com	0%	11	11	9	9	25	84
srp4-0.austtxrdc-rtr4.texas.rr.com	0%	10	10	12	8	18	31
pop2-hou-P6-1.atdn.net	0%	10	10	39	15	26	41
bb1-hou-P0-3.atdn.net	10%	9	10	52	15	25	52
bb1-dal-P6-0.atdn.net	0%	10	10	26	23	38	132
pop2-dal-P0-0.atdn.net	0%	10	10	54	20	32	54
iar3-so-2-1-0.Dallas.cw.net	0%	10	10	30	21	30	54
agr1-loopback.Dallas.cw.net	0%	10	10	46	24	33	48
dcr1-so-6-0-0.Dallas.cw.net	0%	10	10	54	23	29	54
dcr1-loopback.Washington.cw.net	20%	8	10	57	57	68	105
bhr1-pos-10-0.Sterling1dc2.cw.net	0%	10	10	79	56	69	111
csr03-ve240.stng01.exodus.net	0%	10	10	80	56	71	87
216.35.210.122	0%	10	10	58	57	68	94
w1.rc.vip.dcx.yahoo.com	0%	10	10	61	56	64	79

Figure 7-6: Results of the `trace-route` utility.

Each line of your `traceroute` results represents a *hop*. This command helps illustrate the concept I explain earlier in this chapter, of packets being *routed*, or handed off to carriers along the way to move your package closer to its destination. Each hop is a physical machine that reads your packet address and forwards it. You also notice a latency time associated with each hop. You can identify heavy network congestion, or a weak router along the way, by identifying the relatively larger numbers in the list.

Sometimes, especially when you're troubleshooting, the reason that you can't access your intended Web site, you perform a `traceroute` that times out somewhere along the way. This situation usually indicates that a "traffic accident" has occurred somewhere along the information superhighway. Give it a few minutes and try again. TCP/IP is an amazingly robust networking protocol that was designed to reroute packets efficiently in the event of a failed network segment.

If, as you get close to your own network, your `traceroute` command abruptly stops and doesn't tell you anything, a *firewall* may be in the way, blocking that information from being shared.

Chapter 8

Surfing the Web and Managing E-Mail

Give a man a fish and you feed him for a day; teach him to use the Net, and he won't bother you for weeks.

—Anonymous

Assuming that your Internet connection is configured (which I discuss in Chapter 7), you can now get on with doing something interesting on the Internet. In this chapter, I introduce you to a few useful communication utilities that provide you with the tools of the Internet trade.

Many people attribute the explosive growth of the Internet to the graphical Web browser. The Internet has been around for much longer than the invention of the browser. It's just that most of the work done on the Internet was in plain old text, which held little attraction for those of us who are more spatially oriented (that is, we preferred picture books as young children).

Several graphical Web browsers are available for Linux. The most popular of these browsers is Mozilla, which does far more than just display Web pages. You can also use Mozilla to manage your e-mail and newsgroup subscriptions. Mozilla is also the browser included with Fedora Core 1, which is on the CDs that come with this book.

A multitude of e-mail programs is available for Linux users. Fedora Core 1 has included Ximian Evolution as the default in its distribution, and you may agree that Evolution is a worthwhile choice.

Configuring Mozilla

You can start surfing right now, if you want. However, you may want to take a moment to customize Mozilla with preferences, such as a home Web site, font sizes, colors, and many other options.

Mozilla provides an entire menu of Help documents. To access the online Help options, click the Help menu on the menu bar at the top of the Mozilla screen.

The following steps introduce you to the Preferences dialog box, where all the Mozilla configuration parameters are stored:

1. **Start Mozilla by clicking the planet or dinosaur icon on your Panel.**

   Mozilla starts after a moment. Be patient; Mozilla is a large program, and it usually takes a few seconds to load from the disk into memory.

2. **Choose Edit⇨Preferences.**

   The Preferences window appears, as shown in Figure 8-1.

Notice that many configuration options are available. Throughout the rest of this chapter, I guide you through configuring a few of the essential settings. I encourage you to explore the many options available along the way.

Use the left pane of the Preferences window to access the various preferences categories. You can expand any of the major categories by clicking the small plus sign (+) next to them, and contract them again by clicking the small minus sign (-). Each of the categories also has its own menu, so don't forget to look at those too. If you get tired of reading through menus, just click OK or Cancel at any time to close the Preferences dialog box and get back to surfing.

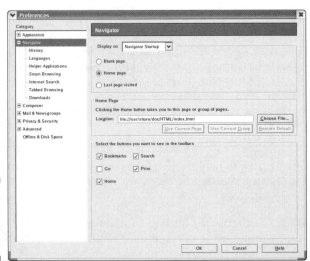

Figure 8-1:
The Mozilla
Preferences
window.

Appearance preferences

Selecting the Appearance option — Figure 8-2 — allows you to determine how you want Mozilla to start when it loads. Navigator (the browser part) is selected by default. If you use Mozilla primarily for e-mail, you may want to select the Composer check box instead. Keep in mind that you can still get to your browser and newsgroups by using the Window menu. Selecting your startup preference is a matter of speed and convenience.

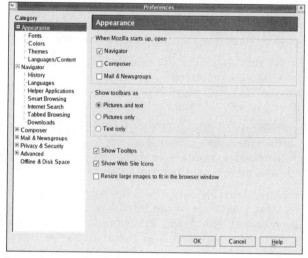

Figure 8-2:
The Mozilla
Appearance
Preferences
window.

The other check box items in the Appearance option window enable you to determine the cosmetics of your toolbar, such as whether to display ToolTips (those little pop-up help texts) or show Web site icons. The option categories in the Category pane on the left are shown in this list:

✔ **Fonts:** Enables you to set your preferred typeface. For desktop resolutions of 1024 x 768 and higher, I recommend jacking up your font sizes immediately. (Otherwise, become very familiar with the key combinations Ctrl-+ to make all the fonts in the browser bigger, and Ctrl-- to make them smaller. Use the + and – on your number pad and not your main keyboard.)

✔ **Colors:** Sets your text colors and whether you want to override explicit Web page settings. This setting is an important one for color-blind people.

✔ **Themes:** Allows you to put a custom paint job on your Mozilla installation.

✔ **Languages/Content:** Allows you to set the sidebar preferences of your browser to a particular locale's language.

Navigator preferences

The Navigator category enables you to select the behavior of your browser when it's first started. You can choose to not show anything, show a specified home Web page (entered into the Location text box), or show the last Web site you visited during your last session. Note that the Location text box also holds the Web site you're transported to whenever you click the Home button on the browser. The following options allow you to personalize your browser with some additional personal preferences:

- **History:** The History text box enables you to designate how many days you want your browser to remember where you have been. You can click the Clear History button to clear the history manually at any time.

- **Languages:** No, this option doesn't automatically translate the content of a Web page into the preferred language. Rather, some Web page authors provide their Web pages in more than one language. If it's an option, this one merely lets you decide language preference.

- **Helper Applications:** In this table, you designate applications to intercept special file types. An example is a .pdf file, which requires the Adobe Acrobat Reader in order to view it. You can specify the application and optional arguments that need to be passed to the program.

- **Smart Browsing:** With this option, you can set the characteristics of the What's Related tab, which is on the Sidebar (located in the left pane of the browser window). The What's Related tab provides a drop-down menu listing sites that may be related to the displayed Web site.

- **Internet Search:** Search engines have become an integral part of Web browsing. To accommodate this, Mozilla can integrate your favorite search engine right into your browser. You can click the drop-down button under Default Search Engine and choose your preference.

- **Tabbed Browsing:** This option reflects the latest craze in Web browser capabilities. It allows you to have multiple surfing destinations, all in one window, and change between them by clicking tabs.

- **Downloads:** Mozilla provides you with a helpful download manager that lets you watch the progress of multiple files, all in a single window. You can even see the last items you downloaded.

E-mail and newsgroup preferences

The Composer category (Figure 8-3) allows you to set preferences for the editor when you compose e-mail messages, and the Mail & Newsgroups category (Figure 8-4) is where you provide your cosmetic e-mail preferences — although if you're using Fedora Core 1 from the DVD or CDs that come with this book, see the Evolution section to find out how to make use of that e-mail client as well.

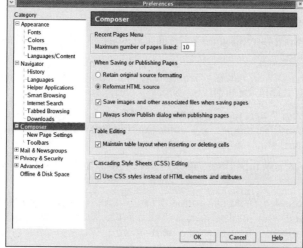

Figure 8-3:
The Mozilla
Composer
Preferences
window.

Previous versions of Mozilla enabled you to configure your e-mail servers and identity, but this feature has moved to an e-mail subsystem. I cover this topic later in this chapter, in the section "Evolving into E-Mail."

The following list shows a few optional pinstripes and chrome for your e-mail preferences:

- **Windows:** You can choose how to format the windows created for working with your mail.

- **Message Display:** You can choose the font type and fixed or variable width, along with how you want to display those emoticons, such as ☺.

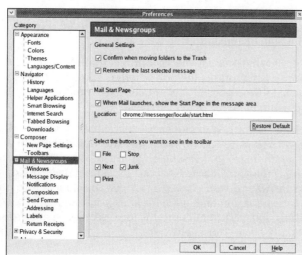

Figure 8-4:
The Mozilla
Mail &
Newsgroups
Preferences
window.

✔ **Notifications:** Do you want sounds to play when a new message arrives? If so, which ones?

✔ **Composition:** Do you want to attach forwarded messages or cut-'n'-paste inline?

✔ **Send Format:** You can determine whether you want to send messages in plain text, HTML, or both.

✔ **Addressing:** When you address a new e-mail message, Mozilla searches your local address book or a common directory server (if you're on a network and share a common contact directory).

✔ **Labels:** You can label messages with colors. This feature is a nifty way to identify them.

✔ **Return Receipts:** You can request a *return receipt* to tell you if someone has opened your mail or not, and also set how return receipts are handled when someone requests one from you.

Other preferences

Other preferences you may want to check out before you start using Mozilla include

✔ **Privacy & Security:** Network security has become a very big issue for everybody connected to the Internet. Although the typically nontechnical media often sensationalizes this issue, security should still be a consideration for all users of the Internet. Every time you send an e-mail or click a Web site, you're exchanging information across a network. Although you don't need to lose sleep over it, you should be conscious of every request you make on the Internet. Even though completely securing your information is impossible, you can feel reasonably safe that your exchanged Internet information is safe because of the default options that Mozilla has provided. See the Popup Windows section (Figure 8-5) for how to keep these annoyances from cluttering your screen.

✔ **Advanced:** This category provides options that affect the entire Mozilla user environment. Options include whether you want to enable Java applets or XSLT Web pages. This area is also where you can flush your cache and establish your proxy settings:

• **Cache:** Visiting a Web site entails establishing a network connection with the site and downloading the Web document and included images for viewing on your browser. The browser *caches* (stores) this information on your local hard drive. By doing so, your browser doesn't have to retrieve the same information from the Internet again and again for sites you frequent. This option enables you to set limits on this local storage space. You can also manually clear your cache here.

- **Proxies:** If you're part of a Local Area Network (LAN) that has a connection to the Internet, you likely connect to a proxy server. Your system administrator provides you with this information. You can safely ignore this option if you're using a dial-up account.

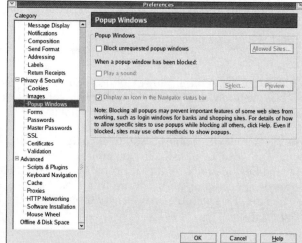

Figure 8-5:
The Mozilla
Popup
Windows
Preferences
window.

Them Dad-Gum Browser Plug-Ins

Do you ever get irritated at those Web sites that insist that you download a *plug-in*, or additional piece of software, just to view the site? The difference between a plug-in and an external program is this: A plug-in displays the results in the browser, and an external program runs outside the browser. Although these plug-ins are annoying if you're just looking for some basic information, they can provide some pretty cool stuff, such as streaming video and music through your Web browser.

Plug-ins provide *browser capability extensions*, which are programs that interface with the browser to provide nonstandard features, such as sound and video. The digital age is still in its infancy, so the industry hasn't yet adopted these multimedia formats as standard. In turn, the developers have chosen not to build support into the Mozilla browser. Rather, the plug-in architecture enables software developers to innovate without requiring the supporting browser to know what to do with newly emerging media formats.

Each plug-in may require manual setup steps, and Linux doesn't support all available plug-ins for Mozilla — yet. (Apple QuickTime is one good example, though you should see Chapter 15 for ways to get around this glitch.) Your Mozilla installation includes some plug-ins. To view which plug-ins are installed, choose Help➪About Plug-ins.

The general rule for plug-in installation is to move the required file, which usually has a `.so` file extension, into the `plugin` directory, located below the Mozilla installation. A likely place for the default Fedora Core 1 installation is `/usr/lib/mozilla-1.4.1/plugins`.

To associate a file with a program or plug-in, choose Edit➪Preferences to open the Preferences window, and in the Navigator category, click Helper Applications. The File Types pane appears, as shown in Figure 8-6.

This window provides you with a simple way to associate a particular file type with a specific program or plug-in. For example, a file with a `.ram` extension denotes a file in Real Media format that probably contains an audio or video presentation. A special plug-in (program) from Real Media is required in order to play this file. This window enables you to match up the file type with the required program.

Luckily, Mozilla comes preconfigured for many common multimedia file types. Any new plug-ins you're required to download come with instructions for configuring them for Linux and Mozilla.

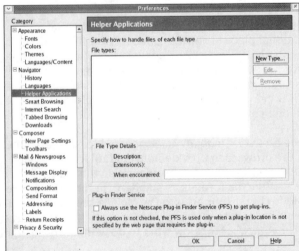

Figure 8-6: The Helper Applications window in Mozilla.

Shifting Mozilla into Gear

After you fine-tune your graphical Internet vehicle, you can take it for a road test. In this section, I cover some righteous maneuvers with your Mozilla browser.

Steering the monster

Mozilla is your viewing window into the wonderful World Wide Web. Mozilla's primary purpose is to fetch Web pages on your command, download all their graphics and related files into your computer's memory, and, finally, render the page for your interactive viewing pleasure.

If you're used to using Internet Explorer or Netscape, using Mozilla should be a snap. It has all the familiar navigation tools, such as an address bar; Back, Forward, Reload, and Stop buttons; and a feature that stores links to your favorite Web sites (bookmarks).

Mozilla, like Netscape, also has a Sidebar feature — press F9 to add and remove it — which you can use to find sites related to the one you're visiting, search for a word or phrase on the Internet, access bookmarked Web pages, or access a Web page you recently visited (via the History option). The pane at the bottom of the Mozilla browser window contains a few buttons that allow you quick access to Navigator, Mail & Newsgroups, Composer, and Address Book, and so does the Window menu.

Perusing newsgroups

Although e-mail is usually directed at an individual, you can think of *news-groups* as public-message bulletin boards where people with similar interests come together to discuss a topic. Newsgroups are also great places to find technical support.

With the newsgroup server information that your ISP provided, follow these steps to access the world's largest cork board:

1. **Choose Window⇨Mail & Newsgroups.**

   The message center window appears with your Inbox selected by default. The first time you open this menu option, you immediately see the Account Wizard shown in Figure 8-7. However, from now on you have to choose Edit⇨Mail & Newsgroups Account Settings before you'll be able to return to this dialog box.

Figure 8-7:
The Mozilla
Account
Wizard.

2. **Select the Newsgroup Account radio button and click Next.**

3. **Continue your newsgroup server configuration by answering the
   remaining questions presented to you via dialog boxes.**

   Note that your ISP probably provided this information when you signed
   up for service. When the configuration is complete, you return to the
   Inbox window.

4. **Right-click the newsgroup server that's highlighted and choose
   Subscribe.**

   When you add your Newsgroup servers in the Preferences dialog box,
   you indicate a default news server. As your default server, it's automatically highlighted.

The first time you do this, you're in for a wait as an index of all the newsgroups downloads to your browser. Tens of thousands of newsgroup titles
are out there, so even though the browser is downloading only the newsgroup names, the process takes some time. The status bar at the bottom of
the dialog box indicates progress.

After all the newsgroup titles have loaded into your browser, you can scroll
through the list for topics of interest. To subscribe to a newsgroup, highlight
the group name and click the Subscribe button to the right.

Subscribe to the newsgroup `comp.os.linux.announce` to see how this
process works. Don't worry; by subscribing, you aren't flooded with e-mails
and don't announce to the world that you're a member of this group. Rather,
the subscription is merely telling your browser to remember this group for
you. Follow these steps to subscribe to a newsgroup:

1. **In the Newsgroup text box, type the name of the newsgroup you want to subscribe to.**

   For example, if you want to subscribe to the Linux announcements newsgroup, type **comp.os.linux.announce**. The group is then highlighted.

2. **Click the Subscribe button.**

   A check mark is placed next to the selected newsgroup you want to subscribe to.

3. **Click OK.**

   You're now back at the Message Center and see an extra item, listed under your news server, labeled `comp.os.linux.announce`.

4. **Double-click the item for your newsgroup in the Message Center.**

   The Mail & Newsgroups window pops up with a message stating that it's loading headers for this group. If it's a busy newsgroup, you may be prompted for the number of message headers you want to download.

After the message headers are loaded, you can scroll through the messages and read or contribute to this newsgroup. Seeing what your peers are doing around the world is educational!

You need to be aware of the written and unwritten rules for newsgroup etiquette, which vary wildly from group to group. I recommend that you read the Frequently Asked Question (FAQ) page for the newsgroup and lurk for a while before posting questions and comments.

Evolving into E-Mail

Although you can utilize Mozilla for e-mail, the default mail client in Fedora Core 1 (the distribution included with this book) is Ximian Evolution. If this product doesn't come with your distribution, you can find it at `www.ximian.com`, although these days it comes with nearly all versions of Linux.

Setting up Evolution

The first time you open Evolution, the program walks you through the setup process, so be sure to have the following information on hand:

✔ Your assigned e-mail address, in the format `username@example.org`.

✔ The type of mail server used for incoming mail: for example, `POP`.

✔ The name of the mail server used for incoming mail, in the format `servername.example.org`.

✔ The type of mail server used for outgoing mail: for example, SMTP.

✔ The name of the mail server used for outgoing mail, in the format servername.example.org. This name may be the same as for the incoming mail server.

✔ Any special type of authentication required, for both mail coming in and going out. This authentication is typically just passwords for coming in, and may be nothing for going out.

After you start Evolution for the first time, follow these steps:

1. **Click Forward to proceed past the Welcome screen.**

   The Identity dialog box (Figure 8-8) opens.

2. **Change the Full Name field, if you want, and then change the E-Mail Address field if it doesn't match the address your ISP gave you. Then click Forward to proceed.**

   The Receiving Mail dialog box opens, as shown in Figure 8-9.

3. **Select in the Server Type list box the type of e-mail server your ISP uses.**

   Leave it as None if you don't want to receive e-mail on this machine. Depending on which item you choose, the dialog box changes to ask for the appropriate information. I assume that you're using a POP mail server to receive mail.

4. **Enter the full name of the POP mail server in the Host text box.**

   The name may be something like pop.example.com.

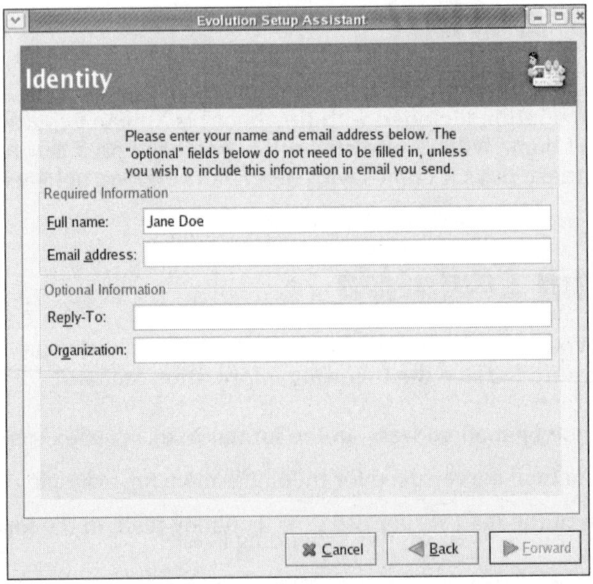

Figure 8-8:
The Ximian
Evolution
Identity
dialog box.

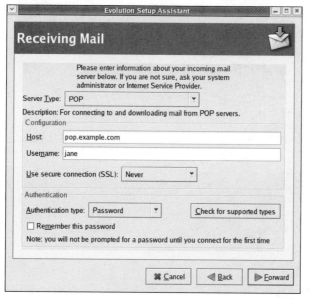

5. **Enter your login name for checking mail in the Username text box.**

    If your e-mail address is jane@example.com, your username is pat.

6. **If you were told to use SSL for security, check the Use Secure Connection (SSL) check box.**

    If you don't know what kinds of authentication your mail server uses, click the Check for Supported Types button.

7. **Select the appropriate authentication option.**

    Typically, it's Password.

8. **If you aren't concerned about someone else using your login session when you turn your back, check the Remember This Password check box. Otherwise, do not.**

9. **Click Forward to proceed to the second Receiving Mail dialog box (Figure 8-10).**

10. **Set how often you want to check for new mail automatically, if you want to do so.**

    If you don't have a permanent connection to the Internet, you may prefer to check mail manually.

11. **If you check mail from multiple machines, you may want to check the Leave Messages on Server check box so that you can access the same messages from all your machines.**

    Click Forward to proceed to the Sending E-Mail dialog box, shown in Figure 8-11.

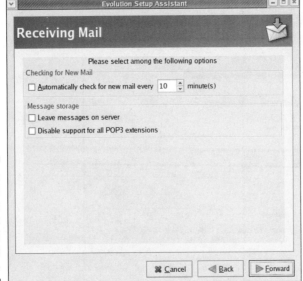

Figure 8-10:
The second
Ximian
Evolution
Receiving
Mail dialog
box.

12. **Change the Server Type entry if yours isn't SMTP.**

    I assume that you're sending e-mail with SMTP.

13. **Enter the full name of the SMTP mail server in the Host text box.**

    The name may be something like `smtp.example.com`.

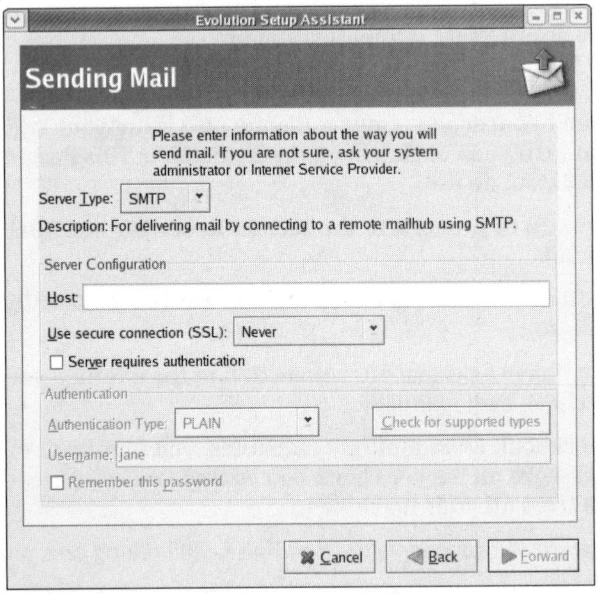

Figure 8-11:
The Ximian
Evolution
Sending
Mail dialog
box.

14. **If you were told to use SSL for security for outgoing mail, check the Use Secure Connection (SSL) check box.**

15. **If you were told to use additional authentication for sending mail, check the This Server Requires Authentication check box.**

    Typically, nothing is required here. You have to fill out the appropriate information if you do activate this section.

16. **Click Forward to proceed to the Account Management section, shown in Figure 8-12.**

    If the account you just set up wasn't your default e-mail account, deselect the Make This My Default account check box.

    You need to add another account later.

17. **Click Forward to proceed to the Time Zone dialog box.**

    This dialog should easily remind you of the Time Zone selection portion of the Fedora Core 1 installation routine.

18. **Click your continent to zoom in, and then click the closest city to where you live, time-zone-wise.**

    Your time zone is selected. You can also click the drop-down list box and choose your time zone manually.

19. **Click Forward to proceed to the Done dialog box.**

20. **Click Apply.**

    That's it! Ximian Evolution finally opens, as shown in Figure 8-13.

Figure 8-12:
The Ximian Evolution Account Management dialog box.

Sending and checking e-mail

The following steps outline how to create a new e-mail message and send it to the President of the United States:

1. **Click Inbox.**

   The Inbox window appears, as shown in Figure 8-14.

2. **Click the New Message button.**

   A Compose a Message window appears, which contains a work area to create your e-mail message.

3. **Complete the message, as shown in Figure 8-15.**

4. **When you finish typing your message, click the Send button.**

   Watch for MIBS (Men In Black Suits) to show up at your door and haul you away for interrogation. Just kidding! This e-mail address gets millions of messages.

   Within a few minutes, you have mail in your inbox waiting to be read. No, the President of the United States isn't constantly reading and replying to everyone's e-mail. A program called an auto-responder is running on the computer that has responsibility for the President's e-mail. When a message is received, the auto-responder returns a form letter to the e-mail address of the sender. Your message is queued up, and the Presidential staff eventually reads it (or so I'm told).

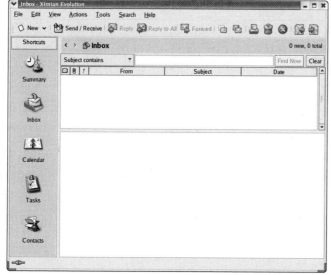

Figure 8-14:
The
Evolution
Inbox
window.

5. Click the Send/Receive button.

Your e-mail goes out. Wait a minute or so and then click the button again. You should have a message waiting for you from the President of the United States.

Take some time to really explore Evolution. As you can see just from the figures in this chapter, there's much to see in this program.

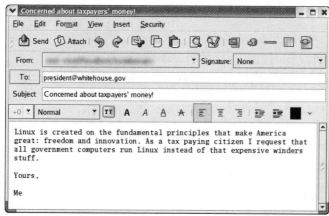

Figure 8-15:
An e-mail
message
to the
President of
the United
States.

Chapter 9

Cool Internet Tools

● ●

In This Chapter

▶ Getting the message out instantly

▶ Browsing with other Web browsers

▶ Mail, mail, and more mail

▶ Exchanging files quickly with FTP

● ●

> *In case you haven't heard, the Internet is not a superhighway.*
>
> —Bill Washburn, *Internet World magazine*

The *Internet* is a vast network of computers that spans the globe. Many different types of computers and operating systems work together to allow you access to information across the Internet. Linux, along with its related Unix operating system, has long supported and worked with the Internet. Practically all the different services available on the Internet are available from your Linux desktop.

When Fedora Core 1 is installed using the Personal Desktop option, several Web browsers, mail programs, and instant messaging tools are installed in your Linux system. In this chapter, I introduce you to some tools you can use to access different services on the Internet, such as accessing Web sites, using e-mail, investigating newsgroups, and utilizing FTP.

Your Linux system has other tools in addition to the applications I mention here, and I suggest that you take the time to explore these tools. You may find that an application I don't cover works better for you. Also, if you don't like any of the Internet-related tools in your Linux system, you can always find lots more on the Internet and install them on your Linux system. But those are topics for Chapters 17 and 19.

Instant Messaging

Instant messaging between people is like using a telephone — except that you type your conversation rather than speak it. In addition, you can simultaneously hold multiple instant messaging conversations without the need for additional connections to the Internet. America Online (AOL) provides one popular instant messaging service, named AOL Instant Messenger, or AIM. Others are ICQ and MSN. A wide variety of computer operating systems, including Linux, support these various services. Kit and Gaim are two instant messaging software packages that are installed by default on your Fedora Core 1 system when you select the Personal Desktop installation option. Because Gaim supports more than just a single instant message (IM), I cover this one in detail. Kit supports only AIM.

In other distributions, if you select the GNOME desktop during installation, Gaim is installed. If you select KDE during installation, Kit is installed in the system. If you select both GNOME and KDE, Gaim and Kit are both installed. In Fedora Core, however, both are installed by default, although Gaim is the main selection.

Gaim

You can launch Gaim by choosing Main Menu➪Internet➪Instant Messenger to open the application shown in Figure 9-1. After the application starts, you need to enter your current IM account, or screen name, or create a new screen name. Gaim supports AIM, ICQ, MSN, and even more services.

Figure 9-1:
The Gaim
IM client.

For a quick start, if you're now an AIM user, enter your screen name and password and click the Sign On button. Make sure that your Internet connection is already established before you use the AIM service.

If you use types of messaging services other than AIM, or if other users want to use this same instance of Gaim, you need to use the Account Editor to set things up (unless you give them their own login, which is the best solution):

1. **Click the Accounts button in the Gaim main window.**

   A window containing the current accounts is displayed, as shown in Figure 9-2.

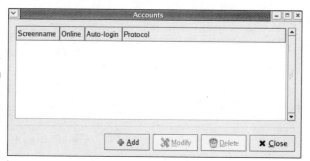

Figure 9-2:
The Gaim
Accounts
window.

2. **To add an IM screen name or account type, click the Add button.**

   The Add Account window appears, as shown in Figure 9-3.

Figure 9-3:
The Gaim
Account
Editor Add
Account
window.

3. **Select the IM service type in the Protocol drop-down list.**

   You have the option to choose AIM/ICQ (these use the same network, so if you want to add either one of these types of accounts, select this one), TOC (another aspect of AIM you need if you want to use AIM chats), Yahoo!, MSN, IRC, Jabber, Napster, Zephyr, and Gadu-Gadu.

4. **Enter your IM name in the Screenname text box.**

5. **Enter your IM password in the Password text box.**

6. **If you want to use a nickname with your IM name, enter that in the Alias text box.**

7. **If you're the only person using this account (and this is Linux, after all — if other people want to use IM, give them their own login accounts and let them set up Gaim for themselves!), select the Remember Password check box.**

   If other people have access to this account, don't check this box. Otherwise, someone may accidentally or intentionally, have a bit of fun with your IM at your expense.

8. **If you want Gaim to automatically log you in to this account when you start the program, check the Auto-Login check box.**

   More settings exist, but these are the basics. Continue on and click the triangle next to Show more Options to see more. If you don't want Gaim to automatically log you in, follow the remaining steps to manually connect Gaim to IM.

9. **Click the OK button to return to the Account Editor window.**

10. **If you want to create another IM account, return to Step 2. You can log in to multiple IM accounts at the same time with Gaim.**

11. **After all your accounts are created and you're back in the Account Editor window, select the Online check box for each one you want to connect with.**

    Gaim attempts to connect to each of your specified accounts.

Troubleshooting Your IM Connections

If you have been using AIM or MSN with other operating systems, after your Linux system has successfully connected to the IM service, you see your buddy lists and any buddies now connected. If you haven't ever used AIM or MSN, you can now set up buddy lists. *Buddy lists* contain the usernames of people you want to communicate with through the instant messaging service. Your buddy list lets you know when your "buddies" are online and available to receive an instant message.

If you're using ICQ, your buddy list isn't stored on the Internet for you. This list is stored on your machine and not in a central location online.

Sometimes, your Linux system is unable to properly connect to the IM service. When this happens, an error message pops up on your screen and indicates a failure to connect. You may be unable to connect to the IM service for several reasons:

✔ You may have entered the wrong password for your IM account or chosen the incorrect IM account name.

✔ Your computer may not be connected to the Internet. Try opening Mozilla or another Web browser to see whether you can get to a Web site, which tells you whether you're connected to the Internet.

✔ If you can open a Web site but can't get IM to work, the IM system may be unavailable. This problem occurs at times because of maintenance of the IM service or an excessive amount of traffic on the Internet or on the IM service.

✔ If you attempt to access the IM service from your computer at work, your company or organization may block the IM service for security or productivity reasons. If using IM at your work is permitted, check with your network administrator to see whether he can help you out.

✔ Often, companies use firewalls between the company's network and the Internet to keep out unwanted traffic on the company's network. If the firewall is configured to block IM traffic, you cannot use IM across the Internet.

Other Browsers to Consider

There are three kinds of death in this world. There's heart death, there's brain death, and there's being off the network.

—Guy Almes

In Chapter 8, you can explore a Web browser named Mozilla that includes lots of features to access Web sites, work with e-mail, and perform other services. In addition to Mozilla, other graphical Web browsers are available for Linux. Another popular Web browser, Konqueror, is also included with Fedora Core 1 on the DVD that comes with this book, and on the CDs you can order. In addition to browsing the Web, you can use Konqueror to manage your e-mail and newsgroup subscriptions. There's also Firebird, a version of Mozilla that is Web-only and therefore a bit less cumbersome.

Konqueror

Some Linux systems, including Fedora Core 1, come with a Web browser named Konqueror. You can launch Konqueror by choosing Main Menu⇨ Internet⇨More Internet Applications⇨Konqueror Web Browser to see the tool shown in Figure 9-4.

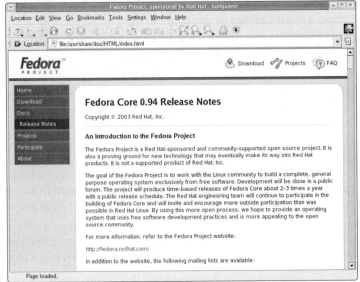

Figure 9-4:
The
Konqueror
Web
browser.

To set up the Konqueror preferences, choose Settings⇨Configure Konqueror. The Settings window, which is shown in Figure 9-5, contains many options, some of which are similar to Mozilla preferences. You can explore each configuration area by clicking the area icons in the left pane of the Settings window.

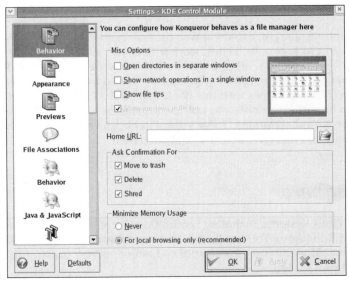

Figure 9-5:
The
Konqueror
Settings
window.

E-Mail Client: KMail

Most Web browsers provide e-mail support so that you can read and send e-mail to other people. In addition, several e-mail applications, or *e-mail clients,* that deal with only e-mail are available. As an example, I look at the e-mail application named KMail, which is part of KDE.

KMail is a simple e-mail program that is available in many distributions of Linux, including Fedora Core 1. (If KMail isn't installed by default, see Chapter 17 for information on how to add software to Linux.) You can launch KMail by choosing Main Menu⇨Internet⇨More Internet Applications⇨KMail from the main menu.

The first time you launch KMail, you must set up your e-mail environment:

1. **Choose Settings⇨Configure KMail.**

   The Configure window appears as shown in Figure 9-6. It allows you to set your name, your e-mail signature, the storage location for your e-mail, and the name and port number of the Simple Mail Transfer Protocol (SMTP) server. If you don't know the settings for your SMTP server, check with your ISP, or if you're at work, check with your network administrator.

Figure 9-6:
The Configure – KMail dialog box.

2. After you make all desired settings, click OK.

You return to the KDE Mail Client window.

The KDE Mail Client application window contains a series of labeled buttons across the top of the window (as shown in Figure 9-7). To create a new message, select the New Message button, and the Composer window appears. Enter the e-mail address of the recipient of your message, a subject line, and the main body of the message in the window. When you have completed your message, click the Send button to send the message on its merry way.

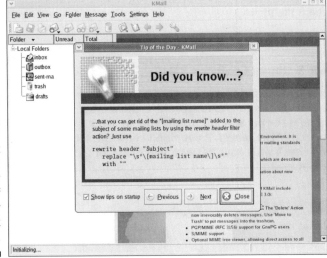

Figure 9-7:
The KDE
Mail Client
application
window
with Tip of
the Day
dialog box
open.

Before sending a message, you can also attach a file, such as a picture, by using the Attach File button. The Attach File button displays a miniature file system navigator so that you can browse to and locate the file you want to attach to your e-mail. You can also spell check your message before delivery by choosing Edit➪Spelling in the Composer window.

Transferring Files with FTP

One of the first types of services designed for networks were *file services*. People needed a way to get files to and from file servers quickly and reliably. File Transfer Protocol (FTP) was designed to provide this type of service. FTP has been around for ages and is still one of the best ways to get files to and from systems in a network. In addition, most current Web browsers support FTP for downloading, so you no longer need to memorize commands to transfer files if you never need to upload. Sometimes, as you point your browser to a Web site and download an update to a software package, you're receiving the file by way of FTP. Applications, such as gFTP, provide a nice graphical interface to facilitate FTP file transfers without needing to use your browser.

Using a Web browser for FTP

To access a FTP service with a Web browser, open up your Web browser and, in the Address field, type **ftp://** followed by the address of the FTP location. For example, if `ftp.redhat.com` is the name of an FTP service, type **ftp://ftp. redhat.com** in the Address field of your Web browser.

Figure 9-8 shows the Mozilla Web browser software FTP interface. In the browser view of FTP, you click directories to navigate up and down the file structure. If you click a file, you're given the option to open the file or download and save it in your file folders.

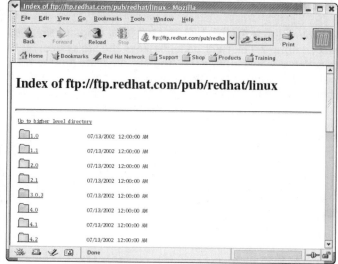

Figure 9-8:
A Web
browser
software
FTP
interface.

Checking out gFTP

Fedora Core 1 includes a graphical FTP application named gFTP.

To access the application, follow these steps:

1. **On the Panel, click the Main Menu button at the left to open the Main Menu.**

2. **Choose Internet⇨More Internet Applications⇨gFTP.**

   The gFTP application window appears, as shown in Figure 9-9.

3. **In the Host field in the upper-left corner, type the address or URL of the FTP server.**

   For example, type **ftp://ftp.redhat.com**.

4. **In the User field at the top center, type the name of an account to access the FTP server.**

   If an account isn't necessary, enter **anonymous** for the account name.

5. **In the Pass field at in the top upper-right corner, type the password for the account.**

   If you're using anonymous to access the FTP service, enter your e-mail account for the password.

6. **To connect, click the two-computer button in the upper-left corner of the screen.**

   In the bottom area of the display, you see messages and status indicators as the connection to the FTP server is processed.

After the connection is established, the left pane displays the file system on your Linux computer. The right pane displays the file system on the FTP server to which you just connected. You can navigate around both systems and upload and download files by using the right and left arrows that are located between the two panes.

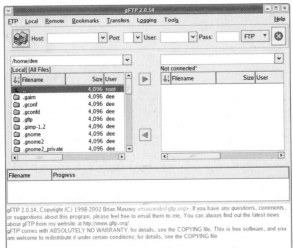

Figure 9-9:
The gFTP application window.

Part III
Getting Up to Speed with Linux

The 5th Wave   By Rich Tennant

Principal

"I found these two in the multimedia lab morphing faculty members into farm animals."

In this part . . .

In this part of the book, I expand my coverage of Linux beyond what's part and parcel of the operating system to include its many other facilities and capabilities. These components are critical to making Linux the raging monster of productivity that a well-constructed, properly configured system can represent.

Here you read about the Linux file system and how to manage its constituent files and directories, as well as how to control which users or groups are permitted to access these vital system resources. Next, you can read about using the Linux command-prompt environment, known as the *shell,* along with some key capabilities that should be part of any savvy Linux user's standard repertoire. After that, you explore two common graphical user interface (GUI) tools for Linux: GNOME (the GNU Network Object Model Environment) and KDE (the K Desktop Environment). With a GUI to use, you also review how to spiff up the look and feelof your Linux desktop. Finally, I explore a variety of text editors, the increasingly popular OpenOffice suite, and take a whirlwind tour of Multimedia Wow.

Chapter 10

Manipulating Files and Directories

There is no need to do any housework at all. After the first four years, the dirt doesn't get any worse.

—Quentin Crisp

There's no avoiding it. At some point, you have to work with the files and directories in your system. Fortunately, after you get familiar with the rules and commands, you feel more comfortable (even if you find yourself being reminded from time to time of working in good old MS-DOS). Because many people find that working at the command line is easier when dealing with files, in this chapter I cover both the typed commands and the graphical tools you have at your disposal.

Comprehending File Types

You find lots of different file types out there in the Linux world. By types, I'm not referring to extensions, such as .exe or .doc. Linux sees everything within its file system — even directories — as "files." As a result, assigning a type to a file is merely a Linux machine's way of keeping track of what's what. In the following sections, I show you how to see what's in your file system, describe each of the file types used in Linux, and explain how to figure out which type you're looking at.

Listing directory contents

One of the most basic skills any computer user needs is the ability to see what's where in her file system. In Linux, you use the ls (short for *list*) command to do this. If you use this command by itself with no *options* — special extras that let you control the behavior of a command — all the command tells you is which files and directories are in the specified directory.

Suppose that you're at the base of the Fedora Core directory tree (which is referred to as *the root,* or /). The ls command lists the contents of the current directory by default. So, if you type ls at the command prompt in the root directory, you see the following output, which lists all subdirectories inside the root:

```
bin    dev   home    lib          misc   opt    root   tmp   var
boot   etc   initrd  lost+found   mnt    proc   sbin   usr
```

But this is only the tip of the iceberg for the ls command. The ls command has a bunch of options you can mix and match to get the results you need. I list the most interesting of these options in Table 10-1. *Remember:* Linux is case sensitive; when an item is shown in uppercase, it must be used in uppercase, and vice versa.

Table 10-1	ls Options
Option	*Purpose*
-a	Displays all files, including hidden files (files whose names start with a period)
-c	Displays the last time the file was changed
@hycolor	Color codes items by type
-l	Displays a long format file listing
-R	Displays the contents of the directories in this directory
-S	Lists the files by size
-t	Lists the files according to how long ago they were changed
-u	Lists the files according to how long ago they were accessed

In this table, -a and -l are by far the most commonly used options. If you're in a brand-new home directory and type ls, you see nothing. However, if you type `ls -a`, you may see something like this because of the hidden files (those starting with periods):

```
.    ..    .bash_logout   .bash_profile   .bashrc
```

What are the first two entries? The first entry — the single dot — always refers to "right here." It points to the directory you're in now. (Don't worry if this stuff doesn't make any sense to you at the moment. As you work with other commands and get more familiar with Linux, it makes sense.) The second part of the line (the two dots) refers to the *parent directory,* or the directory one level up from where you are now. For almost all user home directories (for example, `/home/dee`), the parent is `/home`. I discuss file system structure in more detail in "Working with the File System," later in this chapter.

If you type `ls -l` in this same brand-new home directory, you get nothing, just like you did when you typed `ls`.

Type one of the most commonly used combinations and you get much more information. If you type `ls -la`, for example, you see something similar to the following:

```
drwx------ 2 dee   dee   4096 Jul 29 07:48 .
drwxr-xr-x 5 root  root  4096 Jul 27 11:57 ..
-rw-r--r-- 1 dee   dee     24 Jul 27 06:50 .bash_logout
-rw-r--r-- 1 dee   dee    230 Jul 27 06:50 .bash_profile
-rw-r--r-- 1 dee   dee    124 Jul 27 06:50 .bashrc
```

You may find some parts of this format easier to understand, at a glance, than others. The first item in each listing (the part with the letters and dashes — for example, the `drwx ------` in the first line) is the *permission set* assigned to the item. Briefly, permissions define who can read the file, change it, or run it if it's a program. You can read more about permissions in "Haggling with Permissions," later in this chapter. The second item in the first line (in this case, 2), is the number of links to the item.

A *link* is a fake file listing that points to another file, making a kind of shortcut. You use two kinds of links in Linux and Unix:

- ✔ **Soft link:** This link is like a Windows shortcut in that the link points back to the original file, and anything you do to the link happens to the original file. Erase the original file, and the link remains, but it becomes unusable. The link is broken without the original file.

- ✔ **Hard link:** This link doesn't have a counterpart in the Windows world. A hard link isn't just a shortcut; it's another instance of the file itself. The data in this file is saved in only one place, but you can edit either the original or the link, and the edit is saved for both instances of the file. Erase the original, and the file still exists as long as the link is there. It's like two doors to the same room!

The third item (dee) is the file's *owner,* and the fourth (dee) is the *group* — depending on which version of Linux you're using, both these items may or may not be identical. You can find out more about both of these in "Haggling with Permissions," later in this chapter. The fifth item is the file's size in bytes. All directories show up as 4,096 bytes. Everything else has its own size. You can tell an empty file from the size of 0 bytes.

The sixth, seventh, and eighth entries are all related to the last time the file was changed: the month (Jul), the date (29), and the time in 24-hour format (07:48). Finally, the ninth item is the filename (for example, bash logout, in the third row).

Getting information about specific files

You can zoom in and focus on specific files too. As you may guess, one tool used for this purpose is the ls command. Typing ls *filename* gives you the short listing, where *filename* is the name of the file you're interested in. The short listing isn't all that useful unless you're just checking to see whether the file exists. What's more useful is typing ls -l *filename*, which gives you a single line in the ls -l format, which I examine in the preceding section.

When you type any form of ls *directory*, you actually see the contents of the directory instead of the directory and its permissions (unless you add the -d flag to the mix). For example, typing ls -ld *directory* gives you the long format listing for just the directory itself.

The first letter in any long format file listing (the result of a ls -l command) tells you which type of file you're dealing with. In Table 10-2, I list the types you're likely to run into.

Table 10-2		Linux File Types
Label	*Type*	*Description*
-	Regular file	The item is an everyday file, such as a text file or program.
b	Block device	The item is a driver (control program) for a storage medium, such as a hard drive or CD-ROM drive.
c	Character device	The item is a driver (control program) for a piece of hardware that transmits data, such as a modem.

Label	Type	Description
d	Directory	The item is a container for files, also referred to as a folder in some operating systems' lingo.
l	Link	The item is a soft link.

Linux has additional commands that can give you something a bit easier to understand than a raw listing of information. The first of these commands is simply named `file`, which directly tells you which kind of file you're dealing with. For example, if you type `file /home`, you see the following result:

```
/home: directory
```

The `file` command even traces links for you! You can use it with links in two different ways:

✔ If you use just the `file` command and a filename or directory, the command tells you about the exact item you listed. For example, if you type `file /usr/src/linux`, you may (depending on your Linux distribution, if you have particular packages installed, and other issues) see the following line:

```
/usr/src/linux: symbolic link to /usr/src/linux-2.4.18
```

✔ When you use the `-L` *flag* (often the same thing as an option) with `file`, it traces a link back to the original and gives you an answer based on the original. For example, if you type `file -L /usr/src/linux`, you see the following line:

```
/usr/src/linux: directory
```

Working with the File System

It was an accident, Phyllis.

Oh, you know, so was Chernobyl.

—*From the movie* Quick Change

You need to know how to move within the directory structure, how to find out where you are, and how to add and remove things. I suggest logging in to a user account to experiment with what you read about throughout the rest of this chapter. Don't use `root`. You don't want to delete or move something vital!

Moving through the file system

Linux has two commands you may find useful for moving around in the file system. The first of these lets you see exactly where you are. You may think that you wouldn't need a command like this one. After all, shouldn't your location be obvious? Many Linux distributions, however, have the habit of giving you a prompt like the following:

```
[dee@myhost dee]$
```

This prompt tells you that your login name is dee, and that the machine you're on is myhost. The directory you're in, however, is /home/dee, not just dee. Linux uses this format mostly because the full location can get pretty huge: A prompt showing the full path can take up half the line or more. To see exactly where you are, type **pwd**.

You move through the file system with the cd (change directory) command. If you're in the /home/dee directory and you want to go to the temporary directory (/tmp), you type cd /tmp.

Another thing that you need to be aware of — and that can save you lots of typing — is that you can type file system locations in two different ways:

- ✔ **Type the whole thing.** If you're in /home/dee and you want to switch to the subdirectory files, you can type cd /home/dee/files. You have another way to do it, though.

- ✔ **Type a *relative* location.** If you know where you are and where you want to go *relative* to where you are, you can use the *relative location* rather than type the whole thing. For example, to switch to the files subdirectory of /home/dee from inside /home/dee, you can just type cd files. The cd command understands that you're already in /home/dee, so it looks for the files directory inside it.

Maybe you're logged in as root and checking up on a few different user directories. You're in /home/dee and you want to go to /home/ralph. You can either type cd /home/ralph or cd ../ralph. Remember that the .. always refers to the directory that contains the one you're in. Using ../ralph tells the cd command to back up one directory (into /home) and then move forward into ralph.

Just want to change to your own home directory? Type **cd ~** and you get there immediately! In fact, you can just type cd with nothing else if you want. If you want to change to your own text subdirectory (maybe it's /home/ralph/text), you could type cd ~/text.

Creating files and directories

As you work with your Linux machine, two things you probably want to do immediately are

- ✔ **Create your own files:** If you're using the Linux machine for serious work, you probably will want to create files for a variety of reasons. You may have a personal journal to keep or want to make a tip sheet for yourself with the things you find out about Linux during your experimentation.

- ✔ **Create directories:** Eventually, those files add up! Directories are there for organizational purposes. Make the most of them.

Making new files

In Linux, you have essentially three ways of creating new files. One is the wonderfully straightforward `touch` command, and I get into the details here. The others are a bit more complex and involve things you get into as you continue with your explorations or with this book.

You can create a new, empty file at any time by using the `touch` command. Because the file contains nothing (it just has a name), all you're really doing is making an entry in a directory. But this technique does have its uses. You use `touch` in the format `touch` *filename,* where *filename* is the name of the file you want to create. You can either be inside the directory in which you want to create the file, in which case you just type `touch` *filename,* or use the techniques I discuss in the preceding section. If you're in `/home/mike` and want to create the file `today` in your journal subdirectory (`/home/mike/journal`), you type `touch journal/today`. Or, if you're in `/home/mike/journal` and want to create the file `note` in `/home/mike`, you type `touch ../note`.

When you get to the "Haggling with Permissions" section of this chapter and start experimenting with file permissions, use the `touch` command to make expendable files that you can mess with without causing yourself problems later.

The other methods of creating files depend on which kind of files you want to make. If you want to create a text file, you can use one of many text editors available for Linux. A *text editor* is a small program that lets you work with raw text with no formatting, such as Notepad in Windows. In Chapter 13, I cover one of the text editors that comes by default with all Linux distributions and point you to additional ones.

Finally, the *nontext files* are items like word processing documents that have lots of formatting codes, image files (such as GIFs) that are chock-full of formatting stuff and have no readable text, and more. You create these files by using the appropriate program for them. To make a word processing file, you use a word processing program, such as WordPerfect or OpenOffice.org (see Chapter 14).

Making new directories

As you add more and more files to your home directory and elsewhere, you realize that you need to organize them before you get completely buried and can't find anything quickly. Directories are the perfect tools for filling this need. You create new directories in Linux with the mkdir command. Again, you can use it in more than one way. If you're in /home/mike and want to create the directory /home/mike/pictures, you can type mkdir pictures. If you need to create a temporary directory outside your home directory with files to share with others, you type mkdir /tmp/pictures. This is a perfect use for those hard and soft links, since you'll want to keep a copy of those files in your own home directory. The contents of your /tmp directory are removed pretty regularly!

Moving, renaming, and deleting files and directories

One of the facts of life is that things change. Suppose that you create a file named text one day. Then, the next day, you have a pile of text files and need to make a new directory for them. You make the new directory and then move the files into it. Or, suppose that you make a filename too generic and you can't tell the difference between text and text5 at a quick glance. You need to rename them. Fortunately, Linux has commands to do all these things easily.

Moving and renaming

You need to be careful if you're using the root account. Renaming, moving, or deleting system files can wreak total havoc! This is just one more reason that I constantly beg people not to use root at all unless they have to.

You use the mv command for both moving and renaming files. To move a file from one location to another, you type mv *originallocation newlocation*, where *originallocation* is the directory in which the file starts, and *newlocation* is where you want to move the file. Suppose that you want to move the file /home/mike/text into the directory /home/mike/textfiles. When you're inside /home/mike, you type mv text textfiles. This command is the same as typing mv /home/mike/text /home/mike/textfiles or even mv /home/mike/text /home/mike/textfiles/text. If you make the destination the name of an existing directory, the mv command assumes that you want to put the file into that directory with the same name.

Renaming files is remarkably similar. If you want to rename /home/mike/ text as /home/mike/grocerylist, you type mv text grocerylist from inside /home/mike.

You can even move and rename at the same time. You can move /home/mike/ text into /home/mike/textfiles while renaming it grocerylist, all from inside /home/mike by typing mv text textfiles/grocerylist.

Getting rid of the junk

In any operating system, cleaning out your files occasionally is a good idea. If you don't, you're on the road to having no drive space left, which is definitely no fun. Linux has two different commands for deleting. One is rm (short for *remove*). If you use this command by itself, it deletes files. For example, if you type rm ~/test.tif, the test.tif file may just be deleted without question, or you may see the following line, depending on how your distribution has the rm command set up:

```
rm: remove 'test.tif'?
```

Press **N** or Enter to cancel the operation. Otherwise, press **Y** to delete the file. Linux contains a number of options, as shown in Table 10-3, that you can use to make the rm command behave according to your preferences. The default preferences may differ between your root account and your user accounts.

Table 10-3	Options for rm
Option	*Description*
-d	Removes a directory, even if it's not empty
-f	Removes items without asking for confirmation
-i	Asks for confirmation before removing anything
-r	Continues into subdirectories and removes items there too
-v	Prints status information during the removal process

You can use these options individually or in combinations. If you use the -d option, you can use rm to remove a directory as well as a file. For example, if you want to delete /home/mike/textfiles, you type rm -d textfiles from inside /home/mike. This command removes both the directory and its contents, but you may be prompted for each item, depending on how your distribution has rm set up. You can override either behavior (prompting or no prompting) with the proper flags. If you type rm -df textfiles, you don't have to answer any questions; if you type rm -if textfiles, you do.

Suppose that you have a series of subdirectories you want to get rid of. Maybe you have /home/sally/files, and the files directory has the sub-directories /text, /images, /programs, and more. You can type rm -r files in /home/sally to get rid of all of them. Once again, though, you're prompted frequently during this removal process. To eliminate the constant prompting, type rm -rf files.

The command rm -rf is perhaps the most dangerous thing you can type on a Linux or Unix system, especially if you're logged in as root (rm -rf * is the worst possible command because it's a great way to accidentally delete your entire file system). *Be quadruply sure* that you're typing this command in the right place if you're logged in as root and that you really want to get rid of everything in the subdirectories. Many people have typed rm -rf in the root directory accidentally, only to feel sick as they listen to the drive churn and churn as it deletes everything. You can press Ctrl+C to cancel out of this com-mand, but you can't get back the already deleted files.

Another way you can get rid of directories is to use the rmdir command. This program deletes only *empty* directories. Many people prefer to use a combina-tion of rm to delete the files, and then rmdir to remove the directories, just to ensure that they aren't making a colossal mess of things. You use rmdir in the format rmdir *directory*. Suppose that you have a temporary directory, /tmp/mikesfiles, that you want to remove. After typing rm -r or rm -rf in that directory for each of the files, you type cd .. to back up to /tmp (you can't delete a directory if you're now in it) and then type rmdir mikesfiles.

Haggling with Permissions

Take a look at some long format file listings on your machine by typing **ls -l** within a directory. If you find yourself scratching your head, don't worry. The "Comprehending File Types" section, earlier in this chapter, gives you a feel-ing for the first letter on each line, but nine more characters are attached to that item before you get to the next column. This group of nine is the set of *permissions* (also called a *permission set*) for the file or directory. Linux, Unix, and even Mac OS X use permissions as a way of providing file and directory security by giving you the means to specify exactly who can look at your files, who can change them, and even who can run your programs. You need this capability when you have a bunch of different users on the same machine, networked to the world.

Checking out the triads

Each permission set consists of three triads. Each of the triads has the same basic structure but controls a different aspect of who can use what. Consider the long format listing for /home/dee in the following code:

```
total 20
drwx------ 2 dee   dee   4096 Jul 29 07:48 .
drwxr-xr-x 5 root  root  4096 Jul 27 11:57 ..
-rw-r--r-- 1 dee   dee     24 Jul 27 06:50 .bash_logout
-rw-r--r-- 1 dee   dee    230 Jul 27 06:50 .bash_profile
-rw-r--r-- 1 dee   dee    124 Jul 27 06:50 .bashrc
-rw-rw-r-- 1 dee   dee      0 Jul 29 07:48 lsfile
```

The first character in the permission set refers to the type of file. For a directory, the character is shown as a d, as you see here for the first two items in the preceding list; files are designated with a dash (-) instead. Each file or directory's permission set is a group of nine characters — that is, the nine characters that follow the first character (for a total of ten). But this group of nine is really three groups of three, as shown in Figure 10-1.

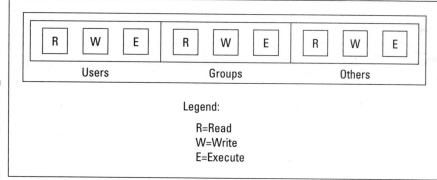

Figure 10-1:
Breakdown
of the nine
permission
characters.

The three triads are read as follows:

✔ The first triad consists of the second, third, and fourth characters in the long format file listing. This triad sets the permissions for the *user*, or *owner*, of the file. (Owners are discussed in the "Beware of owners" section, later in this chapter.)

✔ The second triad consists of the fifth, sixth, and seventh characters in the long format file listing. This triad sets the permissions for the *group* that is assigned to the file. (Groups are discussed in the "Hanging out in groups" section, later in this chapter.)

✔ The third triad consists of the eighth, ninth, and tenth characters in the long format file listing. This triad sets the permissions for *other*, or everyone who isn't the file's owner or a member of the owning group.

Although each triad is often different from the others, the internal structure of each one is made up in the same way. Focus specifically on how to read one triad before looking at the set of them together. Each triad includes three characters:

- ✔ The first character is either an r or a dash. The r stands for *read* permission. If r is set, the triad allows the entity it stands for (user, group, or other) to view the directory or file's contents.

- ✔ The second character is either a w or a dash. The w stands for *write* permission. If w is set, the triad allows the entity it stands for to add or edit items to, or in, this directory or file.

- ✔ The third character is either an x or a dash. The x stands for *execute* permission. If x is set, the triad allows the entity it stands for to run programs contained in this directory or to run the particular program in this file.

In all cases, if the dash sits in place of r, w, or x, the triad doesn't allow the entity the read, write, or execute permission.

The following sections describe owners and groups in more detail.

Beware of owners

You may have noticed by now that I talk a great deal about owners (users) and groups in Linux. Every file and directory has both of these components: a user from the /etc/passwd file that's assigned as its owner and a group from /etc/group assigned as the group.

Although an everyday user probably doesn't need to change file ownerships often, the root user does so regularly. If you add the file comments, for example, to /home/tom while you're logged on as the *superuser* (another term for the administrator, who is the person who owns the root account), root owns that file. The user tom can't do anything with it unless you have set the last triad's permissions to allow the *other* folks (those who aren't the file's owner or in the specified group) to read and write to the file. But this method is a pretty sloppy way of doing things because the whole idea of permissions is to reduce access, not to give everyone access. Instead, remember to change the file's owner to the user tom. You do this with the chown (*change owner*) command. For example, by typing chown tom comments, root changes the ownership over to tom. Then tom can work with this file and even change its permissions to something he prefers.

Hanging out in groups

Groups are more interesting to work with than owners. You use groups to allow the root user to assign to multiple users the ability to share certain file system areas. For example, in many versions of Linux, all users are added to a group named *users*. Then, rather than a long format file listing such as the one shown in "Reading a long format file listing" section, later in this chapter, you may see the following:

```
total 20
drwx------ 2 dee   users 4096 Jul 29 07:48 .
drwxr-xr-x 5 root  root  4096 Jul 27 11:57 ..
-rw-r--r-- 1 dee   users   24 Jul 27 06:50 .bash_logout
-rw-r--r-- 1 dee   users  230 Jul 27 06:50 .bash_profile
-rw-r--r-- 1 dee   users  124 Jul 27 06:50 .bashrc
-rw-rw-r-- 1 dee   users    0 Jul 29 07:48 lsfile
```

In distributions such as Red Hat Enterprise Linux and Fedora Core, both the user and group are the same by default (you would have owner dee and group dee, for example). This isn't always the case, however, as you see from the preceding code listing, which has owner dee and group users. Various Linux distributions have their own philosophies about this issue.

As the root user, you can create new groups or add users to groups:

✔ To create a group, you use groupadd *groupname*, specifying the name of the group you want to create (for example, groupadd labteam).

✔ To add a user to an existing group, you use usermod -G *group user*, specifying the name of the group to which to add the user and the user you want to add to this group (for example, you type usermod -G labteam dee).

Changing permissions

Permissions and ownerships are assigned to all files during the installation process. From there, every directory and file you create has permissions assigned to it automatically (what these default permissions are depends on your Linux distribution's default settings). But you may not like the permissions that are already in place. Maybe you want to change them to make your data more secure or even more accessible. In the listing in the preceding section, for example, I don't see the need for everyone on the system to be able to view the contents of lsfile. So, I can use the chmod (*change mode*) command to deal with this issue in the format chmod *new permissions filename*, where *newpermissions* indicates that you want to change the existing permissions for whatever file you specify as *filename*. For example, for lsfile, you type chmod newpermissions lsfile at the command prompt.

You can express the *newpermissions* component in two different ways: by the letters or by the numbers, as described in the following sections.

Permissions by letters

One method of telling Linux how you want to change a set of permissions is to use letters. You have two groups of characters to use here. The first group consists of

- u for user
- g for group
- o for other, or everyone
- a for all (or ugo has the same effect)

The second group consists of the familiar characters that Linux uses for the permission triad: r, w, and x. (See "Checking out the triads," earlier in this chapter.) Next, you have the *operators,* which are characters that tell chmod what to do with the permissions relative to the triad you're referring to:

- + to add a permission
- - to remove a permission
- = to set the permissions to the exact value

Now that you have all the pieces, you can begin putting them together. Start with the example chmod *newpermissions* lsfile. Your goal here is to allow no users — outside of yourself or your group members — to view the contents of lsfile. From this clue, you know that you're referring to the third triad (the o triad). The permission used to determine whether people can view the contents of a file or directory is the r position, and the operator used to take away this permission is the dash (-). So, you type chmod o-r lsfile. The deed is done: None of the users in the o (other) group can view the contents of lsfile. It really is that easy!

You can change multiple triads at the same time in a couple of different ways. For example, if you want to change lsfile so that only the owner (dee) can read its contents, you type chmod go-r lsfile to change both the group and other settings simultaneously. Getting even more complex, if you want to make sure that only the file's owner can read, write, or run that file, you type chmod go-rwx lsfile.

Technically, you can even type the full set of permissions, if you want. If you want both the owner and group to be able to read lsfile, but only the owner to be able to write to it, you can type chmod rw-r----- lsfile.

Permissions by numbers

Another method that Linux users commonly use to change permissions is numbers. Because this format is used all over the place in Linux documentation, from books to courses to manual pages and online references, I truly thought that I should include the information for you here — even though it's a bit technical.

To put it simply, permission numbers allow you to deal with just a raw *octal number* — octal is a numbering system in base 8, meaning that you only use the numbers 0 to 7 instead of 0 to 9, which is the more familiar base 10 system. The nice thing is you don't need to know any more than that about octal in order to use this method.

Look at the following permission set:

```
-rw-rw-r--
```

In the following list, the preceding line of code is broken into its three triads:

- ✔ Triad 1: rw-
- ✔ Triad 2: rw-
- ✔ Triad 3: r--

In each position in each triad, the important thing to notice is whether a letter or a dash is there. The numeric values for each possible item are

- ✔ Every r is worth 4
- ✔ Every w is worth 2
- ✔ Every x is worth 1
- ✔ Every - is worth 0

Each triad keeps its own total. All you need to do is add the values. So, in the case of the sample permission set, you have the results shown in Table 10-4:

Table 10-4	Results of Sample Permission Set
Triad	*Conversion to Numbers*
rw-	4 + 2 + 0 = 6
rw-	4 + 2 + 0 = 6
r--	4 + 0 + 0 = 4

The numeric permission set is basically set so that the value for the first triad is the first number, the second value is the second number, and the third triad is the third number. The permission set rw-rw-r-- works out to 664.

If you know exactly what you want to change your permissions to, you use the format chmod *newpermissions* file with numbers for the permissions. For example, to change the lsfile's permission to rw-------, you type chmod 600 lsfile.

Reading a long format file listing

A long format file listing (`ls -l`) is quite easy to read after you get a handle
on each of the elements within it. I go through the following example — line
by line — in the following sections:

```
total 20
drwx------ 2 dee   dee   4096 Jul 29 07:48 .
drwxr-xr-x 5 root  root  4096 Jul 27 11:57 ..
-rw-r--r-- 1 dee   dee     24 Jul 27 06:50 .bash_logout
-rw-r--r-- 1 dee   dee    230 Jul 27 06:50 .bash_profile
-rw-r--r-- 1 dee   dee    124 Jul 27 06:50 .bashrc
-rw-rw-r-- 1 dee   dee      0 Jul 29 07:48 lsfile
```

Line One

```
total 20
```

The first line specifies how many *blocks* (a unit of file system usage) the files
in this directory use.

You can find out how large the blocks are on a particular partition by typing
`dumpe2fs -h partition`, where `partition` is the device information for
that part of the drive. To get the list of partitions on your system, you type
`df`. For an example, you can type `dumpe2fs -h /dev/hda1` for the first partition on your first IDE hard drive.

Line Two

```
drwx------ 2 dee   dee   4096 Jul 29 07:48 .
```

The first letter here is a `d`, so it immediately tells you that this entry is a directory. Now, move to the permissions. Only the first triad has anything turned
on here, so the owner (that's `dee`) is allowed to view the contents of the directory (thanks to the `r`), save files to that directory (thanks to the `w`), and run
programs in the directory (thanks to the `x`). No one in the group (including
`dee`), can do any of these tasks in `/home/dee`. After this entry is the number of
links to the item, which in this case is `2`. Then, you have the user who owns
this item, `dee`, and the group that owns this item, also `dee`. Next is the item
size (directories often show 4,096 bytes, but can be larger if the directories
contain a huge amount of data). Then comes the creation or last change date
and time. Last, you see the item name. In this case, it's a period, which stands
for the *current directory,* so the first entry tells you about `/home/dee` itself.

Line Three

```
drwxr-xr-x 5 root root 4096 Jul 27 11:57 ..
```

Once again, the first letter is a `d`, so you're looking at a directory. As for the
permissions, the first triad refers to the root user, who has all three (`rwx`)

enabled, so root can do anything she wants to do in /home. The second triad is r-x, so anyone in the group (also root, in this case) can read the contents of /home and execute programs in there. The third triad is identical to the second, so the same rules apply to everyone else. This item has five links, and it's owned by the user root and the group root. After the size and creation/modification date and time comes the name of the item. The .. stands for the directory above this one, so the second entry tells you about /home.

Okay, the root user can do anything she wants within the Linux file system. If you're using a Red Hat Linux-related distribution such as Fedora Core, every user has her own group with the same name as the user account; other distributions, such as SuSE, have all users assigned to the group user.

Lines Four, Five, and Six

```
-rw-r--r-- 1 dee   dee    24 Jul 27 06:50 .bash_logout
-rw-r--r-- 1 dee   dee   230 Jul 27 06:50 .bash_profile
-rw-r--r-- 1 dee   dee   124 Jul 27 06:50 .bashrc
```

Now you get to the files, which you can recognize by the dash (-) as the first character. Files are always listed after directories when you use ls -l. The permissions for all these items are the same. Their first triad is rw-, which means that the owner (dee) can view the file's contents and edit them. The second and third triads for these three are r--. Anyone in the dee group can view the contents of these files, and everyone on the entire system can too. Each file has only one link, is a different size (in bytes) and was created at the same time — in this case, when the account itself was created. The names for these files are .bash_logout, .bash_profile, and .bashrc.

Line Seven

```
-rw-rw-r-- 1 dee   dee     0 Jul 29 07:48 lsfile
```

This last item is also a file. You can tell because the first character is a dash. Because its first two triads are identical (rw-), the owner (dee) and members of the group (dee) can both view the file's contents and change them. Every-one else, however, can only read the contents because the last triad is r--. Only one link exists, and this item is owned by the user and group dee. It's empty too, indicated by the file size — 0 bytes. After the creation or last modification date and time, you see the file's name: lsfile.

Wildcards, or Legal Cheating

Working at the command prompt involves lots of typing. This fact becomes painfully obvious if you want to deal with a bunch of files and have to type their names one by one. Fortunately, you don't have to do that. You have wildcards at your disposal.

Wildcards are characters that represent one or more characters. Table 10-5 lists the wildcards you have available when working with files and directories.

Table 10-5	Wildcards for File and Directory Manipulation	
Character	*Name of Character*	*Purpose*
?	Question mark	Stands for a single missing character
*	Asterisk	Stands for a group of characters
[]	Square brackets	Allows you to specify a range or group of characters

Suppose that you have a directory with the following short file listing:

```
afile   cfile   file1file   file2file   fileafile
bfile   file1   file2       file3       filebfile
```

Table 10-6 shows you how you can use wildcards to access those files:

Table 10-6	Using Wildcards to Access Files
If You Type . . .	*Then You Get*
ls ?file	afile, bfile, cfile.
ls file?	file1, file2, and file3.
ls file*	file1file, file2file, fileafile, file1, file2, file3, and filebfile.
ls *file	afile, cfile, file1file, file2file, fileafile, bfile, and filebfile.
ls file[1-3]	file1, file2, and file3.
ls file[1-3]*	file1, file2, file3, file1file, and file2file.
ls file[1,a]*	file1, file1file, and fileafile.

You may also find filename and command completion useful. The bash shell (the default Linux shell; see Chapter 11) has a feature that finishes a filename for you. If you're working at the command prompt and typing a long filename, press the Tab key and bash does the rest. You can also complete commands by pressing the Tab key. You have to type enough letters, however, to make the item unique so that nothing else can come up during the completion.

File Managers

Tired of typing stuff at the command prompt? If you prefer, the GUI contains a bunch of file managers for you to use. A *file manager* is a program, such as Windows Explorer, that enables you to dig through and manipulate your files and directories with your mouse rather than at the command prompt. In this section, I take you on a tour of the file managers that, by default, come with popular Linux distributions.

In both GNOME and KDE, the file managers can do more than just work with your files. Have some fun and experiment with the programs covered in this section!

Sailin' with Nautilus

In the GNOME desktop environment (and anywhere in Fedora Core 1), the default file manager is *Nautilus*. You can find this program by double-clicking the Home icon on your desktop. Figure 10-2 shows an example of what you can see with Nautilus open in a default Fedora Core 1 GNOME setup.

The workings of this file manager should seem similar to those you're used to in other operating systems. If you like to have the full file system tree available to you in a pane on the left, you can change the default setup by following these steps:

1. **Choose the Information drop-down list box.**

   The list box expands, displaying your options.

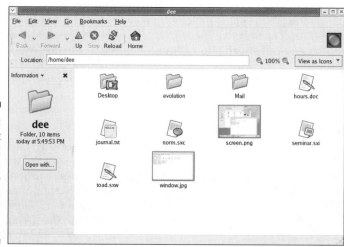

Figure 10-2: The default GNOME Nautilus file manager displaying dee's home directory.

2. Select Tree.

Nautilus now gives you the same two-panel layout with click-and-drag functionality you find in Microsoft Windows Explorer.

The default Nautilus setup varies according to which Linux distribution you're using. In some distributions, this tree panel is set up by default.

Browsing your files

Moving through the file system is pretty easy in Nautilus after you have the tree open — the tree lets you do a lot of drag and drop stuff. The main thing you need to keep in mind is that your directories are on the left (if you have activated the side pane and have both activated and selected the Tree tab), and your files are on the right. You can do the following file management tasks in Nautilus:

- ✔ **Open a directory on the left:** To open a directory within the left panel, locate it in the list and click the right-facing arrow next to it. The arrow pivots to point down, and if subdirectories exist, they're now listed beneath the current directory.

- ✔ **Open a directory on the right:** To open a directory within the right panel, locate it in the window and double-click it. Linux automatically displays the files in this directory.

- ✔ **View a directory's contents:** To view the files in a directory, click the directory's folder icon or the name in the left panel, and its contents appear in the right panel.

- ✔ **Look at files and run programs:** To view a file's contents or run a program, double-click the item in the listing.

Are you getting too much information about each file or not enough? Experiment with the View As Dropdown list box in the upper-right side of the Nautilus window; the options include View As Icons (the default), View As List, or View As. The first two items pull up a view on the right that gives you a different amount of information about the files and directories. The third item opens the View As Other dialog box, which allows you to set the default viewing behavior for the current folder or to alter which programs are opened for which file types.

Copying and moving files

You can copy and move items using two different methods in Nautilus (assuming that you have added the side pane and activated the tree view). The first is by using the usual drag-and-drop method you're probably familiar with from Windows or the Mac OS — but only within the right pane — and the other is by using the program's menus. To move a file by using the drag-and-drop method, first click the file you want to move in the listing on the right. Then drag it to the folder you want to drop it into within the left pane.

You do the same to copy, except that you click the item and then hold down the Ctrl key while you drag and drop.

Deleting files and directories

To use Nautilus to delete either a file or a directory from the file system, follow these steps:

1. **Browse to the file or directory's location.**

2. **Select the file or directory.**

   Click the item to highlight its name, whether it's in the left (if you have activated it and the tree view) or right pane.

3. **Click the Delete button.**

   The file or folder vanishes from view. Keep in mind that if the folder contains other files or folders, they go right along with it.

These deleted items are not fully deleted yet. Deleting from the command line is a one-step operation, but deleting by using Nautilus puts the files in the Trash folder, which you can open by double-clicking the Trash icon on your desktop. You can delete the contents of the Trash at any time by following these steps:

1. **Right-click the Trash icon.**

   This action opens a shortcut menu with options listed.

2. **Choose Empty Trash from the shortcut menu.**

   A confirmation dialog box opens.

3. **Click Empty in the confirmation dialog box to delete the contents of the Trash folder.**

   Linux permanently removes the items in the Trash folder.

Viewing and changing permissions

If you have experimented with the different file views, you already know that neither the Icon view nor the List view shows you a file's permissions. To view and change a file or directory's permissions, you need to follow these steps:

1. **Browse to the file or directory's location.**

   You need the file or directory to appear in the right pane, so click the folder in the left pane (if you have activated it and the tree view) that contains the item.

2. **Select the file or directory.**

   Click the item in the right pane to highlight its name.

3. **Right-click the file and choose Properties from the shortcut menu that appears.**

   The Properties dialog box opens with the Statistics tab open.

4. **Click the Permissions tab.**

   The Permissions portion of the Properties dialog box appears, as shown in Figure 10-3.

5. **Set the new permissions and ownerships.**

   As you can see, Nautilus offers some pretty handy tools for setting the permissions exactly the way you want them without having to remember their structure or which numbers go with which letters. You can also change owner and group information here.

6. **Close the dialog box.**

   When you have everything set the way you want it, click the Close button to close the dialog box and put the changes into effect.

Figure 10-3:
The Permissions tab of the GNOME Nautilus file manager's Properties dialog box.

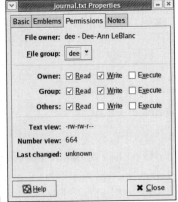

Rulin' with Konqueror

In KDE, the default file manager is Konqueror. You can find this program in Fedora (as I discuss in Chapter 9) by choosing Main Menu⇨Internet⇨ More Internet Applications⇨Konqueror Web Browser. After it's open, click the button with the house to go to your Home directory. Figure 10-4 shows an example of what you can see with Konqueror open.

In default GNOME and KDE setups, the Main Menu button in the lower-left corner is a footprint (in GNOME) or a big K (in KDE). If you installed Fedora Core 1, the Main Menu button is the Red Hat fedora icon in both GNOME and KDE. In other KDE-setup distributions, Konqueror is your default file manager.

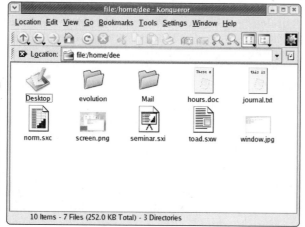

Figure 10-4:
The KDE
Konqueror
file
manager,
displaying
the home
directory.

The workings of this file manager should seem similar to those from other operating systems. After you click Window⇨Show Navigation Panel to open the directory tree on the left, you have the two-panel setup you're probably already used to from Windows Explorer or the Mac OS. From here, you can move about and utilize the usual drag-and-drop features.

Browsing your files

Konqueror allows you to move through your file system with ease. The main thing you need to keep in mind is that your directories are on the left (if you have opened the directory tree on the left), and your files and subdirectories are on the right. File management tasks you can do in Konqueror are described in this list:

- ✔ **Open a directory using the left pane:** To open a directory using the left pane, locate it in the list and click the plus-sign (+) symbol next to it. The graphic changes to a minus-sign (–); and if the directory has subdirectories, they're now listed beneath the current directory.

- ✔ **Open a directory using the right pane:** To open a directory using the right pane, locate it in the window and click it. Linux automatically displays the files in this directory.

- ✔ **View a directory's contents:** To view the files in a directory using the left side, click the directory's folder icon or the name.

- ✔ **Look at files and run programs:** To view a file's contents or run a program, click the item in the listing. If the system is unsure of which program should be used to open a file, it offers you the Open With dialog box so that you can select the appropriate application.

If you double-click a file to open it and get an unexpected and useless result, click the back (left-pointing) arrow and then right-click the file you want to open. A shortcut menu appears. Click Open With and from the pop-up sub-menu, choose the program you want to use to view this file.

Changing file views

Are you getting too much information about each file or not enough? Konqueror has a collection of settings that lets you tweak how file information is presented. The Icon View and Tree View buttons appear to the right of the first row of icons when you're viewing a directory's contents. These buttons have the following set of functions:

- To move between a general Icon view to a more detailed file listing, click the Icon View and Tree View buttons.

- To select which layout of icons you want in Icon view, click and hold the Icon View button until the drop-down menu with Icon View and Multicolumn View appears. Then click the option you want to use.

- To select which combination of details you want in Tree view, click and hold the Tree View button until the drop-down menu with Tree View, Info List View, Detailed List View, and Text View appears. Then click the option you want to use.

Take some time to experiment with these sets of options to see which one you like the best. The last layout you choose remains as your default until you close Konqueror.

The Settings menu contains a number of entries that allow you to customize Konqueror so that it remembers your preferences.

Copying files

In some versions of KDE and Konqueror, you can open a file just by single-clicking it. You may think that it's hard to drag and drop when just clicking an item opens it. You can, however, still use this feature! Just make sure not to click and release the item you want to move. You have to click it and hold the mouse button down as you drag the item.

For copying and pasting without using drag and drop, follow these steps:

1. **Right-click the item and choose Copy from the shortcut menu that appears.**

   Your computer copies the item to its memory.

2. **Navigate to where you want to put the copy.**

3. **Right-click in the destination directory and choose Paste from the shortcut menu that appears.**

Your computer copies the file to this location.

Moving and deleting files

Moving a file or directory is suspiciously similar to copying one:

1. **Right-click the item and choose Cut from the shortcut menu that appears.**

   Your computer copies the item to its memory and grays out the icon to indicate that it's on its way out.

2. **Navigate to where you want to put the file or directory.**

3. **Right-click in the destination directory and choose Paste from the shortcut menu that appears.**

   Your computer moves the file or directory to this location.

Fortunately, deleting files and directories is pretty easy in Konqueror. You just browse to the item you want to delete, right-click it, and choose either Move to Trash or Delete from the shortcut menu! Or, you can even use the Delete key.

You can delete the contents of the Trash at any time by following these steps:

1. **Right-click the Trash icon.**

   This action opens a shortcut menu of options.

2. **Choose Empty Trash from the shortcut menu.**

   A confirmation dialog box opens.

3. **Click Empty to delete the contents of the Trash folder.**

   Linux permanently removes the items in the Trash folder.

Viewing and changing permissions

You work with permissions in Konqueror almost exactly the same way you do in Nautilus. To view permissions, change to any of the Tree View listing formats. To modify a file's permissions in this file manager, follow these steps:

1. **Browse to the file or directory's location.**

2. **Right-click the file or directory and choose Properties from the shortcut menu that appears.**

   The Properties dialog box appears.

3. **Click the Permissions tab.**

The Permissions tab of the Properties dialog box opens, as shown in Figure 10-5.

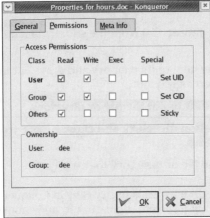

4. **Set the new permissions and ownerships.**

   As you can see, Konqueror offers you some handy tools for setting the permissions exactly the way you want them without having to remember the structure or which numbers go with which letters. You can also change owner and group information here.

5. **Click OK to close the dialog box.**

Chapter 11

Working without the GUI

Whom computers would destroy, they must first drive mad.

—*Anonymous*

*M*any computing old-timers speak fondly of the command line. Others who developed their skills by pointing and clicking refer to the command line as some antiquated tool used by crusty old-timers. The truth is that most skilled computing professionals recognize the merits of both the graphical user interface (GUI) and the command-line interface (CLI). You must understand that the command line provides a powerful lever for operating your computer. If you ever watch over the shoulder of a skilled Linux geek, you notice that, after logging in, he doesn't take long to start tapping out seemingly cryptic instructions on a command line.

In this chapter, I explore the Linux program that provides the CLI, which is called the bash shell. Although many shells are available for Linux, bash is the most common, and for good reason. Basically, the creators of bash rolled all the good features of all the other shells into one terrific program.

Each shell has its own way of handling commands and its own additional set of tools. I start by explaining what a shell really is, and when you understand that, you're ready to get down and dirty with bash. I cover specifically what you can do with some of the best features of the bash shell. Then, I continue with working at the command prompt and get into bash shell interior decorating.

Shells come equipped to perform certain functions. Most of these features have evolved over time to assist the command-line jockey with a myriad of tasks. Although I only scratch the surface here, you're encouraged to read the man page for bash because it's likely one of the more complete and readable man pages in existence. You can read all about how to use man pages (the online Help system in Linux) in the "Help!" section, later in this chapter.

Playing the Shell Game

You need a way to tell the computer what you want it to do. In Linux, one of the ways to communicate with the computer is through something called the shell. A *shell* isn't a graphical thing; it's the sum total of the commands and syntax you have available to you to do your work.

The shell environment is rather dull and boring by graphical desktop standards. When you start the shell, all you see is a short prompt, such as a $, followed by a blinking cursor awaiting your keyboard entry. In just a moment, I show you a couple of methods for accessing the shell.

The default shell used in Linux is the bash shell. This work environment is based on the original Unix shell, which is called the Bourne shell and is also referred to as sh. The term bash stands for the *Bourne again sh*ell. The bash shell comes with most Linux distributions.

If you installed your Linux distribution to log in to a graphical desktop, such as GNOME or the KDE environment, you're likely not looking at a shell prompt. Rather, you interact with your computer via a mouse. You can start a bash session from within the GUI desktop in a couple ways.

The quickest method to activate a bash session is to click the computer monitor icon on the GNOME panel, located at the bottom of your screen, or in Fedora Core, choose Main Menu⇨System Tools⇨Terminal. If successful, you should be looking at a screen similar to the one shown in Figure 11-1.

The prompt may include some helpful information. For example, if you're logged in as evan on the machine deepthink in Fedora Core 1, your prompt looks similar to this:

```
[evan@deepthink evan]$
```

Before surveying a few of the shell capabilities, I need to tell you about another method for starting a shell session. First of all, notice that your shell prompt is merely inside a window that is part of your GUI desktop. Suppose you want to start a shell session in a character-only or text environment.

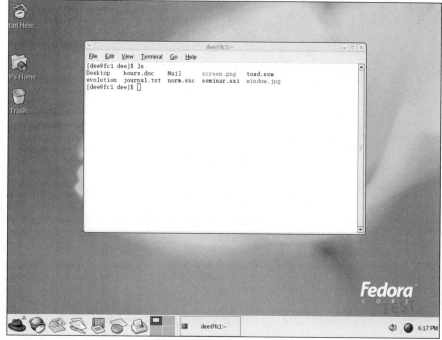

Figure 11-1:
Fedora Core
1 GNOME
desktop
with an
open bash
instance.

To switch to a text environment, press Ctrl+Alt+F2. Don't be alarmed when your familiar graphical desktop disappears. It's still running in the background, and you can get back to where you left off in a moment. But first, a few words about the boring text screen you're looking at now (I hope).

You're looking at a virtual terminal, one of several available with your default installation. You probably see something like this:

```
deepthink login:
```

Go ahead and type your username and password, which you're prompted for. You see a message indicating your last login date followed by the bash prompt:

```
[evan@deepthink evan]$
```

Notice the similarity between this prompt and the open window you left behind in the GUI desktop. Both prompts are an indication that you have a bash session open. Note that, although it's accurate to say they're both the results of using the bash shell, they're distinct and separate *instances* of the same program. In other words, the environment you're working with here is exclusive of the bash environment you still have open in the GUI terminal window.

"Which login am I in?"

One of the most confusing concepts about Linux shells is that you're continually moving in and out of them. Each time you log in, you open a shell instance — a specific shell with its own settings. If you're logged in twice on two different virtual terminals, therefore, you have two shells going. If you change the settings in one of the shells, those settings don't apply to the other. However, if you make the changes permanent, any new shells you open may have the new settings.

Are you wondering where your GUI desktop has gone? Just to settle your nerves a bit, do some jumping around. The GUI desktop is located at virtual terminal (VT) number 7 by default. You now have VT-2 open. Position your piano-playing fingers and strike the chord Ctrl+Alt+F7. Within a second or two, your screen should flash and return you to your graphical desktop, and your terminal window with the bash prompt should still be patiently awaiting your command. Neat huh? And guess what? The bash session you left open on VT-1 is still there; you never logged out. Go back again by pressing Ctrl+Alt+F2. Voilà! — right where you left it. Feel free to jump back and forth a few times, and try some other VTs, (F1 through F6). Whoopee! This virtual terminal stuff rocks.

Okay, when you have grown weary and bored with this little trick, exit or log out from all the VTs you may have opened and return to the graphical desktop and your bash prompt. Then you can explore what all the fuss is about with this *shell* doohickey.

Understanding bash Command Syntax and Structure

Many people happily skip through their Linux use without understanding the fundamentals of commands in the bash shell. Note that this approach makes you lose out on some cool capabilities available in bash. The more you know about how this shell's "language" works, the more interesting things you can do with it.

The basics of using bash at the command prompt often involve typing a command and any of its flags and values. For example, you enter the ls -la ~ command to see a long-format listing of all files in your home directory, including those that start with a dot (.), which are typically configuration files and directories. That other mysterious squiggle character is technically called a tilde. The *tilde* is a bash shortcut character that points to a user's home directory. For this example, I merely list the contents of my home directory.

You can break a command into three distinct components:

✔ The command name

✔ The options or flags

✔ The arguments

Consider this example.

Start with a simple command. The du command lists the contents of the directory you're now in, and its subdirectories, and how much hard drive space each item takes up, with a total at the end. Try typing just the du command by itself:

```
du
```

That's neat, but it probably raises more questions than it answers. The output gives you a long listing of data, but of what? Are those numbers in bytes, kilobytes, or messages from outer space? To clarify, try adding a simple option to your command:

```
ls -h
```

You're still issuing the same command, but now you're providing additional direction on what you want displayed. The -h option tells du to show you the information in terms that humans can read more easily. Now *M*s, *K*s, and *G*s appear next to the numbers so that you can see how big these numbers actually are. But, wait — there's more. What if you just want to know the total amount of disk space this directory and its subdirectories are taking up? That calls for the -s flag:

```
du -s
```

What if you want the total for a different directory? Or just one of your subdirectories? In my case, I keep a Music subdirectory for the items I have copied from my CDs into Oggs (see Chapter 15). I can type the following command to see how much hard drive space that directory takes up in a human-readable way rather than have to count zeroes:

```
du -sh ~/Music
```

In this example, du is the command name, -sh indicates the flags (options), and ~/Music is an argument. The -sh flags can be accompanied by many more flags that provide various options applicable to the command.

Are you wondering where to find all the available options and arguments of a particular command? Most commands offer `man` pages, which are discussed in the "Help!" section, later in this chapter. Another good place to turn is the `-help` option, available with many commands. Note that `-help` displays a terse list of options, but it's nice and quick if you already know about an option but just can't remember exactly which one it is. Try it by entering the following command:

```
du -help
```

Cool, huh?

Starting Programs from the Shell

The most obvious, and perhaps not so apparent, use of the shell is to start other programs. Most utilities you use in Linux are separate and distinct executable programs. Users need a method to start these programs. In the GUI, you can associate an icon with a particular program, and the graphical environment contains the intelligence to start the program. Note that programs often require information drawn from environment variables, which are a part of the shell environment. (I discuss environment variables in more detail later in this chapter.) For this reason, the GUI often calls the intended program via the `bash` shell. So you see, even the GUI finds the shell a necessity — although the GUI does its best to hide this detail from users.

For example, after you have a terminal window open, type the following command at the prompt:

```
mahjongg
```

After a few seconds, the Mahjongg game is displayed. You can start any program at a command prompt that you can click from the GNOME menu if you know what the underlying program name is. Note that if you're in a virtual terminal (press Alt+F1), you may see an error message. Some programs require a graphical environment in which to run, which a character-based terminal obviously doesn't have.

Putting Wildcard Expansion to Good Use

Computing life would be tedious if you had to repeat the same command on multiple files. After all, aren't repetitive tasks what the computer was designed to do? *Wildcard expansion* refers to the ability of one command to be executed against many files. The asterisk (*) and the question mark (?) are two wildcard characters that are used to match any filename, or a portion of a filename. For example, you can use the following command to see a long directory listing that includes only files that end with a .doc filename extension:

```
ls -l *.doc
```

The files listed may include resume.doc, cover_letter.doc, and to_editor.doc, for example. (Refer to Chapter 10 for more on wildcards.)

If you're used to using Microsoft Windows, be aware that, in Linux, no special meaning is assigned to file extensions, such as .doc, .exe, and .txt. For example, in a Linux filename, the dot character in a .doc extension is treated like any other character in the filename. However, the . extension convention is rather handy and widely used to easily identify file types; just remember that, unlike the Windows file system, the Linux file system doesn't require anyone to follow this convention.

Working with Long Commands

As you become used to the command line, you should learn some shortcuts to ease your typing chores. In this section, I show you some features of the bash shell designed to make your life on the command line as pleasant as possible. These features include command-line completion, editing, and using the history of previously entered commands.

Asking Linux to complete a command or filename for you

Considering that you do much more typing on the command line in Linux than you may normally do in a GUI environment, a feature that provides typing shortcuts wherever possible is great. Command completion is a function of the shell that completes filename and system commands.

The capability of the Linux file system to deal with practically unlimited sizes of filenames means that many filenames can become huge. Typing these long filenames can become cumbersome. Fortunately, with command completion, typing a command or a long filename is short work.

You may want to use command completion in two situations: to enter a command or to complete a filename.

Completing a command

Suppose that you want to type a command, but you can remember only that it begins with the letters up and is supposed to return the length of time that has passed since the system was rebooted. Type **up** at the command prompt and then press Tab:

```
[evan@deepthink evan]$ up[TAB]
```

One of two things happens:

- ✔ If only one matching command is in the *search path* (directory locations for searching for programs), your command line is completed with that command, and the system waits for you to press Enter to execute the command.

- ✔ If you hear a beep, it means that more than one command begins with up. Simply press Tab a second time, and all the possibilities are displayed. Locate the command on the list and continue typing it until the first letters are unique, at which point you can press the Tab key to complete the command.

Completing a filename

Command-line completion isn't only for commands; if you're typing a filename on your command line, you only need to type the first few characters and then press Tab. The shell usually searches the current working directory for filenames that match what you have typed and subsequently completes the filename on the command line. This feature behaves the same way as the command-completion feature in that, if more than one file contains the letters you type, you hear a beep and need to press Tab again to see a list of choices.

It takes a little getting used to, but after you have control of the Tab key and the shell command-line completion feature, you may wonder how you ever got along without it.

Accessing your command history

It's nice of the shell to remember what you have done, for better or worse. Having the shell keep track of the commands you enter makes it easy to return to those gawd-awfully long commands you pecked at a while ago — even days ago! Let me give you an example. Suppose that yesterday you managed to issue a command to find all the *core dump* files in your system (core dump files are massive files containing debugging data that only an expert programmer or your computer can understand) and delete them. The command looked something like this:

```
find / -name core -exec rm {} \;
```

To re-execute the command, all you need to do is fish it out of your shell history and rerun it. The simplest way to read through your command history line by line is to press the up-arrow key repeatedly until you locate the command you want to re-execute. Then just press the Enter key to run the command again. That's all there is to it!

You can access your command history in two ways:

✔ **Press the up-arrow key:** This technique is the easiest way to access the history. As soon as you press the up-arrow key, you see all your previous commands light up on the command line. When you find what you're looking for, just press Enter and you're cookin'.

✔ **Enter the** history **command:** The history command lists your last 20 commands (by default) when you enter it at the prompt.

Creating aliases for commands

Pretend for a moment that you're one of those crusty old DOS users who enjoys wielding commands, such as dir to display a directory listing. You can use the alias feature of bash to create new commands that resemble the commands you're used to. For example, to create an alias that generates a long directory listing similar to what you have become accustomed to with dir, you can enter this line:

```
[evan@deepthink evan]$ alias dir='ls -l'
```

Then, whenever you type dir, you see a long directory listing.

You can also use the alias feature to create shortcuts to very long commands you use frequently. To see which aliases Red Hat is kind enough to provide by default, simply type the alias command. The list includes a few prepackaged aliases along with the dir alias you just created.

Note that the next time you log out or create an additional shell instance, your newly created aliases disappear. I show you later how you can put these aliases and other shell commands into a bash startup file that runs each time you begin a new bash session. (See "Altering the Shell Environment," later in this chapter.)

Working with Variables

Variables in the bash shell are words or strings of text that computers use to represent a piece of data. An example of using a variable is setting the variable fruit to contain the text apple. A number of variables contain information about your account and environment settings.

Variables versus environment variables

The first thing I need to make clear is that the bash shell has two classes of variables:

- ✓ **Variables:** A variable can be referenced in a program or shell session, but it's visible and available to only that session or program.

- ✓ **Environment variables:** An environment variable can also be referenced by the shell or program. However, it has the added behavior of having its value copied to any other program or shell that is created from its environment.

You can usually tell at a glance the difference between a variable and an environment variable in bash. The normal convention is to name local variables in all lowercase or in mixed-case characters. An environment variable, however, is usually always in all uppercase letters.

Checking out commonly used environment variables

The bash shell has many environment variables. You may be amazed at the range of items these variables store. The handy thing is that, if something is stored in a variable, you can change it to suit your needs! In Table 11-1, I list the environment variables you're most likely to want to work with.

Table 11-1	Commonly Used bash Environment Variables	
Environment Variable	*Purpose*	*Value*
HISTSIZE	Determines the number of previously typed commands that are stored.	Number of commands
HOME	Sets the location of your home directory.	The path to your home directory
MAILCHECK	Sets how often the bash shell checks for new mail in your mailbox. If mail has arrived, you see a message similar to You have new mail the next time you do something at the command prompt.	Number of seconds to wait between checks

Environment Variable	Purpose	Value
PATH	Sets the directories that bash looks in, and the order to look in them to find a program name you type at the command prompt.	Colon-separated directories
PS1	Sets your command prompt.	Command and formatting characters used to form the prompt

Most environment variables are established for you by the system administrator or perhaps by the shell itself. These variables are mostly read by programs to gather information, and you don't need to change their values. However, you may want to alter the value of some environment variables. For example, in Table 11-1, the first entry, HISTSIZE, determines the number of lines of command-line history that are kept on file. You may remember the discussion, earlier in this chapter, of re-executing a command from yesterday (refer to the section "Accessing your command history" earlier in this chapter). By setting a higher number for HISTSIZE, you can save an even longer list of previously executed commands.

Storing and retrieving variables' values

To assign a value to a variable, you just use the variable name followed by an equals sign (=) followed by the value to store:

```
MyVariable=MyValue
```

To retrieve the value being represented by that variable, you need to precede the variable name with a dollar sign ($). Look at a variable, created by the shell, that determines what your prompt looks like. This variable is named PS1. First, you view the value being held by PS1:

```
echo $PS1
```

You likely see something like the following line:

```
[\u@\h \W]\$
```

Each of the characters preceded by a backslash represents a special instruction to the shell to return specific information when the shell prompt is referenced. See Table 11-2 for examples of special slash-characters you can use in customizing your prompt.

Table 11-2	Pieces of the PS1 Puzzle
Component	**Result**
\!	Prints the position of the command in your history list.
\#	Prints the number of commands you have used during the current shell session.
\$	Prints a $ for user accounts or a # for the superuser.
\d	Prints the date in the following format: day month date.
\h	Prints the name of the machine you're logged in to.
\n	Moves down to the next line.
\s	Prints bash for the bash shell.
\t	Prints the time in 24-hour format.
\u	Prints your username.
\w	Prints the lowest current directory level.
\W	Prints the entire current directory.

Okay, on with the example; to change your shell prompt to something more amusing, enter the following line:

```
PS1='Hello \u, what can I do for you? => '
```

Note the single quotes. (I get to those later in this chapter.) Immediately after pressing the Enter key, you see that your prompt has changed into something more inviting. Don't worry if you would rather have the original prompt: You can either reassign to the original prompt the value stored in PS1 or simply log out and log in again, and you're back to familiar territory.

Are you wondering which other variables your system has in store for you? You can view all environment variables at one time by typing env. Note that you may not have any reason to access variables on the command line as a casual use of Linux. However, after you get more proficient, you may want to journey into the shell programming capabilities of bash, in which case variable storage is quite handy, just as it is in any computer programming language.

What's with those single quotes? You have to be careful of some details when changing environment variables. If you're just assigning something to a number, you could just use, for example, HISTSIZE=250. However, if you want to use something with spaces in it, you need to use quotes. Which kind of quotes you use depends on what else you want to do.

If you want to display *exactly* what you have specified, use single quotes to create a *literal text string*. For example, type the following line at a command prompt:

```
echo 'Hello, my name is $USER'
```

Kinda goofy, huh? Take a look at a different kind of string that the shell interprets differently: an *interpolated string*. An *interpolated* value is one in which the shell interprets special characters before processing the value. Rather than use single quotes, this time you use the same example with double quotes:

```
echo "Hello, my name is $USER"
```

Notice what the output is this time. Rather than display the exact text you provided, the shell replaces the variable name, designated with a dollar sign, with the actual value stored in that variable.

Why did I use single quotes in the PS1 example? The items with the backslashes (\) are *interpreted* one way or another. However, if you use double quotes with PS1 they are interpreted only once, so that item that lists what directory you're in changes only the first time. With a single quote, the variables are interpreted every time you do something.

If you're going to play around with environment variables, I recommend that you start by using the methods I discuss in this section. After you have decided that you're comfortable with any changes you have made, you can make your changes permanent by opening the ~/.bash_profile file and adding the same text there. The next time you log in, the changes go into effect. I talk more about making changes permanent in an upcoming section.

Don't be too discouraged if you don't understand all this variable stuff right now. As you become more proficient with Linux, you should explore *shell scripting*. Shell scripting is the art of creating computer programs with just the shell. Most Linux and Unix administrators speak shell script language like you and I speak our native tongues.

Using Redirection and Pipes

Redirection and pipes facilitate the flow of information. A *pipe* is exactly what it sounds like: It directs the output of one program to the input of another program. A pipeline may consist of several utilities that are plumbed together by pipes. At either end of this pipeline is, optionally, a redirection.

Almost all Linux utilities that require input and output have been plumbed with the following common interfaces: stdin (standard in), stdout (standard out), and stderr (standard error). By having a common method to feed input to a program or read data from the output of a program, you can glue utilities together into sophisticated solutions.

Redirecting command output

I discuss redirecting command output here because it's by far the most common form of information detouring. One example of *output redirection* involves telling a command to send its results to a file rather than to the screen, as you probably have been used to seeing. Start in some familiar territory by typing `ls -la ~` and then pressing Enter, to produce something like the following:

```
total 20
drwx------ 2 sue   users 4096 Oct 30 07:48 .
drwxr-xr-x 5 root  root  4096 Oct 30 11:57 ..
-rw-r----- 1 sue   users   24 Oct 30 06:50 .bash_logout
-rw-r----- 1 sue   users  230 Oct 30 06:50 .bash_profile
-rw-r----- 1 sue   users  124 Oct 30 06:50 .bashrc
-rw-rw-r-- 1 sue   users    0 Jan 2 07:48 wishlist
```

Want to send this information to a file instead? You can use the > redirection operator to tell `bash` to send the data into a file instead of onto your screen. Enter the following command to send the information to a file named `listing`:

```
ls -la ~ > listing
```

Notice that nothing displays on the screen, as you normally would expect. That's because the shell has rerouted the output to a file named `listing`. To verify that the directory listing is there, enter the following command:

```
cat listing
```

The `cat` command displays the contents of the listing file.

Note that if you type `ls -la ~ > listing` again, the data is overwritten, meaning that the file's contents are wiped out and replaced with the new output. You can avoid this situation by using >> as your redirection operator, which tells `bash` to add the command's output to the end of the specified file. If you type `ls -la ~ >> listing` in the same directory after making no changes, the contents of `listing` are as follows:

```
total 20
drwx------ 2 sue  users 4096 Oct 30 07:48 .
drwxr-xr-x 5 root root  4096 Oct 30 11:57 ..
-rw-r----- 1 sue  users   24 Oct 30 06:50 .bash_logout
-rw-r----- 1 sue  users  230 Oct 30 06:50 .bash_profile
-rw-r----- 1 sue  users  124 Oct 30 06:50 .bashrc
-rw-rw-r-- 1 sue  users    0 Jan  2 07:48 wishlist
total 20
drwx------ 2 sue  users 4096 Oct 30 07:48 .
drwxr-xr-x 5 root root  4096 Oct 30 11:57 ..
-rw-r----- 1 sue  users   24 Oct 30 06:50 .bash_logout
-rw-r----- 1 sue  users  230 Oct 30 06:50 .bash_profile
-rw-r----- 1 sue  users  124 Oct 30 06:50 .bashrc
-rw-rw-r-- 1 sue  users    0 Jan  2 07:48 wishlist
```

Laying pipes

Another `bash` shell feature enables you to connect commands so that the output of one becomes the input for the next one. This feature is referred to as a *pipe*. Suppose that you want to look over the details of all files in the /etc directory in long-listing format. If you type `ls -la /etc` to do so, a massive listing appears, and much of the information scrolls right past you. Although you can back up a bit by pressing Shift+PageUp, you may not be able to see everything.

To see all the information, you can do one of two things:

✔ Send the data to a file with redirection by typing something like `ls -la /etc > ~/etclisting` and then review the contents of `~/etclisting` with your favorite editor.

✔ Pipe the output to the `more` command. This command ensures that text doesn't show more than one screen at a time. It waits until you press the spacebar before showing you the next screen. Many Linux users find this command quite useful.

To pipe the output to `more`, type `ls -la` *directory_path* `| more`, where *directory_path* is the directory for which you want to list the contents. The | symbol (which on the keyboard looks more like two vertical bars stacked on top of each other rather than just one solid line) tells `bash` that you want to use a pipe.

The `more` utility is a *pager*. There's another utility that behaves like `more`, but has additional features and ability. Guess what it's called? It's called `less`. The `less` utility allows you to scroll information both forward and backward and search for keywords. So, `less` can be used in place of `more`. At least in this example, `less` is better than `more`.

Altering the Shell Environment

You can change several configuration files to alter your bash environment. Each of the following files is text and can be edited with any available editor. You can simply alter or add the settings your want in each of these files:

- ✔ /etc/profile: The system-wide settings. When any user logs in to a bash session, this file is read first.

- ✔ .bash_profile: The user-specific login settings, run after the /etc/profile file is evaluated.

- ✔ .bashrc: The subshell configuration file that is read each time a subshell instance is created. A subshell is called every time a new program is executed. This file merely provides another level of shell configuration for this event.

- ✔ .bash_logout: The file that's evaluated when a user logs out of a bash session. This file is handy for deleting temporary work files or other housekeeping you may want to perform after closing up shop for the day.

Note that these last three files are kept in a user's home directory and are hidden, which the dot at the beginning of the filename indicates.

If you experiment heavily with these files, create a separate user account so that you can do whatever you want without messing up your own login. This advice especially goes for /etc/profile. You can damage everyone's logins with this one! To create a separate /etc/profile, you can make a backup by typing cp /etc/profile /etc/profile.original. Then, edit /etc/profile knowing you can always delete it with the rm command and use the mv command to rename /etc/profile.original to /etc/profile.

Your Handy Command Toolkit

Now that you may have a little more respect for that command prompt and what it can do, you're ready to take a look at a few commonly used tools.

"I'm lost"

Want to know whom you logged in as last? Or, perhaps you have chanced upon a terminal with no user nearby. A few key commands can give you information about who and where you are:

- ✔ whoami: By typing whoami on the command line, you can find out to whom the current shell belongs.

✔ who: The who command is related to the whoami command, but it displays not only who owns the session, but also the controlling terminal and date logged in along with every other user logged in to the system.

✔ uname: You can find out more about the system you're running by using the uname command. Try adding the -a option on the end for information regarding your current kernel version and when it was compiled.

✔ pwd: Knowing whom you're logged in as is only part of the mystery — knowing *where* you are is the other vital clue. As you find out in Chapter 10, much of navigating Linux is in working with files and directories. Unless you're an astral traveler, you can likely be in only one place at any time. In the Linux file system, this place is known as the current working directory. To determine your current working directory, type **pwd**.

"Help!"

The *man page* system is the electronic manual for Linux (*man* is short for *man*ual), designed to provide users with a convenient reference to all the detailed command information. This information includes command prompt options, file formats, and program function usage.

The syntax for drawing a man page is man <command name>.

Don't know the command you're looking for or need basic information about using the man page system? Just type man man to get started.

Tracking memory and disk space

Other useful information for inquiring minds is how much memory and disk space is being used. The df command returns a list of all your mounted partitions and how much space is used and available of each one. As with many commands, you can see a terse listing of helpful options by including the —help option on the end of the command. Use the df —help command to determine which command option you need to use to display the information in a much more familiar byte-size, rather than block-size, number (it's -h).

That's all fine and good, but perhaps you're running out of disk space and you want to find some files to delete, or at least know where all your space is being used. The du command stands for *d*isk *u*sage. The command by itself simply returns the number of blocks allocated in the current working directory. If you include an argument of a directory path, du returns that directory and all subsequent directories, listing the number of blocks used in each one.

I don't want to overwhelm you right now, but if you type the command top, you can see a second-by-second update of how your system is allocating resources, such as memory, and to which processes. Enjoy it as long as you like, and just press Q to exit when you're done.

Clearing the screen

The clear and reset commands are handy to know about when you're working in a shell. The clear command simply wipes the bash screen clean. Don't worry; it's not deleting any files or changing and settings — it's just tidying up so that you can start dumping new stuff to the screen again.

The reset command is a little more interesting. Suppose that you try listing a binary file to the screen with the cat command. After the computer finishes puking the result of executing the cat command on a binary file, you may get lucky and still be able to read your prompt. More likely, your prompt has been rendered into box characters of no special meaning, and typing on the keyboard gives you more of the same. To get back to normal, just type reset and press Enter. Note that it doesn't look like you're typing the word reset, but rest assured that the computer understands the series of characters and, after a couple seconds, should restore your shell environment to your native language.

What's cookin'?

A few more status commands can help you keep tabs on your system:

- ps: While top is useful for watching what's happening, the ps command lets you take a snapshot of what's happening on the system. This command returns statistics on all of your processes, or even every process on your system.

- kill: One handy use of virtual terminals and the ability to start a shell session is the ability to sneak up from behind and kill a process that is misbehaving. (It sounds much harsher than it really is.) The kill command is usually executed (no pun intended) with the following parameters:

  ```
  kill -signal process_id
  ```

  The -signal is a number that indicates the message you want to send to the process. Not all messages are designed to destroy the process: Some graciously request that the process stop what it's doing and return the resources to the kernel. The deadly signal is -9, the equivalent of vaporizing the process from the system regardless of the process's intentions.

- killall: The killall command, related to the kill command, allows you to kill a process based on the name of the command that's running the process. For example, I at one time routinely jumped to a virtual terminal and entered killall netscape because some bugs in the software seemed to allow the Netscape program to run amok. This problem hasn't occurred lately, though, with all the work being poured into Mozilla.

Chapter 12

Gettin' Gooey with the GUIs

. . . .

In This Chapter

▶ Adding applets to the Panel

▶ Adding programs to the desktop

▶ Downloading and setting up themes

▶ Configuring the X Window System

. . . .

*T*he X Window System (or X) opens a world of possibilities. X is, in general, a set of applications that work together to provide a graphical interface. Some applications draw windows, some manage the look and feel of the interface, and others handle other aspects of the graphical world for you. In the Linux world, you can configure all these aspects, which is where many people start to get overwhelmed.

In Chapter 6, I introduce the two major players in the Linux GUI market: GNOME and KDE. In this chapter, you get a chance to alter the GUI's behavior to suit your own needs. For example, if you have a hard time reading text in those small command-prompt windows in the GUI, you can make both the windows and their fonts larger. A wealth of other things can be changed too, so read on and take a look.

If something goes terribly wrong in the GUI and you need to exit in a hurry, press Ctrl+Alt+Backspace. This key combination does one of two things. If you boot into the GUI, it collapses your GUI session and takes you to the GUI login prompt. However, if you boot to the command line, this key combination collapses the GUI immediately, taking you to the command line.

However, press Ctrl+Alt+Backspace only in an emergency. This key combination doesn't cleanly stop the programs involved. You'll end up with all kinds of bits and pieces of programs, files, and more on your system.

Changing GNOME's Look and Feel

Change is inevitable, except from a vending machine.

— Anonymous

The GNOME desktop environment has an amazing set of features for you to explore, including lots of ways to change the GUI's look and feel. Some of these customization features are nice and practical, and others are just plain fun. I tried to group the types of changes into related topics so that you can peruse them easily.

How do ya like them applets?

Applets — a collection of miniprograms that do anything from display the time to show system status — are available out there in the great big world of computer programming. A number of people got it in their heads to write some of these applets specifically for use in the GNOME desktop environment in Linux. So these applets are included with your GNOME installation. Some of these miniprograms are more useful than others. Then again, everybody needs a bit of entertainment too, right?

If you're using Red Hat Enterprise Linux or Fedora Core, GNOME is your default environment.

Adding an applet icon to the Panel

You can have fun sifting through to see what kinds of applets are available to you. To look through your options and perhaps add an applet to the Panel (remember that the Panel is the bar along the bottom of your screen), follow these steps:

1. **Right-click any free space on the Panel and choose Add to Panel.**

   The Add to Panel submenu opens.

2. **Browse the following submenus: Accessories, Amusements, Internet, Multimedia, and Utility.**

   Each of these submenus contains a collection of applets you can add to your panel.

3. **To install an applet, click it on the submenu.**

   The applet is now on your Panel.

Configuring an applet

After you have an applet placed and running, you may be able to play with configuration options. Some of these options enable you to change what information is displayed. Others have a variety of look-and-feel settings.

To check for which configuration and other options are available for your applet, follow these steps:

1. **Right-click the applet and examine the shortcut menu that appears.**

   This shortcut menu is different from applet to applet. The bottom portion is always the same: Remove from Panel and Move. Common entries for the top portion are Help and About. The rest of the items are either configuration options (see Step 2) or special applet features, such as the ability to copy the date from the Clock applet.

2. **Choose Preferences from the shortcut menu.**

   Not every applet has a Preferences dialog box. If this one does, the dialog box opens when you choose this option, and whichever configuration features this applet has are displayed.

3. **Alter the selections in the Preferences dialog box to customize this applet's behavior.**

   Now you get to have some fun. Make changes so that you can see what this applet can do. Each applet has its own set of features, so I cannot do a general walkthrough here. Just remember that you can always go back and change the settings or remove the applet from your panel later.

4. **Click Close to put your changes into effect and close the dialog box.**

An option available for all applets is to choose Move from the bottom of the shortcut menu. This action allows you to move the applet to another spot on the Panel.

Ditching an applet

You only have room for so many applets. And, if you're like me, you probably don't want to have every bit of free space cluttered with icons. To remove an applet from the Panel, simply right-click the applet you want to remove and choose Remove from Panel from the shortcut menu that appears. With nary a whimper, the applet vanishes from the Panel.

Don't forget the programs

You may be looking at your panel and wondering whether you can make any changes to the programs listed there, like you can with applets. The good news is that you *can* change the programs on the bar! They fit in the same empty spaces that applets do. You can also add a program to the desktop, if you want.

Adding a program to the Panel

If you have a program you end up using often, you can add it to your panel by following these steps:

1. **Click the Main Menu button and browse to the program you want to add to the bar.**

   Don't open the program. Just point to the menu item with your mouse pointer.

2. **Right-click the program and choose Add This Launcher to Panel.**

   An icon for this program appears on your Panel.

After you have your program on the Panel, you can run the program just by clicking its icon.

Removing a program from the Panel

If you want to remove one of the programs on the Panel, just right-click the icon you want to remove and choose Remove from Panel from the shortcut menu that appears. The icon vanishes from the Panel. That's it!

Adding a program to the desktop

The panel has only so much room. Maybe you would rather have your program shortcuts lined up on the desktop as you do in Windows. To add a program to the desktop, follow these steps:

1. **Click the Main Menu button to open the GNOME main menu.**

2. **Browse to the submenu containing the program you want to add to the desktop.**

   For example, if you want to add The GIMP, you open the Graphics submenu.

3. **Select the program you want to add to the desktop.**

   Don't open the program — just move your mouse pointer to it. For example, to add The GIMP, you move your mouse to the words _The GIMP_ so that they're highlighted.

4. **Click the program name and drag it to the desktop.**

   Be sure to drag this item to the side (not up through the menu). A little piece-of-paper graphic follows your mouse pointer until you release the mouse button. After you do so, your new shortcut is added to the desktop.

If you're not happy with where a desktop icon is placed, click it and then drag it to a new location.

Removing a program from the desktop

To get rid of an icon you have on your desktop, right-click the icon and choose Move to Trash from the shortcut menu that appears.

Customizing KDE

Don't worry, you KDE users: You have plenty of options too. You can customize your KDE setup in lots of ways, from the fun to the practical, so that you truly enjoy using it. As with GNOME, in fact, you can choose from far more features than I have room to cover in this chapter, so if you enjoy fiddling with the look and feel of your GUI, do some exploring on your own!

Applets keep fallin' on my head

Applets are miniprograms that do all sorts of things. An applet may display the time, show system status, or even offer a little frivolous fun. All kinds of applets are available out in the great big world of computer programming. A number of applets are included with your default KDE installation, though some of them are more useful than others.

Adding an applet icon to the Panel

An interesting combination of applets is available in KDE, and you can easily add and remove these little gems from your KDE Panel as suits your needs. To add an applet to the Panel (remember that the Panel is the bar along the bottom of your screen) in KDE, follow these steps:

1. **Right-click a blank spot on the Panel.**

   The Panel's menu opens.

2. **Choose Add⇨Applet.**

   You find yourself looking at the Applet submenu's contents.

3. **Select the applet you want to add to the Panel.**

   If the applet has any configuration options available, a Preferences dialog box opens after you have completed this step.

On a particularly crowded panel bar, you may have to use the right and left arrow bars at the Panel's ends to see the applet. You may need to delete from the Panel, in fact, any items you don't use, to ensure that everything can show up (see the section "Removing an applet," later in this chapter).

See those vertical bars between various Panel entries? Hover your mouse pointer over them, and the pointer changes into a two-headed arrow. You can drag those vertical bars left and right to expand and contract various parts of your panel.

Configuring an applet

Some applets have options that let you customize how they behave. Others are more boring and just do the same old thing no matter what you would prefer. To check which configuration and other options are available for your applet, follow these steps:

1. **Right-click the applet and examine the shortcut menu that appears.**

   This shortcut menu is different from applet to applet. In fact, there doesn't seem to be any real consistency in the menu options! (And not every applet even has a shortcut menu.) Look for entries such as Preferences, Settings, and the word *Configure*.

2. **Select the appropriate item from the shortcut menu.**

   If you see a Configure or Preferences dialog box, make your changes and click Apply to see how that affects your applet without closing the dialog box. You may see more than one configuration dialog box or sub-menu, as is the case for the KNewsTicker applet.

3. **Alter the selections in the dialog box to customize this applet's behavior.**

   Experiment as much as you want. Just remember that you can always go back and change the settings or remove the applet from your panel later.

4. **Close the dialog box.**

   In a Preferences dialog box, click OK to close the window. Settings dialog boxes typically have a button, aptly named Defaults, that enables you to restore your defaults.

Removing an applet

You have room for only so many applets. And, if you're like me, you probably don't want to have every bit of free space cluttered with icons. To remove an applet from the Panel, follow these steps:

1. **Right-click the Panel on an empty spot.**

2. **Choose Remove➪Applet.**

   The series of submenus opens, and you finally are looking at a list of the applets you now have on your Panel.

3. **Choose the applet you want to remove from the Panel.**

   The applet is no longer on your panel.

Cluttering the desktop with icons

KDE allows you to alter which applets and programs appear on your Panel, and on your desktop. Managing these shortcuts is a simple operation after you understand how it works.

Adding a program to the desktop

The Panel has only so much room. Maybe you would rather have your program shortcuts lined up on the desktop as you do in Windows. To add one of these shortcuts, follow these steps:

1. **Click the Main Menu button to open the KDE main menu.**

2. **Open the submenu containing the program for which you want to make a shortcut.**

   For example, if you want to add The GIMP, you open the Graphics submenu.

3. **Select the program for which you want to make a shortcut.**

   Don't open the program. For example, to add The GIMP, you move your mouse to the program and then click and hold the mouse button.

4. **Drag the program to the desktop.**

   A little piece-of-paper graphic follows your mouse pointer until you release the mouse button, at which point you're asked whether you want to add the shortcut to the desktop but not remove it from the menu (Copy Here); add the shortcut to the desktop and remove it from the menu (Move Here); or make an obvious shortcut that looks more like a Windows shortcut (Link Here). After you make your selection, your new shortcut is added to the desktop.

If you're not happy with where a desktop icon is placed, click it and then drag it to a new location.

Removing a program from the desktop

If you want to remove one of the programs from the desktop, just right-click the icon you want to remove and choose Delete. The icon vanishes from the Panel or desktop. That's it!

Prettying Up Your Desktop

You may be familiar with the ability to install desktop themes under Microsoft Windows. A *theme* in the desktop world refers to color schemes, images, and sounds applied to all portions of the desktop — window borders, fonts, icons, sound effects, and more — as part of a single, centralized entity. Many people are happy to find out that themes are available in the Linux world too.

Downloading themes

A large number of themes is available on the Internet for both GNOME and KDE. To find and grab these themes for your own use, follow these steps:

1. **Point your Web browser to** `http://themes.freshmeat.net.`

   You're taken to the Themes Web site, where any number of GUI customization items is offered.

2. **If the Section drop-down list box isn't already selected, select it and choose Themes.**

   You're taken to the Themes section of the site.

3. **For GNOME themes, click GTK; for KDE themes, click KDE.**

   This action brings you to the appropriate section, to ensure that you choose themes that work with your system.

4. **For GNOME, select the GTK 2.X area; for KDE, select KDE 3.X.**

   Now you're in the section for the latest versions of GNOME or KDE.

5. **Browse and choose the theme you want to try.**

   You can use the Sort Order drop-down list box to change the order in which the items are displayed. Keep your eye out for the requirements that go with the theme. Some themes require additional "engines" (software that runs behind the scenes), and you want to avoid them if you're uncomfortable with finding and adding software at this point. You're safe if it mentions Metacity — that's part of the Fedora Core GNOME GUI.

6. **After you have chosen your theme, click its name to go to the theme-specific page.**

   There, you can find any comments someone has about the theme.

7. **Scroll down if necessary and click the link under Tar/GZ.**

   Your browser asks for specifics on where you want to place the file. If you want to use this theme only for yourself, place it in your home directory or a subdirectory within your home. If you want to share the theme with others, place it in a directory that everyone can reach — make one, and set its permissions appropriately.

In the next two sections, I cover how to set this new theme as your current theme.

Setting your theme in KDE

Most Linux distributions are installed with a collection of themes already assembled. In Fedora Core (the distribution that comes with this book), you can tour the available themes in KDE and select one by following these steps:

1. **Open the main menu.**

   In default GNOME and KDE setups, the Main Menu button in the lower-left corner is a footprint in GNOME or a big K in KDE. If you installed Red Hat Linux, the Main Menu button is the Red Hat fedora icon in both GNOME and KDE.

   The appropriate menu opens.

2. **Choose Control Center⇨Appearance & Themes⇨Theme Manager.**

   This action opens the KDE Control Center, shown in Figure 12-1. If you didn't download a theme because you want to use one of those already included, skip to Step 7.

3. **Choose Main Menu⇨System Tools⇨Terminal.**

   A command-line terminal window opens.

4. **Use the** cd **command to go to the directory where you stored the theme.**

5. **Type** gunzip *themefile* **to uncompress the theme.**

   This step leaves you with a file of the same name, with .tar at the end.

Figure 12-1:
The KDE
Control
Center with
the default
theme
selected.

6. **Type** tar xvf themefile **to unpackage the theme.**

This step brings you down to a single file with .ktheme at the end.

7. **In the Control Center, click Add.**

The Add Theme dialog box appears.

8. **Browse to the** .ktheme **file and select it, clicking OK to add it to the Control Center's menu.**

If your theme is fully compatible with your version of KDE, the theme is added to the list of choices.

9. **Click the theme you want to sample.**

Look in the Preview pane, toward the top of the window — not all themes can be previewed. If the theme can be previewed, the Preview pane's contents change to represent what the various components of your screen look like if you use this theme. Notice how the window shown in Figure 12-2 is different from the window shown in Figure 12-1.

10. **Continue previewing themes until you find one you like.**

You're still not committing at this point, so don't worry.

11. **Click the Apply button to see how this theme looks when you apply it to your desktop.**

This process may take some time, depending on the speed of your computer. The changes you see may be minor, or your desktop may look incredibly different. If you want to go back, you need to click your preceding theme (Default if you never chose one) and click Apply again.

12. **Click the X in the upper-right corner to close the Control Center.**

Figure 12-2:
The KDE
Control
Center with
a different
theme
selected.

Setting your theme in GNOME

Most Linux distributions are installed with a collection of themes already assembled. In Red Hat Linux (the distribution that comes with this book), you can tour the available themes in GNOME and select one by following these steps:

1. **Click the Main Menu button.**

   The appropriate main menu opens.

2. **Choose Preferences⇨Theme.**

   This action opens the GNOME Theme Preferences dialog box, shown in Figure 12-3.

3. **If you downloaded a theme, add it to the Theme Preferences dialog box.**

   Double-click your user's Home directory icon on your desktop to open the file manager, and then browse to where you stored the theme. Select the theme file (yes, while it still has the `.tar.gz` extension) and drag it into the left (Installer) pane of the Theme Preferences dialog box. If your theme is fully compatible, the installer dialog box opens. Click Install, and your new theme is added to the list of choices.

   The Theme Preferences dialog box allows you to install the theme even if it isn't compatible with your GUI! This is bad since said theme *doesn't work.* Once you have added the theme, if it doesn't show up in the themes list in Step 4, the theme isn't compatible.

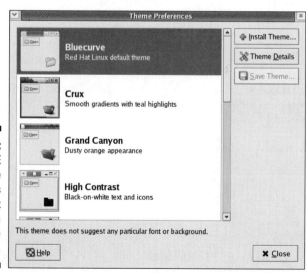

Figure 12-3: The GNOME Theme Preferences dialog box with a theme selected.

4. **If you installed a new theme, click Details to open the Theme Details dialog box, click the theme you want to sample, and click Close to return to the main dialog box.**

   If you like this theme and want to keep it in your list, click Save Theme. You're asked to give the theme a name, and then it shows up in the Theme Preferences dialog.

5. **Click the theme you want to sample.**

   Your desktop items change to match the theme. What a handy way to preview!

6. **Continue previewing themes until you find one you like.**

   You're still not committing at this point, so don't worry. You're not committed until you close the dialog box, and even then you can always come back and change it later.

7. **Click Close when you're finished, and the Theme Preferences dialog box closes.**

Tweaking the GUI's Innards

Behind GNOME and KDE lurks the X Window System, or "X." X provides the skeletal GUI structure and functionality. GNOME and KDE make use of this skeleton to provide you with a pleasant GUI environment. Whenever you configure hardware or other basic GUI features like resolution, you actually work with X, and not GNOME or KDE. In this section, I introduce you to the critical components of X and point you to some useful X configuration tools.

The /etc/X11/XF86Config file contains your X configuration. Although this file is just a normal text file, the format is complicated and confusing. Rather than make you work with this file by hand, the various Linux distributions provide a number of tools. The following table can help you identify which tool or tools you can use to change your X configuration for a few different Linux distributions:

Linux Distribution	Tool
Red Hat	Xconfigurator and redhat-config-xfree86
SuSE	sax and sax2
Mandrake	drakx

The X Window System searches for the XF86Config file in several places, reading the first one it finds. The filename XF86Config-4 takes precedence over XF86Config in the distributions where it occurs, so if you find both, go with XF86Config-4.

Additional X configuration tools come with every Linux distribution. They're not quite as easy to use as those just listed, but if you need them, here they are:

- XF86Setup: A popular, graphical X Window System setup tool. It uses a simple GUI, so it can run on any VGA setup and has a useful graphical interface for configuring X. Note that VGA is just an older graphics standard and has fewer capabilities than the SVGA cards that are common in most personal computers today.

- xf86config: A text-based X configuration tool.

If you really enjoy experimenting with GUIs and fiddling with them, you can do a number of things. Go to www.linuxdoc.org and read the various X Window System and XFree86-related HOWTO files. Some are quite technical, but some are a bit more friendly, and you may be surprised by just how much you can tweak the Linux GUI. You can also find www.gnome.org and www.kde.org, and dozens of other useful sites out there.

Chapter 13

Putting the X in Text

. . . .

In This Chapter

▶ Viewing the contents of text files

▶ Manipulating text files in vi

▶ Manipulating text files in gedit

. . . .

*F*rom text editors to word processors, Linux offers a wide variety of options for working with words. In this chapter, I take a look at different ways to view the contents of a text file, using some simple text editors in both the non-GUI and GUI environments. In Chapter 14, I take a look at office suites for those who would rather do word processing!

Viewing the Contents of a Text File

Almost all configuration files in Linux are text files. In addition, many pseudo-programs (called *shell scripts*), all HTML documentation, and many other items in your system are text files. Fortunately, if you just want to see what's in a text file and don't want to do anything to its contents, you don't have to use an editor or word processor. You can use three commands to view text files: cat, less, and more. I would bet that you will grow to love them.

Yes, that first command is cat, and it's taken from the word *concatenate*, which means "to bring together end to end" — you can use the cat command on multiple text files to have their text joined, one file's contents directly after another's. Typically, you use this command in the Linux world in the format cat *filename,* where the contents of the file *filename* are displayed on the screen. For example, if you create the short text file greetings and then type cat greetings, you see the following:

```
$ cat greetings
These are the contents of the greetings file.
Meow!
$ _
```

Of course, if the file contains more than a screen's worth of information, cat spews it all out at one time like a big hairball, and all but the last screen of text scrolls off the screen. It's a good thing that you have some other choices. The one you're likely to choose is less, which displays the contents of a file a full screen at a time. Then you press the spacebar to continue to the next screen. You can also use the arrow keys to move up and down one line at a time, if you want.

An alternative to less is more. The main difference between the two is that with more, you can move only forward through the file, and see only a screen's worth of information at a time. You can't back up.

To use either less or more, the format is similar to the format used with the cat command: less *filename* or more *filename*.

Getting Prehistoric with vi

People tend to have a love-hate relationship with the vi editor. Some think of vi as a wonderful, efficient, fast-moving tool (usually, those who know how to use it); others find it cryptic and confusing. Whether you love it or hate it, you can't get around the fact that if something is wrong with your Linux computer, vi may be the only editor you have access to. The entire program is small enough to fit on a single floppy disk — a rare thing these days! I suggest that you take the time to get familiar with vi and then try out other editors and decide which one you like best.

Many text editors are available in the Linux world. You probably already have vi, pico, emacs, and mcedit on your system, which you use from the command prompt. If you prefer the GUI, you can use gedit (GNOME default), xedit, and kedit (KDE default). Each of these editors has a different set of features and a different look and feel. Drastic differences exist among the various non-GUI editors.

Opening files

Because vi is a text-based text editor, opening a file is straightforward. You just type vi *filename* (replacing *filename* with the name of the particular file you want to see), and the file opens. If the file's content already exists, you can see it in the file. Otherwise, you get a blank screen, as shown in Figure 13-1.

Looking for menus? You don't see any. The vi editor has help information, but no menus. Instead, it has *modes*. vi has three basic modes:

- **Command mode:** vi assumes that everything you type is a vi command.

- **Insert mode:** vi interprets everything you type in this mode as text that goes in the file.

- **ex mode:** If you have ever used the old ex editor, you can use those old ex commands in this mode. You can recognize ex commands in various resources when you see something that starts with a colon (:).

TIP

If you have a file open in vi, you can get help information by pressing F1. To close the help screen, type **:q** (that's a colon and the letter *q*) and press Enter, which takes you back to vi in Command mode.

Entering text

To type text in vi, you need to enter Insert mode. To enter Insert mode, follow these steps:

1. **Press Esc to enter Command mode from any mode you may now be in.**

   The layout of this screen should look similar to the one shown in Figure 13-1.

2. **Press i to enter Insert mode from Command mode.**

   Notice that the screen changes slightly from mode to mode, but it mostly looks similar to the image shown in Figure 13-1.

From here, you simply type text until you're finished.

Figure 13-1:
The initial vi screen in a KDE terminal window, displaying an empty file.

Editing text

You have a number of ways you can edit text in the vi editor. You can do it the old-fashioned way by entering Insert mode and manipulating the text by using the Delete key, Insert key, and more from your keyboard. However, vi does have some fancier options available. To use any of these options, follow these steps:

1. **Press Esc to enter Command mode from any mode you may now be in.**

   The layout of this screen looks familiar (refer to Figure 13-1).

2. **Use the arrow keys to properly position the cursor for the option to work.**

   Table 13-1 explains proper cursor positioning.

3. **Press the key or sequence of keys that tells vi what you want to do.**

   Table 13-1 shows one group of commands you may want to use.

Table 13-1	Commonly Used vi Editing Commands	
Keystroke(s)	*Initial Cursor Position*	*Result*
A	One space before the place you want to add	vi enters Insert mode directly after text the cursor's position.
P	Directly where you want the text to appear	vi places in the document a copy of the previously copied text.
#o	Anywhere directly above where you want the new line to appear	vi adds a blank line or lines below the cursor's position and then enters Insert mode with the cursor within that blank line.
#r_	Directly on top of the (first) character you want to replace	vi replaces the current character if it's just used as r_ (where _ is the character to replace the item with) or replaces # of characters, including the current one, with _.
#yl	Directly on top of the (first) character you want to copy	vi copies the specified characters into the buffer.
#yy	Anywhere within the (first) line you want to copy	vi copies the specified lines(s) into the buffer.
u	Anywhere in the file	vi undoes what you last did.

The number sign (#) indicates the optional ability to include a number so that the command works on more than one line, word, or character. If you don't include a number, vi assumes a 1. Whenever you see an underscore (_), you need to specify a character for the command to work on. For an example, to replace the current character and the next five after it with dashes, you would type 5r-.

Keep in mind that when an option puts you into Insert mode, you need to return to Command mode before you can use editing commands again.

Deleting text

The vi editor has a large collection of commands that are useful for deleting text. You can use the Backspace or Delete keys, of course, but many other options are available too. To use the vi deletion features, follow these steps:

1. **Press Esc to enter Command mode from any mode you may now be in.**

   The layout of this screen looks similar to the one shown earlier, in Figure 13-1.

2. **Use the arrow keys to properly position the cursor for the option to work.**

   See Table 13-2 for an explanation of proper cursor positioning.

3. **Press the key or sequence of keys that executes what you want to do.**

   Table 13-2 shows some commands you may want to use.

Table 13-2	Commonly Used vi Deletion Commands
Keystroke(s)	**Initial Cursor Position**
#dd	Anywhere within the (first) line you want to delete
#dw	Anywhere within the (first) word you want to delete
p	Anywhere within the line on which you want to paste in the lines that you "yanked" with #y
#x	Directly on top of the (first) character you want to delete
#y	Anywhere within the line on which you want to "yank" (copy) the specified number of lines into the vi "clipboard" (called a buffer), and then delete them (where # is the same number both times)

A # indicates that if you include a number, the command works on more than one item.

Don't forget that when an option puts you into Insert mode, you need to return to Command mode before you can use deletion commands again.

Saving files

Just about every text and document editor has at least two different ways of saving a file. The first way involves saving and closing the document. In vi, you save and close the document by following these steps:

1. **Press Esc to enter Command mode from any mode you may now be in.**

   The layout of this screen looks similar to the screen shown earlier, in Figure 13-1.

2. **Type ZZ to save and close the file.**

   The file closes, and you return to the command prompt.

The second method of saving a file involves saving without closing. To save a file and keep working on it in vi, follow these steps:

1. **Press Esc to enter Command mode from any mode you may now be in.**

   The layout of this screen looks similar to the one shown earlier, in Figure 13-1.

2. **Type : (a colon) to enter Ex mode.**

   The bottom of the screen changes slightly, looking similar to Figure 13-1.

3. **Press w and then Enter.**

   The *w* stands for *w*rite (or *save*). You're now back in the file in Command mode.

Do you want to close the file without saving changes? In the preceding steps, follow the first two steps, and when you get to Step 3, type **q!** rather than w.

Going with gedit

You're not stuck with just command-prompt-based text editors in Linux. Lots of graphical options are available. In this section, I cover gedit because it is the default GUI text editor for Fedora Core 1.

Remember that if you don't automatically boot into the GUI, you can enter it at any time from the command prompt by typing startx.

Starting gedit

To start `gedit` from within GNOME, follow these steps:

1. **Click the Main Menu button.**

   In default GNOME and KDE setups, the Main Menu button in the lower-left corner is a footprint in GNOME or a big K in KDE. If you installed Fedora Core 1, the Main Menu button is the Red Hat fedora icon in both GNOME and KDE.

2. **Choose Accessories➪Text Editor.**

   The program opens, as shown in Figure 13-2.

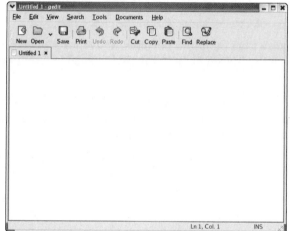

Figure 13-2: The `gedit` window is open, with a blank file.

Entering and editing text

`gedit` is strictly a *text editor,* in that you use it to generate raw text, whereas a *word processor* creates marked-up text that can be opened only by programs that can read that word processor's file formatting. If you want to add bold, italics, underlines, or any other special features to your `gedit` document, you want to read the next chapter.

To enter text in `gedit`, just click within the big white space and start typing. You have access to the standard collection of editing tools, such as cut, paste, and copy. Select the text you want to work with, and then click the appropriate button on the `gedit` toolbar.

The really interesting thing about this particular text editor is its plug-ins. To enable this feature, you need to follow these steps:

1. **Choose Edit⇨Preferences in** `gedit`.

   This action opens the Preferences dialog box.

2. **Locate the Plug-Ins section in the left panel.**

   Plug-Ins is the last entry.

3. **Click the Manager item under Plug-Ins.**

   The Plug-Ins portion of the dialog box opens.

4. **Click each item in the Plug-Ins list box and read its descriptions in the section underneath it.**

5. **Click in the check box for each plug-in you want to use.**

   The plug-in is activated if a check is in the check box.

6. **If the Configure Plug-In button becomes active for a plug-in you have selected, click the button to open the tool's plug-in configuration dialog box.**

   This dialog will be different depending on which plug-in you are using.

7. **When you're finished with each individual plug-in configuration, click OK to return to the Preferences dialog box.**

8. **When you're finished selecting plug-ins, click Close to close the Preferences dialog box.**

You can now access the plug-ins from your `gedit` menus. Each one is placed in its appropriate location: for example, ASCII Table on the View menu.

Saving your work

As with most programs, you have two choices for saving your work. You can save your work and keep going or save it and then close the program. To just save the file and keep going, follow these steps:

1. **Click the Save button.**

   This button looks like a floppy disk. If you haven't ever saved this file, clicking it opens the Save As dialog box.

2. **Browse through the directories in the left pane until you're in the directory where you want to save the file.**

   Double-click the name of a directory to enter it, or click the `. .` in the left pane's listing to move up a level in the directory tree.

3. **Type the file's name in the Selection text box.**

4. **Click OK to save the file.**

   The dialog box closes.

To close gedit, follow these steps:

1. **Choose File⇨Quit.**

   If you haven't saved this file since the last time you changed it, the Question dialog box appears.

2. **If you see the dialog box, click Save to save your work or click Don't Save to abandon it.**

   The program closes, unless you have more than one file open, in which case you see the Question dialog box for each file you have altered but not saved.

Chapter 14

Word Processing and More with OpenOffice.org

Words fly, writing remains.

— Spanish proverb, from *Dictionary of Proverbs,* by Delfín Carbonell Basset

These days, just about everyone who has a computer has at least one office suite at their fingertips. If they're Microsoft Windows users, this suite is probably Microsoft Office, although it may be another worthy contender, such as Corel WordPerfect Office. Undoubtedly, everyone has told you that the biggest problem with Linux is a lack of software: "It has no good office suites," for example.

I have good news for you. They're wrong. A number of office suites are available (see the "Tip" below) but what I cover here is the one that has gobbled up market share like nobody's business: OpenOffice.org. This suite comes with Calc (a spreadsheet), Draw (diagrams and figures), Impress (for presentations), Math (a word processor for writing mathematical formulas), and Writer (for word processing).

After you figure out how to use one of the programs in this suite, you may be happy to find that the others are designed in the same fashion. Menus and features work across each of the programs. You can even save files in Microsoft Office format, if you need to share them with people using it — and you can edit the ones people send you too.

That's enough *about* OpenOffice.org. Let's *actually use* it!

Other office suites available for Linux users are the OpenOffice.org relative StarOffice (`www.sun.com/staroffice`), **Anywhere Office** (`www.vistasource.com/products`), **KOffice** (`www.koffice.org`), and GNOME Office (`http://www.gnome.org/gnome-office/`).

Installing OpenOffice.Org

Many distributions install this office suite by default, but that doesn't mean that it's already on your system. Before you start the huge download unnecessarily, see whether you already have OpenOffice.org installed:

- **In Fedora Core 1:** Look at your Panel. If the OpenOffice.org Writer, Impress, and Calc icons discussed in Chapter 6 are not there, you don't have OpenOffice.org installed.

- **In Mandrake Linux 9.2:** Choose Main Menu⇨Office⇨Wordprocessors and see whether any OpenOffice.org items are listed. If not, you don't have it installed.

- **In SuSE Linux Professional 9.0:** Choose Main Menu⇨Office and see whether Office Suite is listed. If not, OpenOffice.org isn't installed.

If you don't have OpenOffice.org installed, you can do so by using your distribution's package-management tools (see Chapter 17). If you can't stand the thought of not having the latest version, you can first start up any of the OpenOffice.org applications (OpenOffice.org Writer, for example) and choose Help⇨About OpenOffice.org to see which version you have. Then, point your Web browser to `www.openoffice.org`. The latest version is mentioned on the front page. If this version isn't what you have and you want the latest one, read the following section to find out how to proceed.

Getting the software

To acquire OpenOffice.org from the Web, follow these steps:

1. **Open your favorite Web browser.**

   The default browser in Fedora Core is Mozilla.

2. **Go to the URL `www.openoffice.org`.**

   It's the home page for the OpenOffice.org project.

3. **Click Downloads to open the OpenOffice.org downloads page.**

   Note that this Web site changes frequently, so don't be surprised if its organization has changed since the time I wrote this section.

4. **Click the Software and Information link to jump to the New Software Items section.**

5. **Click the OpenOffice.org *version* selection.**

   This action takes you to the OpenOffice.org *version* Download Sites section.

6. **Locate the subsection labeled The Application.**

7. **Click Linux.**

   This action opens the location selector. (Did you notice that you can get this office suite for other operating systems too? — even Windows!)

8. **Look within the table for your particular country.**

   The Linux section is the center column.

9. **Click one of the download server choices offered for your country or the nearest country.**

   If you have problems with this server, try another one within your country or a nearby country. Try to stay at least on the same continent.

10. **When the Downloading dialog box opens, select where you want the file to go and then click Save.**

    I typically create in my home directory a directory named Downloads and put all my new software in there. After you click Save, the Download Manager dialog box opens. It tells you how much of the file you have downloaded, how much more you have to go, and how long this download should take. OpenOffice.org is a huge file. Even if you're on broadband, it takes more than ten minutes to download. In the meantime, feel free to browse elsewhere on the Web or read further into this book.

    After the download is complete, proceed to the following section.

Installing the software

After you have OpenOffice.org downloaded, you need to unpack the software and run the automated installation program, as outlined in the following steps:

1. **Open the File Roller program.**

   Choose Main Menu⇨Accessories⇨File Roller.

2. **Click Open Archive, and then browse to the directory containing the software you just downloaded.**

   The Open Archive dialog box opens. Browse as you would in any other GUI file manager.

3. **Select the file you want to uncompress, and then click OK to access the package's contents.**

For example, if the file's name is
`OOo_1.0.3_LinuxIntel_install.tar.gz`, click that file.

The Open Archive dialog box closes, and you can now see what's inside.

4. **Click Extract, and then browse to the directory where you want to unpack the contents.**

The Extract dialog box opens.

5. **Click OK to extract the file's contents.**

Because this package is so large, the decompression may take a few minutes.

6. **Close File Roller.**

Click the X in the upper-right corner of the window.

7. **Open the Run Program dialog box and choose Main Menu⇨Run Program.**

The Run Program dialog box appears.

8. **Click Append File, and then browse to the directory containing what was in the downloaded file.**

The Choose a File dialog box appears. If you downloaded the file to the Downloads directory, browse to that location; otherwise, browse to where you extracted the file. Then, browse within the extracted directory to the `install` subdirectory, which was created when you unpacked the file.

9. **Select Setup and then click OK.**

The Choose a File dialog box closes.

10. **Check the Run in Terminal check box in the Run Program dialog box, and then click Run to begin the installation.**

After a moment, a terminal window opens, showing you what the installer is doing. A progress dialog box also appears. After the setup program finishes loading, you see the OpenOffice.org installation program initial screen.

11. **Click Next to proceed to information about OpenOffice.org.**

12. **After you have read this information, click Next to proceed to the license agreement.**

13. **After you have read the agreement, click Accept to proceed to the Enter User Data dialog box.**

You can enter as much or as little information as you want.

14. **After you have finished filling out the form to your satisfaction, click Next to proceed to the Select Installation Type dialog box.**

15. **Select Standard Installation and click Next to proceed to the Select Installation Directory dialog box.**

    You can, of course, choose another installation type, if you'd want like. I'm covering the Standard installation herein these steps.

16. **Change the directory in the Installation Directory text box (or by browsing), if you want.**

17. **Click Next to be asked whether you want to create the new directory. Then click Yes to create the directory.**

    This action opens the Start Copying dialog box.

18. **Click Install to begin putting all the proper files into place.**

    You may get asked about Java and JavaScript. If you're not sure what they are or whether you want them, just leave them as unsupported. If you know that you have them, use the Browse button to select them and then click OK to proceed. Then, the installation starts.

19. **When the Installation Completed dialog box appears, click Complete.**

    That's it for the installation!

Word Processing with OpenOffice.Org Writer

Word processors are almost required equipment these days. Kids use them to write letters to their grandparents. Grandparents use them to write letters to their grandkids. Whether you're working on the great American novel or a school book report, OpenOffice.org Writer has all the best features you find in the other word processing packages you have used in the past.

Starting it up

To start OpenOffice.org Calc in the distributions I cover in this chapter, do the following:

- ✔ **In Fedora Core 1:** Choose Main Menu➪Office➪OpenOffice.org Writer. Or, you can click the OpenOffice.org Writer button on your panel.

- ✔ **In Mandrake Linux 9.2:** Choose Main Menu➪Office➪Wordprocessor➪ OpenOffice.org Writer.

- ✔ **In SuSE Linux 9.0:** Choose Main Menu➪Office➪Word processor.

When you first open OpenOffice.org Writer, you see the Address Data Source AutoPilot dialog box. Click Cancel for now. A Paragraph Styles (choose Format⇨Stylelist) dialog box opens too. Click the X in the upper-right corner to close this box. You then see, at some point as you're taking these tours, a Registration dialog box. You now have the option of registering your software. Select the option that suits you and your mood — after all, perhaps you do plan to register but would rather not do so right at this very moment.

After you have closed the dialog boxes, you have a clean screen to work with while getting used to the program.

Taking a tour of OpenOffice.org Writer

Before you proceed, take a look at the GUI layout shown in Figure 14-1.

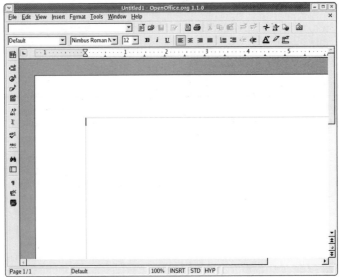

Figure 14-1:
The OpenOffice.org Writer layout.

Main toolbar

Along the left side of the window is the main toolbar. Each icon in this series represents a different functionality. If a button is *extensible* (it has a little green arrow on it), you can click to open a tiny dialog box containing the options therein. Each icon is described in Table 14-1; for an example of what you see when you click and hold the mouse button down over an extensible button, see Figure 14-2. If you determine that you want to remove this toolbar, choose View⇨Toolbars⇨Main Toolbar.

TIP

You can close the small dialog by clicking the X in its upper right corner.

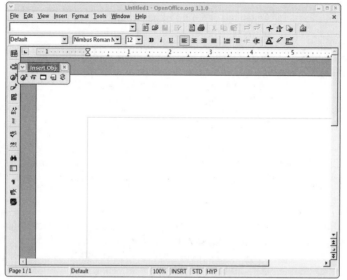

Figure 14-2:
The
OpenOffice.
org Writer's
Insert
Objects
button on
the main
toolbar,
expanded.

Table 14-1	The OpenOffice.org Writer Main Toolbar, from Top to Bottom	
Button	***What You Can Do***	***Extensible?***
Insert	Place an element (a table, another document, or a picture, for example) at the cursor's current location.	Yes
Insert Fields	Place a text element (current date, subject, or author's name, for example) at the cursor's current location.	Yes
Insert Objects	Place an object (a chart, a mathematical formula, or an applet, for example) at the cursor's current location.	Yes
Show Draw Functions	Access the many OpenOffice.org drawing utilities.	Yes
Form	Build forms with their respective special features (text boxes, radio buttons, and more) .	Yes

(continued)

Table 14-1 *(continued)*

Button	What You Can Do	Extensible?
Edit AutoText	Adjust the various settings for commonly used phrases to recall at the click of a button.	Yes
Direct Cursor On/Off	Add or remove special functionality that automatically formats text and objects according to where you click on the page (clicking in the middle centers the item, for example).	No
Spellcheck	Run the spell checker on your entire document or the selected text	No
AutoSpellcheck On/Off	Activate or turn off the automatic spell checker feature.	No
Find On/Off	Open or close the Find and Replace dialog box.	No
Data Sources	Open or close the Data Sources dialog box, which lets you access databases previously specified by using the dialog box accessed through Tools⇨ Data Sources.	No
Nonprinting Characters On/Off	Show all spaces, returns at the ends of paragraphs, and other characters that you don't normally see in your documents.	No
Graphics On/Off	Show embedded images, or just show placeholders so that you can see where they are without seeing the images.	No
Online Layout	Tell OpenOffice.org Writer to show your document as a Web page.	No

Menu bar

Along the top of the window is the Menu bar, something you should be used to if you typically work in Microsoft Windows. OpenOffice.org Writer has all the features you would expect from a modern word processor. It has too many menu options to cover in depth, so I give you instead a (nonexhaustive) summary of what you find on each major menu:

- ✔ **File:** The usual Open, Save, Save As, Print, and Print Preview commands, along with a set of wizards (under the term AutoPilot) plus the ability to send documents through e-mail, create templates, and create Web pages

- ✔ **Edit:** The usual Select All and Find commands, along with change tracking, document merging, and document comparing

✔ **View:** The usual Zoom functions and toolbars, along with the abilities to show or hide formatting characters, to see what the document would look like as a Web page, and to access your database information

✔ **Insert:** The usual page breaks and special characters, along with indexes, tables, bookmarks, headers, footers, and cross-references

✔ **Format:** The usual character, paragraph, and page settings, along with styles, autoformatting capabilities, and columns

✔ **Tools:** The usual spell-checking and thesaurus entries, in addition to hyphenation, autocorrection, an image gallery, and a bibliography database

These menus have more features than what is listed here. Go through and take a look; you may find a new favorite feature in there somewhere.

Function bar

Directly below the menu bar in a default setup is the Function bar, which you can remove at any time by using the View menu. This series of icons allows you single-click access to the most commonly used File and Edit features, among others. Table 14-2 lays out, from left to right, what you find on the default Function bar. The extensible items can all be expanded to show a further set of options.

Table 14-2	The OpenOffice.org Writer Function Bar, from Left to Right	
Button or Item	*What You Can Do*	*Extensible?*
URL Entry drop-down list box	After you type a full URL, including the opening `http://`, open a new window with the Web page's contents displayed.	No
Stop Loading	Tell OpenOffice.org to stop attempting to load the specified Web page.	No
Edit File	Edit the displayed Web page.	No
New	Open new documents of various types.	Yes
Open File	Open an existing file for reading or editing.	No
Save Document	Save the current document. If you have not saved this document before, the Save As dialog will open.	No
Export Directly as PDF	Opens a Save As dialog with PDF selected as the file type.	No

(continued)

Table 14-2 *(continued)*

Button or Item	What You Can Do	Extensible?
Print File Directly	Send a file to the default printer.	No
Cut	Remove the selected text from the document and save it in memory.	No
Copy	Make a copy of the selected document text and save it in memory.	No
Paste	Place the text from memory into the document at the cursor's current location.	No
Undo	Undo the last change you made to the document.	Yes
Redo	Undo the last undone change to the document.	Yes
Navigator On/Off	Open or close the Navigator window, which allows you to jump to specific features within your document.	No
Stylist On/Off	Open or close the Paragraph Styles window, which allows you to select the particular style to apply to selected text.	No
Hyperlink Dialog	Open or close a dialog box that you can use to build complex hyperlinks.	No
Gallery	Open or close a dialog box that provides access to divider bars, bullet types, and more.	No

Object bar

The Object bar is directly below the Function bar in a default OpenOffice.org setup. As usual, you can remove the Object bar at any time by using the View menu. This series of icons allows you to click buttons and expand drop-down list boxes that represent standard word processor functions, such as styles, fonts, font sizes, and formatting instructions. Most features on this bar are identical to what you see in most modern word processors. The button for paragraph background formatting is the only one that's particularly unusual.

This toolbar actually changes depending on what you're doing. If your cursor is within a table, for example, then the Object bar contains useful buttons for working with tables.

Ruler

Directly below the Object bar in a default OpenOffice.org setup is the ruler. All modern word processors offer this item, which marks out the margins and tabs, for example, of your document in the measuring system of your choice. To change which system you want to use, right-click the ruler to open the Measurements pop-up dialog box.

Your document

Oh, yeah — that big, blocked-off white space takes up most of the window. That's where you work on your documents! Just click in there and start typing. You can also access a Formatting pop-up menu by right-clicking in the document section.

OpenOffice.org Writer supports the following file formats (and more): its own "text" format (.SXW), Microsoft Word 95, 6.0, 97, 2000, and XP (.DOC), Rich Text Format (.RTF), Text (.TXT), and Web Page (.HTML).

Spreadsheets with OpenOffice.Org Calc

Some people like to balance their checkbooks by hand. When I first graduated from a university, I decided that it was time to get hold of my finances, and a spreadsheet was the way to do it. These days, I use spreadsheets to keep track of my "time card" when I'm doing consulting or contract work, to help me manage project teams and other tasks. I'm sure that you have your favorite uses for spreadsheets. Let's take a look at OpenOffice.org Calc so that you can get to work.

Starting it up

To start OpenOffice.org Calc in the distributions I cover in this chapter, do the following:

- ✔ **In Fedora Core 1:** Choose Main Menu⇨Office⇨OpenOffice.org Calc. Or, you can click the OpenOffice.org Calc button in the lower panel.

- ✔ **In Mandrake Linux 9.2:** Choose Main Menu⇨Office⇨Spreadsheets⇨ OpenOffice.org Calc.

- ✔ **In SuSE Linux 9.0:** Choose Main Menu⇨Office⇨Spreadsheet.

Taking a tour of OpenOffice.org Calc

Much of what you see here should look familiar, between looking through OpenOffice.org Writer and other spreadsheet programs you have used. Take a look at the GUI layout shown in Figure 14-3.

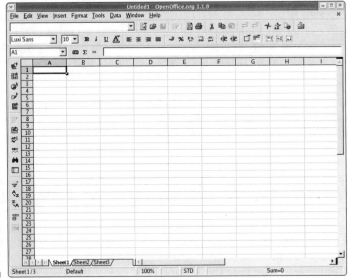

Figure 14-3: The OpenOffice.org Calc layout.

Main toolbar

Along the left side of the window is the main toolbar, which you can remove at any time by choosing View➪Toolbars➪Main Toolbar. Each icon in this series represents a different functionality. If a button is *extensible* (it has a little green arrow on it), you can click and hold the mouse button on it to see the options contained within. Each icon is described in Table 14-3.

Table 14-3	The OpenOffice.org Calc Main Toolbar, from Top to Bottom	
Button	**What You Can Do**	**Extensible?**
Insert	Place an element (a table, another document, or a picture, for example) at the cursor's current location.	Yes
Insert Cells	Place a cell (or column or row) at the cursor's current location.	Yes

Button	What You Can Do	Extensible?
Insert Object	Place an object (a chart, a mathematical formula, or an applet, for example) at the cursor's current location.	Yes
Show Draw Functions	Access the many OpenOffice.org drawing utilities.	Yes
Show Form Functions	Build forms with their respective special features (text boxes, radio buttons, and more).	Yes
AutoFormat	Quickly format a collection of cells in one of a variety of ways.	No
Choose Themes	Quickly assign a color-coordinated look to a sheet.	No
Spellcheck	Run the spell checker on your entire document or the selected text.	No
AutoSpellcheck On/Off	Activate or turn off the automatic spell check feature.	No
Find On/Off	Open or close the Find and Replace dialog box.	No
Data Sources	Open or close the Data Sources dialog box, which brings up the same dialog box as the Tools⇨Data Sources menu selections.	No
AutoFilter On/Off	Quickly sort a selected set of cells in a variety . of ways	No
Sort Ascending	Quickly sort a selected set of cells from ascending to descending order.	No
Sort Descending	Quickly sort a selected set of cells from descending to ascending order.	No
Insert Group	Select a set of rows or columns that you can compress or expand when needed.	No
Ungroup	Remove the group settings.	No

Menu bar

Along the top of the window is the Menu bar, a standard in the GUI world no matter which operating system you're using. OpenOffice.org Calc has all the features you would expect from a modern spreadsheet system. It has too many menu options to cover in depth, so, instead, here's a (nonexhaustive) summary of what you find on each menu:

- ✔ **File:** The usual Open, Save, Save As, Print, and Print Preview commands, along with a set of wizards (under the term AutoPilot) plus the ability to send documents through e-mail, create templates, and create Web pages

- ✔ **Edit:** The usual Select All and Find commands, along with change tracking, headers and footers, and plug-in loading

- ✔ **View:** The usual Zoom functions and toolbars, along with the abilities to show or hide column and row headers and to access your database information

- ✔ **Insert:** The usual page breaks and special characters, along with cells, rows, functions, and external data

- ✔ **Format:** The usual cell and row formatting, cell merging, and page settings, along with conditional formatting

- ✔ **Tools:** The usual spell-checking and thesaurus entries, in addition to hyphenation, autocorrection features, an image gallery, and a bibliography database

- ✔ **Data:** The usual data selection, sorting, and grouping routines in one easy place for quick access

These menus have more features than what is listed here. Go through and take a look; you may find a new favorite feature in there somewhere.

Function bar

Directly below the Menu bar in a default setup is the Function bar, which you can remove at any time by using the View menu. This series of icons allows you single-click access to the most commonly used File and Edit features, among others. Table 14-4 lays out, from left to right, what you find on the default Function bar. The extensible items can all be expanded to show a further set of options.

Table 14-4 The OpenOffice.org Calc Function Bar, from Left to Right

Button or Item	What You Can Do	Extensible?
URL Entry drop-down list box	After you type a full URL, including the opening `http://`, open a new window with the Web page's contents displayed.	No
Stop Loading	Tell OpenOffice.org to stop attempting to load the specified Web page.	No
Edit File	Edit the displayed Web page.	No
New	Open new documents of various types.	Yes
Open File	Open an existing file for reading or editing.	No

Button or Item	What You Can Do	Extensible?
Save Document	Save the current document, either with Save As if you have never saved it or to save over the last saved version if you have.	No
Export Directly as PDF	Open a Save As dialog with PDF selected as the file type.	No
Print File Directly	Send the file to the default printer.	No
Cut	Remove the selected text out of the document and save it in memory.	No
Copy	Make a copy of the selected document text and save it in memory.	No
Paste	Place the text from memory into the document at the cursor's current location.	No
Undo	Undo the last change you made to the document.	Yes
Redo	Undo the last undone change to the document.	Yes
Navigator On/Off	Open or close the Navigator window, which allows you to jump to specific features within your document.	No
Stylist On/Off	Open or close the Paragraph styles window, which allows you to select the particular style to apply to selected text.	No
Hyperlink Dialog	Open or close a dialog box you can use to build complex hyperlinks.	No
Gallery	Open or close a dialog box, which provides access to divider bars, bullet types, and more.	No

Object bar

The Object bar is directly below the Function bar in a default OpenOffice.org setup. As usual, you can remove the Object bar at any time by using the View menu. This series of icons allows you to click buttons and expand drop-down list boxes that represent standard spreadsheet functions, such as styles, fonts, font sizes, and number formatting instructions. Most features on this bar are identical to what you see in most modern spreadsheets.

Formula bar

Directly below the Object bar in a default OpenOffice.org Calc setup is the Formula bar. All modern spreadsheets offer this item, which allows you to enter and edit cell values and contains a few often-used features, such as a single-click Sum button.

Your document

Here's where you work on your spreadsheet! Just pick a cell and start typing. You can also access a Formatting pop-up menu by right-clicking in the document section.

OpenOffice.org Calc supports the following file formats (and more): its own spreadsheet format (.SXC); Data Interchange Format (.DIF); dBASE (.DBF); Microsoft Excel 95, 5.0, 97, 2000, and XP (.DOC); text-based comma-separated values (.CSV), and Web Page (.HTML).

Presentations with OpenOffice.Org Impress

Most people would rather eat glass than speak in front of a group of people. Still, if you have to, you may as well have some cool presentation software to back you up. This program is what I use when I speak at conferences. (I use it even when my clients want me to send in my presentation in Microsoft PowerPoint format. Shh! Don't tell — they don't know the difference!) Give OpenOffice.org Impress a chance to impress you.

Starting it up

To start OpenOffice.org Impress in the distributions I cover in this chapter, do the following:

- **In Fedora Core 1, select:** Choose Main Menu➪Office➪OpenOffice.org Impress. Or, you can click the OpenOffice.org Impress button on your lower panel.
- **In Mandrake Linux 9.2, go to:** Choose Main Menu➪Office➪Presentations➪ OpenOffice.org Impress.
- **In SuSE Linux 9.0, go to:** Choose Main Menu➪Office➪Presentation.

Taking a tour of OpenOffice.org Impress

Before you proceed, take a look at the GUI layout shown in Figure 14-4. The little Presentation dialog box may look like clutter to some, but I personally find it helpful as I'm creating and editing presentations. If you don't need it, just click the X in the upper-right corner of the dialog box. You can bring it back at any time through View➪Toolbars➪Presentation.

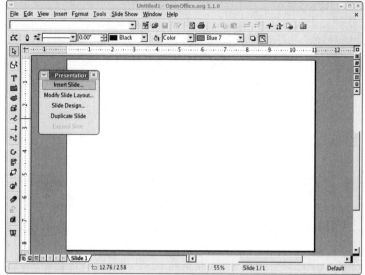

Figure 14-4:
The
OpenOffice.
org Impress
default
layout.

Main toolbar

Along the left side of the window is the main toolbar, which you can remove at any time by choosing View➪Toolbars➪Main Toolbar. Each icon in this series represents a different functionality. If a button is *extensible* (has a little green arrow on it), you can click and hold the mouse button on it to see the options contained within. Each icon is described in Table 14-5. As you can see, this main toolbar is significantly different from the other OpenOffice.org programs.

Table 14-5	The OpenOffice.org Impress Main Toolbar, from Top to Bottom	
Button	**What You Can Do**	**Extensible?**
Select	Set the mouse pointer to select a particular element or section of a slide.	No
Zoom	Use a set of options that let you zoom in and out on the slide.	Yes
Text	Use a variety of methods for entering text on a slide.	Yes
Rectangle	Easily draw various forms of rectangles.	Yes
Ellipse	Easily draw various forms of ellipses.	Yes
3D Objects	Easily draw spheres, cubes, and more.	Yes

(continued)

Table 14-5 *(continued)*

Button	What You Can Do	Extensible?
Curves	Easily draw curvy lines and even freeform.	Yes
Lines and Arrows	Use a selection of connector lines and arrows.	Yes
Connector	Use another set of connector symbols and lines.	Yes
Rotate	Rotate a selected object on a specific axis.	No
Alignment	Shift the selected object to a specific alignment on the page.	Yes
Arrange	Move objects higher or lower in the stack.	Yes
Insert	Insert items, such as graphs.	Yes
Effects	Open the Special Effects dialog box.	Yes
Interaction	Set what should happen when you click with your mouse.	No
3D Controller	Open the 3D Effects dialog box.	No
Slide Show	Begin a slide show with the existing slides.	No

Menu bar

Along the top of the window is the Menu bar, a standard in the GUI world no matter which operating system you're using. OpenOffice.org Impress has all the features you would expect from a modern presentation package. It has too many menu options to cover in depth, so I give you instead a (nonexhaustive) summary of what you find on each menu:

✔ **File:** The usual Open, Save, Save As, Print, and Print Preview commands, along with a set of wizards (under the term AutoPilot) plus the ability to send documents through e-mail and create templates

✔ **Edit:** The usual Select All and Find commands, along with the ability to quickly duplicate a slide

✔ **View:** The usual Zoom functions and toolbars, along with the ability to select whether you're looking at just slides, notes, or another section

✔ **Insert:** The usual new slide, along with charts, frames, graphics, and spreadsheets

✔ **Format:** The usual text formatting features, along with layout, graphics, and style formatting

✔ **Tools:** The usual spell-checking feature, in addition to hyphenation, autocorrection, an image gallery, and a bibliography database

These menus have more features than what is listed here. Go through and take a look; you may find a new favorite feature in there somewhere.

Function bar

Directly below the Menu bar in a default setup is the Function bar, which you can remove at any time by using the View menu. This series of icons allows you single-click access to the most commonly used File and Edit features, among others. Table 14-6 lays out, from left to right, what you find on the default Function bar. The extensible items can all be expanded to show a further set of options.

Table 14-6	The OpenOffice.org Writer Function Bar, from Left to Right	
Button or Item	**What You Can Do**	**Extensible?**
URL Entry drop-down list box	After you type a full URL, including the opening `http://`, open a new window with the Web page's contents displayed.	No
Stop Loading	Tell OpenOffice.org to stop attempting to load the specified Web page.	No
Edit File	Edit the displayed Web page.	No
New	Open new documents of various types.	Yes
Open File	Open an existing file for reading or editing.	No
Save Document	Save the current document, either with Save As if you have never saved it or to save over the last saved version if you have.	No
Edit File	Set file as read-only or read-write.	No
Export Directly as PDF	Open a Save As dialog with the PDF file format selected.	No
Print File Directly	Send the file to the default printer.	No
Cut	Remove the selected text from the document and save it in memory.	No
Copy	Make a copy of the selected document text and save it in memory.	No
Paste	Place the text from memory into the document at the cursor's current location.	No
Undo	Undo the last change you made to the document.	Yes

(continued)

Table 14-6 (continued)

Button or Item	What You Can Do	Extensible?
Redo	Undo the last undone change to the document.	Yes
Navigator On/Off	Open or close the Navigator window, which allows you to jump to specific features within your document.	No
Stylist On/Off	Open or close the Paragraph styles window, which allows you to select the particular style to apply to selected text.	No
Hyperlink Dialog	Open or close a dialog box you can use to build complex hyperlinks.	No
Gallery	Open or close a dialog box, which provides access to divider bars, bullet types, and more.	No

Object bar

The Object bar is directly below the Function bar in a default OpenOffice.org setup. As usual, you can remove the Object bar at any time by using the View menu. This series of icons allows you to click buttons and expand drop-down list boxes that represent standard presentation-software functions, such as arrow styles, colors, line styles, and other formatting instructions. Most features on this bar are identical to what you see in most modern presentation programs.

Ruler

Directly below the Object bar in a default OpenOffice.org setup is the ruler. This item marks out the margins and tabs, for example, of your document in the measuring system of your choice. To change which system you want to use, right-click the ruler to open the Measurements pop-up dialog box.

Your document

Oh, yeah — that big white space takes up most of the window. That's where you work on your slides! Just click in there and start typing. You can also access a formatting pop-up menu by right-clicking in the document section.

OpenOffice.org Impress supports the following file formats (and more): its own presentation format (.SXI), and Microsoft PowerPoint 97, 2000, and XP (.DOC).

Using the AutoPilot Presentation wizard

This discussion of OpenOffice.org Impress gives me a good chance to introduce you to File⇨AutoPilot. When working on any document in OpenOffice.org, you can open this menu and select any of the options available — from Business Cards to Presentation. In this case, select the latter to open the AutoPilot Presentation dialog box shown in Figure 14-5.

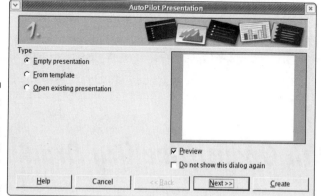

Figure 14-5:
The Open-
Office.org
AutoPilot
Presenta-
tion wizard.

To use this wizard, follow these steps:

1. **Leave the Empty Presentation option selected (unless you have a template you need to work from) and click Next.**

   The Select a Slide Design dialog box appears.

2. **If you want your presentation ultimately to appear on something other than a computer screen, adjust the Select an Output option to its Medium setting.**

   Your choices are Screen, Overhead Sheet, Slide, and Paper.

3. **After you have made your selection, click Next to continue.**

   The Slide Transition and Presentation Type dialog box appears.

4. **Use the Effect drop-down list box to try the various transitions.**

   OpenOffice.org Impress animates these transitions for you as long as the Preview box is checked.

5. **After you have selected an effect, use the Speed drop-down list box to try the various transition speeds.**

   OpenOffice.org Impress animates the transitions again, at the requested speed.

6. **After you have selected a speed, select whether you want to move manually from one slide to the next (the Default option) or have the presentation advance automatically (the Automatic option).**

   If you selected Default, proceed to Step 7. If you selected Automatic, select both the Duration of Page (how long each slide should linger) and Duration of Pause (how long OpenOffice.org Impress should pause between showing slides) options.

7. **After you have your settings selected, click Create to proceed.**

   OpenOffice.org Impress opens to its default layout, as shown in Figure 14-4.

Fine Art with OpenOffice.Org Draw

Whether you're an aspiring graphic artist or just need a tool that lets you generate simple graphics for use on their own, in a presentation, or elsewhere, OpenOffice.org Draw provides a host of drawing functions. If nothing else, it's a whole lot of fun to play with! Not everything in life has to be practical.

Starting it up

To start OpenOffice.org Draw in the distributions I cover in this chapter, do the following:

- ✓ **In Fedora Core 1, select:** Choose Main Menu⇨Office⇨OpenOffice.org Draw.

- ✓ **In Mandrake Linux 9.2, go to:** Choose Main Menu⇨Office⇨Graphs⇨ OpenOffice.org Draw.

- ✓ **In SuSE Linux 9.0, go to:** Choose Main Menu⇨Graphics⇨Vector Drawing.

Taking a tour of OpenOffice.org Draw

Before you proceed, take a look at the GUI layout shown in Figure 14-6.

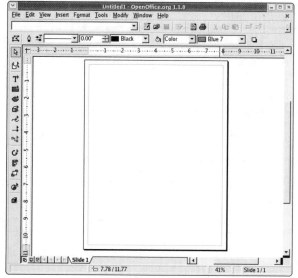

Main toolbar

Along the left side of the window is the main toolbar, which you can remove at any time by choosing View➪Toolbars➪Main Toolbar. Each icon in this series represents a different functionality. If a button is *extensible* (has a little green arrow on it), you can click and hold the mouse button on it to see the options contained within. Each icon is described in Table 14-7. As you can see, this main toolbar is significantly different from the other OpenOffice.org programs.

Table 14-7	The OpenOffice.org Draw Main Toolbar, from Top to Bottom	
Button	*What You Can Do*	*Extensible?*
Select	Set the mouse pointer to select a particular element or section of a slide.	No
Zoom	Use a set of options that let you zoom in and out on the slide.	Yes
Text	Use a variety of methods for entering text onto a slide.	Yes
Rectangle	Easily draw various forms of rectangles.	Yes
Ellipse	Easily draw various forms of ellipses.	Yes

(continued)

Table 14-7 *(continued)*

Button	What You Can Do	Extensible?
3D Objects	Easily draw spheres, cubes, and more.	Yes
Curve	Easily draw curvy lines and even freeform.	Yes
Lines and Arrows	Use a selection of connector lines and arrows.	Yes
Connector	Use another set of connector symbols and lines.	Yes
Effects	Open the Special Effects dialog box.	Yes
Alignment	Shift the selected object to a specific alignment on the page.	Yes
Arrange	Move objects higher or lower in the stack.	Yes
Insert	Insert items, such as graphs.	Yes
3D Controller	Open the 3D Effects dialog box.	No

Menu bar

Along the top of the window is the Menu bar, a standard in the GUI world no matter which operating system you're using. OpenOffice.org Draw has all the features you would expect from a modern drawing package. It has too many menu options to cover in depth, so I give you instead a (nonexhaustive) summary of what you find on each menu:

- **File:** The usual Open, Save, Save As, Print, and Export commands, along with a set of wizards (under the term AutoPilot) plus the ability to send documents through e-mail and create templates
- **Edit:** The usual Find and Replace, Image Map, and other such editing commands
- **View:** The usual Zoom functions and toolbars, along with the ability to select the display quality and place the program in Preview mode
- **Insert:** The usual charts, frames, graphics, and spreadsheets, along with scanning functions
- **Format:** The usual brush and graphics formatting, along with layers and style formatting
- **Tools:** The usual spell-checking, as well as hyphenation, autocorrection, an image gallery, and an eyedropper for grabbing colors

These menus have more features than what is listed here. Go through and take a look; you may find a new favorite feature in there somewhere.

Function bar

Directly below the Menu bar in a default setup is the Function bar, which you can remove at any time by using the View menu. This series of icons allows you single-click access to the most commonly used File and Edit features, among others. Table 14-8 lays out, from left to right, what you find on the default Function bar. The extensible items can all be expanded to show a further set of options.

Table 14-8	The OpenOffice.org Draw Function Bar, from Left to Right	
Button or Item	**What You Can Do**	**Extensible?**
URL Entry drop-down list box	After you type a full URL, including the opening `http://`, open a new window with the Web page's contents displayed.	No
Stop Loading	Tell OpenOffice.org to stop attempting to load the specified Web page.	No
Edit File	Edit the displayed Web page.	No
New	Open new documents of various types.	Yes
Open File	Open an existing file for reading or editing.	No
Save Document	Save the current document, either with Save As if you have never saved it or to save over the last saved version if you have.	No
Edit File	Set file as read-only or read-write.	No
Export Directly as PDF	Open a Save As dialog box with the PDF file type selected.	No
Print File Directly	Send the file to the default printer.	No
Cut	Remove the selected text out of the document and save it in memory.	No
Copy	Make a copy of the selected document text and save it in memory.	No
Paste	Place the text from memory into the document at the cursor's current location.	No
Undo	Undo the last change you made to the document.	Yes
Redo	Undo the last undone change to the document.	Yes

(continued)

Table 14-8 *(continued)*

Button or Item	What You Can Do	Extensible?
Navigator On/Off	Open or close the Navigator window, which allows you to jump to specific features within your document.	No
Stylist On/Off	Open or close the Paragraph Styles window, which allows you to select the particular style to apply to selected text.	No
Hyperlink Dialog	Open or close a dialog box that you can use to build complex hyperlinks.	No
Gallery	Open or close a dialog box that provides access to divider bars, bullet types, and more.	No

Object bar

The Object bar is directly below the Function bar in a default OpenOffice.org setup. As usual, you can remove the Object bar at any time by using the View menu. This series of icons allows you to click buttons and expand drop-down list boxes that represent standard presentation software functions, such as arrow styles, colors, line styles, and other formatting instructions. Most features on this bar are identical to what you see in most modern presentation programs.

Ruler

Directly below the Object bar in a default OpenOffice.org setup is the ruler. This item marks out the margins and tabs, for example, of your document in the measuring system of your choice. To change which system you want to use, right-click the ruler to open the Measurements pop-up dialog box.

Your document

Click in that big white space and start doodling. You can also access a formatting pop-up menu by right-clicking in the document section.

OpenOffice.org Draw appears to have the most limited file type support for saving when you use the Save As dialog, but in fact supports a wide range of graphics formats. You can save images to a format other than the OpenOffice.org Draw format (.SXD) by selecting File➪Export.

Supported graphics formats are: BMP, EMF, EPS, GIF, JPEG, MET, PBM, PCT, PGM, PNG, PPM, RAS, SVG, TIFF, WMF, and XPM.

Calculations with OpenOffice.Org Math

There's nothing like trying to type a math or science report and having to either use multiple lines to show your equations or write them in by hand. OpenOffice.org Math is a great solution to this problem. You can create your equations and more in there and then insert them in any of your OpenOffice.org documents. Whether you're a middle school student or a professional engineer, OpenOffice.org Math just may thrill you.

Many OpenOffice.org Math functions are different from what you're used to if you have looked at all the other OpenOffice.org programs. However, in many ways this program is less complex than some, thanks to its special-purpose nature. Keep in mind that it's not a calculation program. It's for laying out complex formulas on paper. However, you can insert these formulas into OpenOffice.org Calc for some interesting cross-program work.

Starting it up

To start OpenOffice.org Math in the distributions I cover in this chapter, do the following:

- **In Fedora Core 1, select:** Choose Main Menu⇨Office⇨OpenOffice.org Math.

- **In Mandrake Linux 9.2, go to:** Choose Main Menu⇨Office⇨ Wordprocessor⇨OpenOffice.org Math.

- **In SuSE Linux 9.0, go to:** Choose Main Menu⇨Office⇨Office Suite. When the Templates and Documents – New Document window appears, double-click on Formula to open a new OpenOffice.org Math document, or browse to the file you want to edit.

Taking a tour of OpenOffice.org Math

Before you proceed, take a look at the GUI layout shown in Figure 14-7.

Close the Selection dialog box by clicking the small X in the upper-right corner of its window. Keep things as uncluttered as possible. You can get it back at any time by choosing View⇨Selection.Main toolbar.

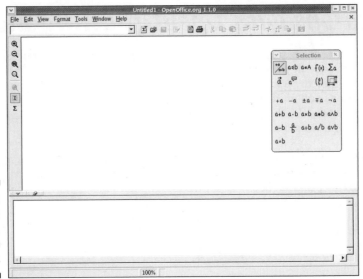

Along the left side of the window is the main toolbar, which you can remove at any time by choosing View⇨Toolbars⇨Main Toolbar. Each icon in this series represents a different functionality. You're likely to find this main toolbar quite different from those in the other OpenOffice.org programs. Mostly, it's just — smaller. Each icon is described in Table 14-9.

Table 14-9	**The OpenOffice.org Math Main Toolbar, from Top to Bottom**
Button	**What You Can Do**
Zoom In	Enlarge the contents of the document section.
Zoom Out	Shrink the contents of the document section.
Zoom 100%	Shrink or enlarge to the contents' original size.
Entire Formula	Enlarge or shrink the formula so that it fits in the full screen.
Refresh	If you have View⇨AutoUpdate Display enabled, update the document area to match the Commands area.
Formula Cursor	Click within the formula in Document view so that your cursor automatically moves to that position in the Commands area.
Symbols	Open the Symbols dialog box, which contains both Greek and other special-purpose mathematical symbols.

Menu bar

Along the top of the window is the Menu bar, a standard in the GUI world no matter which operating system you're using. OpenOffice.org Math may be unlike any program you may have used already, so I don't say anything about what you may expect to find there. I just give you a (nonexhaustive) summary of what you find on each menu:

- ✔ **File:** The usual Open, Save, Save As, and Print commands that you find in most GUI programs, along with a set of wizards (under the term AutoPilot) and the ability to send documents through e-mail, create templates, and create Web pages

- ✔ **Edit:** The usual Select All and Find commands, along with specialized commands for moving within the formula

- ✔ **View:** The usual Zoom functions and toolbars, along with screen update features and more

- ✔ **Format:** The usual font type, font size, spacing, and alignment features and more

- ✔ **Tools:** The usual Configure and Options entries for customizing the program's setup and behaviors, in addition to formula importing and access to the symbol catalog

Function bar

Directly below the Menu bar in a default setup is the Function bar, which you can remove at any time by using the View menu. This series of icons allows you single-click access to the most commonly used File and Edit features, among others. Table 14-10 lays out, from left to right, what you find on the default Function bar. If a button is *extensible* (has a little green arrow on it), you can click and hold the mouse button on it to see the options contained within.

Table 14-10	The OpenOffice.org Math Function Bar, from Left to Right	
Item	*What You Can Do*	*Extensible?*
URL Entry drop-down list box	After you type a full URL, including the opening `http://`, open a new window with the Web page's contents displayed.	No
Stop Loading	Tell OpenOffice.org to stop attempting to load the specified Web page.	No
Edit File	Edit the displayed Web page.	No

(continued)

Table 14-10 *(continued)*

Item	What You Can Do	Extensible?
New	Open new documents of various types.	Yes
Open File	Open an existing file for reading or editing.	No
Save Document	Save the current document, either with Save As if you have never saved it or to save over the last saved version if you have.	No
Edit File	Set file as read-only or read-write.	No
Export Directly as PDF	Open a Save As dialog with PDF selected as the file format.	No
Print File Directly	Send the file to the default printer.	No
Cut	Remove the selected text from the document and save it in memory.	No
Copy	Make a copy of the selected document text and save it in memory.	No
Paste	Place the text from memory into the document at the cursor's current location.	No
Undo	Undo the last change you made to the document.	Yes
Redo	Undo the last undone change to the document.	Yes
Navigator On/Off	Open or close the Navigator window, which allows you to jump to specific features within your document.	No
Stylist On/Off	Open or close the Paragraph Styles window, which allows you to select the particular style to apply to selected text.	No
Hyperlink Dialog	Open or close a dialog box that you can use to build complex hyperlinks.	No
Gallery	Open or close a dialog box that provides access to divider bars, bullet types, and more.	No

Document section

Things get tricky here if you have never used formula editing software. You can't type anything in the main document window in OpenOffice.org Math. Instead, you type in the Commands window. Right-clicking in the Commands window opens a pop-up menu. To help you get used to working with the formulas, I suggest that you play around with this pop-up menu. For example, if you have never used software like this, you might follow these steps:

1. Open the right-click pop-up menu.

You can see this menu shown in Figure 14-8.

Figure 14-8: The OpenOffice. org Math Commands pop-up menu.

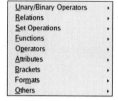

2. Select a submenu to open.

I chose Formats, which you can see in Figure 14-9.

Figure 14-9: The OpenOffice. org Formats submenu on the Math Commands pop-up menu,.

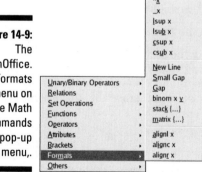

3. Select a formula component within this submenu.

I'm a geek, and I fondly remember taking a class on matrices, so I chose matrix {...}. Immediately, the code that's needed in order to add a matrix to my formula appears in the Commands dialog box. A moment later, because I'm letting the program refresh the rest of the screen as I work, I see what the matrix looks like in the document window. The combination is shown in Figure 14-10.

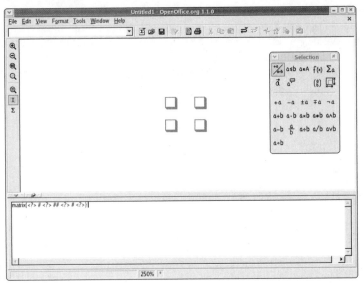

Figure 14-10:
The basic
Matrix
syntax in
OpenOffice.
org Math.

4. **Replace each of the** `<?>` **entries with the letters and numbers for your formula.**

   When I change `matrix{<?> # <?> ## <?> # <?>}` to **matrix{A # B ## C # D}**, I see the result shown in Figure 14-11.

5. **Continue adding components to the formula until you are finished.**

   Suppose that you want to multiply the matrix by 3. You press Enter to go down to the next line, right-click to display the pop-up menu, and choose Unary/Binary Operators⇨a Times b. This choice adds the phrase `<?> times <?>` beneath the matrix code. If you erase this phrase and use it as a guideline, you end up with

   ```
   3 times matrix{A # B ## C # D}
   ```

   This line gives the result shown in Figure 14-12. I could go on, but I hope by now that you're eager to start with your own explorations!

OpenOffice.org Math supports (among others) its own format (.SXM) and MathML 1.01 (.MML), which isn't a program. *MathML* is a standard, similar to HTML for working on the Web, and 1.01 is a specific version of this standard. For this particular version of MathML, see `www.w3.org/TR/REC-MathML/`. The main standard page is available at `http://www.w3.org/Math/`. If you need to add formulas to Web pages, this site can be quite an interesting read!

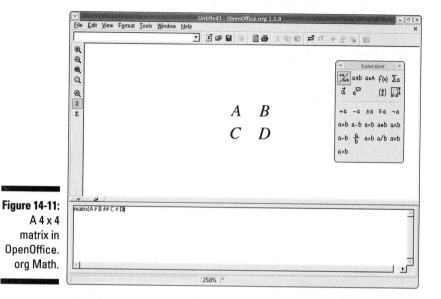

Figure 14-11:
A 4 x 4
matrix in
OpenOffice.
org Math.

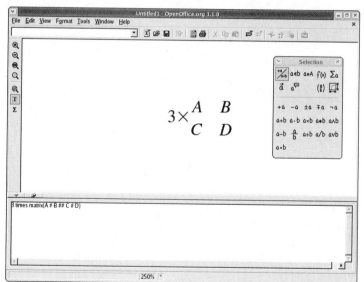

Figure 14-12:
A complete
formula in
OpenOffice.
org Math.

Chapter 15

Multimedia Wow!

The price of freedom is responsibility, but it's a bargain, because freedom is priceless.

—Hugh Downs

*I*n these days of computing in noisy Technicolor, it just doesn't feel like a computer unless you can make it sing and dance. This used to be a weak point for Linux, but these days there's little that I can't do on my Linux desktop machine. From listening to CDs to watching QuickTime movies, you can do just about anything. Sometimes it just takes a bit of elbow grease to get things working.

Time to take a trip on the wild side and get your Linux box doing the macarena.

Some Preliminaries

Because legal complications surround a number of multimedia programs and their use in countries like the United States of America, some multimedia capabilities had to be removed from Red Hat Linux. However, these capabilities are still available if you know where to look — and if you're in a legal jurisdiction that allows listening to MP3s, watching DVDs, or other touchy subjects under patent laws and the DMCA.

If you are in an area where it is legal to use these technologies in Linux and open source, you need to enable the necessary features. Start by using the su command to become the root user (type su - root). Then, use your favorite text editor as discussed in Chapter 13 to open the file /etc/sysconfig/rhn/ sources for editing.

Go to the end of the file and add the following text (where this is all on a single line):

```
yum livna-stable-fc1 http://rpm.livna.org/fedora/1/i386/
yum/stable
```

Right click over the updater icon on the right hand side of your panel, and click Exit. Then, select the main menu⇨System Tools⇨Red Hat Network Alert icon. When the updater icon is back in place, click it, and now when you navigate to the point where you see "channels" for updates, the livna archive is included.

However, this action only makes it possible to update what's already installed. You also want to be able to add items you haven't installed yet, so now open the file /etc/yum.conf for editing in your favorite text editor. Add the following lines at the bottom, where the URL is all on one line (rather than broken up as it appears below):

```
[livna-stable]
name=Livna.org Fedora Compatible Packages (stable)
baseurl=http://rpm.livna.org/fedora/$releasever/$basearch/yum
/stable
[fedora-us]
name=Fedora.us The Non-Red Hat Fedora packages (stable)
baseurl= http://download.fedora.us/fedora/fedora/$releasever
          /$basearch/yum/stable
```

After you have saved this file, you are ready to proceed through the rest of this chapter.

Checking Your Sound Card

Before you can listen to those tunes, you have to make sure that your sound card is working properly. After the configuration issues are dealt with, you can move on to the fun stuff. These days, some people don't bother buying stereos because they can listen to CDs through their computer. There's plenty of support for this under Linux. Internet radio and downloading tunes are also popular regardless of what operating system you're using. Read on to find out more!

Testing and configuring your sound

The first time that you booted Fedora Core, you were asked to listen to a test sound. If you answered that you had, Linux and your sound card are getting along just fine. If you don't remember this step or it didn't pass the first time, I show you how to walk through the test again just to make sure. Then I show you where to find your audio mixer.

Testing your sound and making it work

To test your sound, select the appropriate tool for your distribution:

- **In Fedora Core 1:** Choose Main Menu➪System Settings➪Soundcard Detection.

- **In Mandrake Linux 9.2:** Choose Main Menu➪Configuration➪Hardware➪ HardDrake. Wait for the wizard to detect your hardware, and then select the entry under the Sound Card item.

- **In SuSE Linux 9.0:** Select the SuSE menu, and then choose System➪ Configuration➪YaST➪Hardware➪Sound.

For Fedora Core, after you enter your root password, the Audio Devices dialog box opens (see Figure 15-1). Click the Play Test Sound button, and you should hear a series of guitar strums. If you hear nothing, click No; if you do hear something, click Yes.

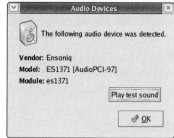

Figure 15-1:
The Fedora
Core Audio
Devices
dialog box.

If your sound isn't working, your card may not be supported. The following strategies can help you to track down a potential solution:

- Proceed to the manufacturer's Web site and locate the page for the specific card that you have. This page often has a link to technical support, drivers, and downloads. If it does, follow these links and see whether a *driver* (the piece of software that tells your operating system how to talk to each piece of hardware) is available for your card in Linux. If drivers are listed by *kernel version* — the version of the Linux core that you're using — type uname -r to see your version number and then choose the closest driver that you can. You also might have to try the central tech support page on that site if there isn't one dedicated to the hardware in question.

✔ Search on www.google.com for the make and model of your card, plus the word *Linux*. For example, I might search for

```
Yamaha YMF-744B Linux
```

You might be lucky enough to find a nice, simple solution to your problem. Or, you might find one that requires you to have a degree in Geekspeak. If so, see the Web sites that I mention in Chapter 1 for where to go for help that you can understand.

✔ Two special sound-related projects in Linux also might be able to help you. One is Advanced Linux Sound Architecture (ALSA), which you can find at www.alsa-project.org/. The other is Open Sound System (OSS) at www.opensound.com/. There's also the Linux Sound & MIDI site at http://linux-sound.org/.

Finding your audio mixer

After you have your sound working, you might want to adjust the base volume or mixer settings like you can in Microsoft Windows. These tools are available at the following:

✔ **Mandrake Linux 9.2:** Choose Main Menu⟹Multimedia⟹Sound⟹KMix.

✔ **Fedora Core 1:** Choose the main menu and then choose Sound & Video⟹Volume Control to see the mixer shown in Figure 15-2.

✔ **SuSE Linux 8.2:** Choose the SuSE (lightning bolt) menu, and then choose Administration⟹YaST2 Modules⟹Hardware⟹Sound. Then click the Volume button.

Figure 15-2:
The Fedora
Core sound
mixer.

Listening to CDs

In Red Hat Linux, many music CDs will start up on their own when you insert them in the drive if you're in the GUI. If that CD is registered in the CD DataBase (CDDB), the title and the song names load so that you can see what you're listening to. (CD DataBase is one of the services that tells your media players what the name of your CD is and what songs are on it; find more at www. gracenote.com/.) What you'll see looks similar to Figure 15-3.

Figure 15-3: The Red Hat Linux CD Player with an album loaded and playing.

If you close this application without clicking the Stop button, the CD will actually continue playing. You can stop it by opening the program again and clicking Stop.

If CDDB doesn't recognize your CD, you can add it to the database by clicking the Open Track Editor button (to the far left beneath the CD display) to open the CDDB Track Editor dialog box shown in Figure 15-4.

Figure 15-4: The GNOME CD Player's CDDB Track Editor dialog box.

Notice the white, right-facing triangles pointing to Show Advanced Disc Options and Show Advanced Track Options. You can click these to expand the amount of information displayed in the dialog box. After you're finished entering the information about your CD, click Save to store the data.

The button to the right of the Track Editor is Open Preferences. Clicking this brings up the dialog box shown in Figure 15-5. Here, you can tell the CD player how to behave when you start and end the program. After you make your changes, click Apply Change and then click Close.

Figure 15-5:
The GNOME
CD Player
Preferences
dialog box.

Listening to Internet radio

Listening to Internet radio stations in Linux is not always the simplest thing in the world, but thankfully, these days it's not as hard as it used to be. Because of various laws, patents, and licensing problems, some formats like MP3 are not always supported out of the box. The best way to see what you're set up to support right now is to simply try and listen. After you're sure that your sound is set up properly, you can try many Web sites with the Mozilla browser:

- ✔ **SHOUTcast** for finding links to thousands of online stations, at `www.shoutcast.com/`
- ✔ **Radio-Locator** for finding "regular" radio stations offering online versions, at `www.radio-locator.com/`

The first place to try is SHOUTcast. This site is the most likely to actually work with a Linux system. When you find a station that you want to listen to, click the Tune In! button. Because this is probably your first time doing this, you receive a dialog box similar to that shown in Figure 15-6.

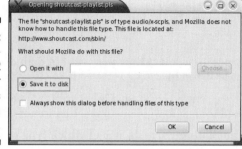

Figure 15-6:
The Mandrake 9.2 looks for Mozilla's Opening dialog box.

Select the Open It With radio button. In the text box, type /usr/bin/xmms. Click OK. The Mozilla download manager dialog box opens. Just minimize this: If you close it, you lose the radio station. Next, XMMS (X MultiMedia System) itself opens (as shown in Figure 15-7). The tool loads the radio station and immediately starts playing (if the file type is supported)!

Figure 15-7:
XMMS in Fedora Core 1.

If the file type is based on MP3, which is a patented type of file format, then you will receive a dialog box from Red Hat informing you that MP3 support was removed due to legal issues. However, if you are in a location where the MP3 functionality is legal to use, you can add this capability. First follow the instructions in the previous section, "Some Preliminaries," and then return here to type:

```
yum install xmms-mp3
```

You may see a lot of information scrolling down your screen. That's just the yum tool grabbing the data it needs on the various files offered through the repositories listed in your yum configuration file. When you see the words Resolving Dependencies, that means this tool is about to get down to business. Before the installation begins, you are asked whether you want to install the package(s) required — you will need any dependencies that are recommended. Press "y" and then Enter.

Now try a trickier one, like Radio-Locator. Not only does this site offer stations in formats that may not work under Linux, but it's also a bit confusing. I recommend that you do the following:

1. **Under the Search By portion, select how you want to drill down to the station that you want to listen to.**

   Choose from format, frequency, U.S. state, Canadian province, or advanced search. I tend to pick *format,* so I'll use that for an example.

2. **Under Available Radio Station Formats, select which type of station you're looking for.**

   Stations are sorted by their content type.

3. **Under the section for your Format, look to the table beneath the featured stations.**

   It's the left-most column that you're interested in. Many of the stations here have blank entries, but some have lightning bolts.

4. **If there is a lightning bolt next to the station that you want, click it.**

   Stations played in a format that you have already told the browser is handled by XMMS or another tool start playing automatically. If this is the case, you're finished with this process.

5. **Otherwise, click the station's call sign if it's marked as a link.**

   This action brings you to the station's own page. If the call sign isn't marked with a link, the station isn't online.

6. **Look for a <u>Listen online</u> link and click it.**

   This action should open the station's streaming feed. If your machine supports this feed, it will play automatically.

If you keep running into stations that your media player won't support, you need to add some software. See the section "Watchin' Movies!" later in this chapter for how to add Mplayer.

Listening to downloaded music

Downloading music off the Internet is a fun activity. A lot of people like to pretend that it's both legal and ethical, when in fact it's often theft. I leave that ethical issue between you and your belief system of choice, but since my own ethics say that it's theft, I'm going to focus on showing you music that you're *welcome* to download. Legally and ethically! Take a look at strategies for finding such music, along with how to listen to it.

One place to find such material is on a band's own Web site. Many groups today realize that offering free downloads of their work is a great PR move — if people love the sample songs, they're more likely to go out and buy the album. For an example, I use one of my own favorite bands, Evanescence (`www.evanescence.com/`).

Evanescence, like many other bands, has its page done mostly with Macromedia's Flash tool. Mozilla will tell you that you can't view the content without the right plug-in, so Evanescence, like many other bands, has its page done mostly with Macromedia's Flash tool. Mozilla will tell you that you can't view the content without the right plug-in, so first you'll have to get the plug-in for Flash. To download and then install this plug-in, perform the following steps:

1. **Point your browser to** `http://macromedia.mplug.org`.

2. **Click the link that best represents your physical location.**

   This link takes you to the Macromedia site with the latest versions of their Flash player, in the most friendly formats available.

3. **Click the** `flash-plugin` **link next to Fedora Core 1.**

   A Save As dialog box opens.

4. **Navigate to your preferred save location and then click Save.**

   The file downloads.

5. **Open a command line terminal.**

6. **Use the** `cd` **command to go to the directory where you stored the file.**

7. **Use the** `su` **command to gain root access.**

8. **Type** `rpm -ivh` *filename*.

   If you receive an error, you may need to install an RPM from your DVD or CD set called compat-libstdc++. You can install this library by typing `yum install compat-libstdc++` and pressing Enter.

9. **Close your browser and then relaunch it.**

10. **Browse to** `www.evanescence.com`.

    If the plug-in still doesn't load, choose the site version that doesn't rely on the particular plug-in in question (if there's one available).

Now, to see whether you can listen to any music here, click the <u>Music</u> link. The songs are in the Flash window on the left. You have the option of clicking `real` for RealPlayer, `windows` for Windows Media Player, or `lyrics` to see the words for this song.

Ripping music tracks from CDs

This is another topic that's impossible to cover without at least acknowledging that both ethics and legal issues are involved. I'm not going to get into legalities here, but my personal ethics are that it's fine to rip (copy) music off my own CDs for my own use. If I want to pull my favorite songs off CDs that I purchased and set them up so I can listen to them collectively in a random playlist, I don't see a problem with this. However, doing this and then taking the CD back for a refund is theft.

So, with that said, a number of music ripping programs are available in Linux. I cover Sound Juicer, which is included on any machine with GNOME installed. You open Sound Juicer by choosing Main Menu⇨Sound & Video⇨More Sound & Video Applications⇨Sound Juicer CD Ripper. Figure 15-8 shows this tool.

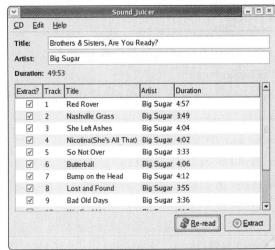

Figure 15-8:
Sound
Juicer
in Fedora
Core 1 with
a CD loaded.

To rip songs from a CD that you already have inserted

1. **For each song that you don't want to rip, uncheck the Extract check box, next to the song.**

   The check mark disappears for each song that you want to digitize.

2. **Select Edit⇨Preferences.**

   The Preferences dialog appears, as shown in Figure 15-9.

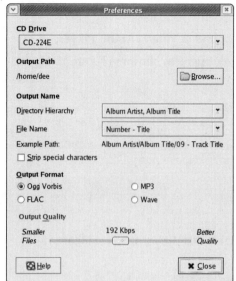

Figure 15-9:
The Sound
Juicer
Preferences
dialog.

3. **Select your preferred sound format.**

   I highly suggest Ogg Vorbis because this format is easily handled on Linux machines without any inherent legal problems, and is also better compressed than MP3 for equivalent sound.

4. **Use the Browse button to select where you want your sound files saved.**

5. **In the Output Name section, select how you want Sound Juicer to name and arrange the files in subdirectories.**

6. **Make any other configuration changes you want to make.**

7. **When finished making changes, click Close.**

   The dialog closes.

8. **Click Extract.**

   The Progress dialog appears, showing you what track you are on and how far within that track you are.

9. **Select CD⇨Eject.**

   The CD tray opens.

10. **Remove the CD and close the tray.**

11. **Close Sound Juicer.**

Want to listen to what you just ripped?

1. **Choose Main Menu⇨Sound & Video⇨Audio Player.**

   The XMMS Media Player opens as shown in Figure 15-10.

Figure 15-10:
The XMMS
Media
Player.

2. **Click PL.**

   This button opens the Playlist dialog box (see Figure 15-11).

Figure 15-11:
The XMMS
Playlist
dialog box.

3. **Click Add.**

   This button opens the Load File(s) dialog box.

4. **Navigate to the directory where your new OGGs are stored.**

5. **Click Add All Files in Directory.**

   This handy trick adds every file in that directory at once to the playlist.

6. **Click Close.**

   The Load File(s) dialog box closes.

7. **Close the Playlist dialog box.**

8. **Click the Play button in XMMS.**

   Isn't that cool?!

Burning CDs

A CD burner is a great way to make data backups (especially if it's a rewrite-able), save and share your digital photos, put together multimedia memento scrapbooks, and more. Many tools are available that allow you to burn CDs under Linux. I'll cover the one that comes with Fedora Core 1, which is xcdroast.

This tool may not be installed by default. It's on your DVD (or CD 2 in the Fedora Core 1 set). See Chapter 17 for how to install new software.

To start this program, use System Tools⇨CD Writer. A number of confusing windows open. The best advice I can give here is to glance them over and keep clicking okay until the tool itself opens. Then, click the Setup button; in the resulting window, you should see your CD burner listed amongst the hardware. Clicking the CD Settings tab brings you to one of the items you might want to edit if you're a CD burning whiz (Figure 15-12).

Then, click the HD Settings tab to bring you to one of the few items that you actually need to edit (check out Figure 15-13). In the Path text box, type /tmp. Then click Add to place this directory in the list of temporary storage options. Now, unless you are a wiz with CD burning and have a ton of things that you want to configure, click Save Configuration. If you know what else you want to do, take your time! After you're finished with all your setup tasks, click the Save Configuration button again if you've made any changes, and then click OK.

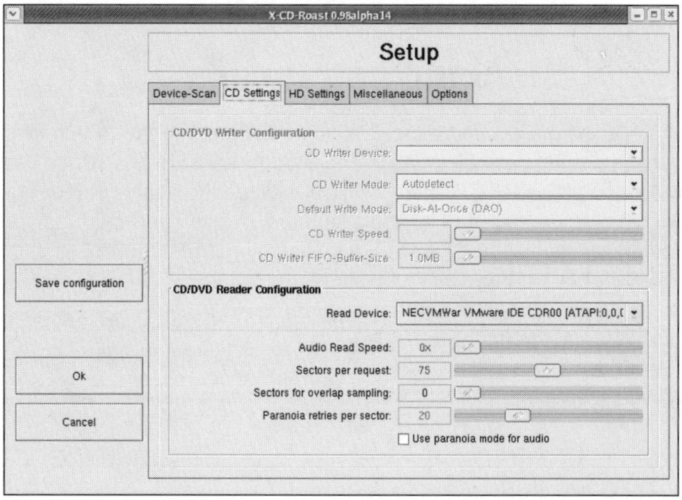

Figure 15-12:
X CD Roast
at its CD
Settings
dialog box.

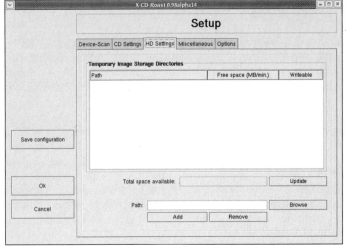

Figure 15-13:
X CD Roast
at its HD
Settings
dialog box.

X CD Roast offers you two options. You can duplicate an existing CD or create one from scratch. Both of these choices offer you an attractive yet simple interface for going through the steps of reading in the existing CD's contents, editing them if desired, and then writing the results onto another CD.

The Tucows download site has a whole section for grabbing Linux multimedia tools. Check out `http://linux.tucows.com/mmedia.html`.

Blocking pop-up ads

The Radio-Locator site gives me another topic for discussion. Every time that you click a link there, you have to deal with pop-up ads. Want to get rid of them? In Mozilla, you can do so by choosing Tools➪Popup Manager➪About Popup Blocking. A dialog box opens asking whether you want to block pop-ups and then configure how this works. Click Yes, and the Preferences dialog box opens to the Popup Windows tab. The defaults here are fine, or you could explore this area more thoroughly. Notice that you have the ability to allow pop-ups from certain sites because there are actually useful pop-ups out there.

After you're finished setting this up, click OK. Suddenly, no more pop-ups!

Creating and modifying graphics with The GIMP

The GIMP is a graphics program that's considered in many ways equivalent to Adobe Photoshop. Many don't consider The GIMP the friendliest program on the planet, but at the very least, it has enough features to keep you busy for weeks experimenting! To open The GIMP, access the main menu and then choose Graphics⇨The Gimp.

When you start The GIMP for the first time, you have to walk through its user setup routine:

1. **In the Welcome dialog box, click Continue.**

   The Personal GIMP Directory dialog box opens.

2. **In the Personal GIMP Directory dialog box, click Continue.**

   Before you proceed, if you're curious, you can click on the various sub-directories and files that will be created during The GIMP setup process. Doing so gives you information about what each file and subdirectory is for. After you click Continue, the User Installation Log dialog box opens.

3. **In the User Installation Log dialog box, click Continue.**

   The box instructs you to read through and look for installation errors. It's worth a quick scroll-through, but I've never run into problems, especially on a package-managed system, such as RPM (see Chapter 17). After you click Continue, the GIMP Performance Tuning dialog box opens.

4. **Alter the value in the Tile Cache Size text box if you want to restrict how much memory The GIMP lets your images take up.**

   The default is just fine for most people, but if you work with large, heavily detailed images, you may need to raise the value. You can do this if you have a lot of RAM on your system (128MB or more). On the other hand, if you really work only with small items, you can lower the value.

5. **If your home directory is on a drive without approximately 500MB of free space (a conservative value to be safe), change the value in the Swap Directory text box to another location, such as** /tmp/ *username*.

Click the icon to open a window that enables you to browse to another location. Again, most people won't need to make any changes. If you're not sure how much room you have, open a terminal window by clicking the Terminal button on the lower button bar (or click the Main Menu button and then choose System Tools➪Terminal) and type df -h to see how much room you have on each of your partitions.

6. **Click Continue to proceed.**

   The Monitor Resolution dialog box opens.

7. **Select the Get Resolution from Windowing System check box.**

   Doing this allows The GIMP to figure your settings automatically instead of forcing you to get down and dirty with the math.

8. **Click Continue to start The GIMP.**

   The full startup is shown in Figure 15-14.

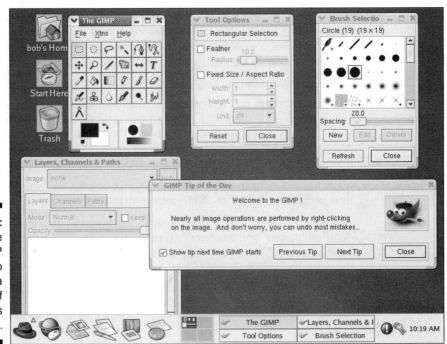

Figure 15-14:
The full GIMP startup includes a collection of dialog boxes and more.

From now on, anytime that you start The GIMP, this is what you'll see unless you close some of the dialog boxes — which The GIMP kindly remembers that you closed the next time. The GIMP is an incredibly complex program, with entire books written for the people who really want to use it heavily. Great starter links for working with The GIMP are

- ✔ **GIMP Tutorials Pointer Page:** `http://empyrean.lib.ndsu.nodak.edu/ ~nem/gimp/tuts/`

- ✔ **RRU GIMP Tutorial:** `www.rru.com/~meo/gimp/Tutorial/`

- ✔ **The official GIMP.org site's tutorials page:** `www.gimp.org/tutorials. html`

- ✔ **The GIMP Savvy Web site (with a full book available for reading online):** `http://gimp-savvy.com/`

Watchin' Movies

These days, you can watch many kinds of movies on your computer. Whether it's a Flash animation, a DVD, or a movie trailer, you've got the tools that you need right at your fingertips (or just a click away). You might have even installed some already while trying to access other multimedia features. Here are some of the tools of the trade.

Watching a DVD in Linux is a bit of a legal quagmire if you live in the U.S. The Digital Milennium Copyright Act (DMCA) and other issues make it tricky for any open source program to navigate the licensing maze when it comes to movies that are encoded or protected in various fashions. However, not all DVDs have such countermeasures enabled: There are DVDs that Americans can watch under Linux with no trouble. (Note that I say _watch_, and not _copy_ or _pirate_.)

For more on the DMCA and the problems it causes, see `anti-dmca.org`.

Perhaps the best media player out there for the Linux community is `mplayer`. You can fetch the latest version of this tool by doing the setup described in the earlier section "Some Preliminaries" and then typing (as root) at the command line:

```
yum install mplayer
```

After you have `mplayer` installed, you'll want to add some frills as well. Type:

```
yum install mplayer-gui
```

After this installation completes, go to the main menu⇨Sound and Video⇨ Movie Player to run your new multimedia player (see Figure 15-15).

This program offers you a feature-rich experience, including the ability to load subtitles and more! Not only that, but it will also come in handy if you want to watch one of the many animations and movies available on the Web.

Figure 15-15:
The
MPlayer
multimedia
tool.

Dealing with Windows-Only Media Formats and Programs

There is little more maddening for the Linux user than to discover that no Linux tool is available for working with a piece of multimedia, a document type, or a program feature that you know is available in Windows but you can't yet find an equivalent for in Linux. Fret not. You're not stuck!

The first thing to do is go to `linuxshop.ru/linuxbegin/win-lin-soft-en/` and see whether there *really* isn't a Linux tool that can do the job. You might be surprised. After this, you have two options. There are commercial packages available that can help you to access these documents and features under Linux, or you can wade in and try to get Wine working, which is the free base beneath all these tools.

Available Software

A growing number of commercially available tools let you work with anything from Microsoft Office to your Windows games. Ultimately, a Linux user's goal is to not have to use any of these extra program layers in order to do what we want to do — but in the meantime, it's nice not to be terribly inconvenienced. I've reviewed or at least used every one of these products, so I'm not just going by their Web sites.

CodeWeavers

CodeWeavers (`www.codeweavers.com`) provides two excellent products that I use from time to time: CrossOver Office and CrossOver Plugin. The Office package allows you to use Microsoft Office (along with a growing number of office applications) directly under Linux, and the Plugin tool helps you to get past those last few hurdles that might be blocking you from accessing various bits of content on the Web (and boy can the Plugin tool, shown in Figure 15-16, help with lots of frustration). It's a bit jarring to run Microsoft Word and QuickTime under Linux at first — because there's no native way to do this for either — but it's certainly handy.

What I most appreciate about CodeWeavers (and all these companies, really) is that they are very upfront about what works really well, what works except for a few features, and what works not so well. All you have to do is check their Web site. You'll have to have your Microsoft Office CDs on hand for CrossOver Office and for the next item. These tools don't come with all the software that they support! They just allow you to run what you have.

CrossOver Office supports Office XP, 2000, and 97 products. See the Supported Applications listing on the CodeWeavers site for more. CrossOver Plugin supports most major Windows multimedia clients along with the Trillian IM client and other items some people just can't do without.

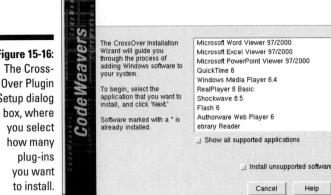

Figure 15-16:
The Cross-
Over Plugin
Setup dialog
box, where
you select
how many
plug-ins
you want
to install.

Win4Lin

Another option is Win4Lin from NeTraverse (www.netraverse.com/). **Although CrossOver Office focuses mostly on serious office tools, Win4Lin extends farther into the multimedia development direction by supporting a larger number of Macromedia and Adobe products. Win4Lin supports Windows 95, 98 (see Figure 15-17), and ME. It also requires you to have your Windows OS CDs on hand.**

WineX

More interested in games than office tools? There's also TransGaming's WineX (www.transgaming.com). **This version of Wine is specifically designed to support Direct X, which is used in Windows to make programming for multimedia and games easier. Subscribers have access to regular updates, allowing them to make use of their favorite games and also add any games they like to the growing list of games that are being tested with the system.**

Selecting the Games link and then selecting the full listing at the bottom of the resulting page allows you to see the full listing of what games are supported and how well they're supported. Figure 15-18 shows an example.

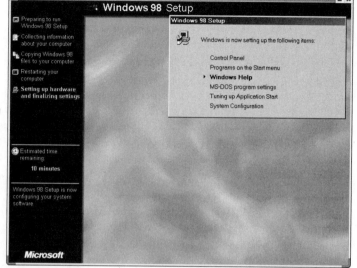

Figure 15-17:
Windows 98 almost finished installing under Win4Lin in a Linux GUI window!

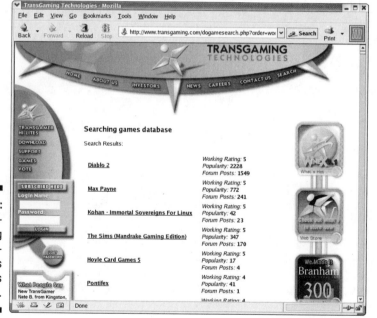

Figure 15-18:
The Trans-Gaming Technol-ogies Games Database.

VMware

Finally, if you absolutely have to do something under Windows itself but only have one machine and it's running Linux (or vice versa, for that matter), there's VMware (www.vmware.com). This is a popular tool in technical support offices where people need access to many different kinds of machines to test things. It's also popular with authors, like myself, because it allows us to grab those tricky screenshots of the boot process and installer screens.

In VMware, you run a full session of another operating system (or even the same one) within your desktop — see Figure 15-19. If your machine is powerful enough, you could have five different operating systems all running in their own windows on a single computer.

All these tools require a bit of extra oomph in your system. Check out their requirements and then try to go as farythem as you can. Each has a nice graphical installer that walks you through the process, and in general can make your life pretty nice if there are things you just can't leave behind from the Windows world.

Figure 15-19:
A VMware window containing Windows XP, but running in Linux.

Installing and Using Wine

And then there's Wine (`www.winehq.org`), a complete rebuild of Microsoft Windows 98 functionality that runs under Linux. Wine is in many ways the mother of everything in the previous section. However, because it's a free and very complicated project, it's not quite as friendly as the commercial versions. It's kind of like the others but with all the makeup and hairspray removed.

Some Linux distributions offer Wine RPMs directly on their installation CDs. If yours doesn't, you can get an RPM from `http://sourceforge.net/project/showfiles.php?group_id=6241`, which you can find by following the Wine download links for the binary versions. Locate your distribution in the list and then get the very latest RPM available for that distribution. It may take a while for the download to complete. This is an entire re-implementation of Microsoft Windows after all!

After you have the file downloaded, access a command line terminal and use the `su` command to become the root user. Then, type `rpm -ivh wine[TAB]` (where `[TAB]` means that you press the Tab key) to install the program.

You'll probably find it useful to return to the Web site soon, at `www.winehq.org/site/docs/wine-user/index`. This is where the Wine documentation is.

The first thing that you must do before you are able to use Wine is, of course, configure it. Fortunately, graphical tools are available to help you out. On the same page where you downloaded the main package, go to the bottom and find the `winesetuptk` RPM. Download this and install it as root. Then type `exit` to return to being a normal user and type `winesetuptk` to start the tool (see Figure 15-20).

Stick with the defaults until you reach the Look and Feel section. Then you'll probably want to choose Windows 98 so you don't feel like you've completely returned to the Stone Age! Click Finish and the tool will do its thing, setting up everything necessary for Wine to do its job.

Now comes the fun part — trying to run your old Windows software. You don't really run Wine, per se. Instead, you first install the Windows software you want to run and then invoke Wine whenever you need to use something from the Windows world. To install a Windows program for Wine, insert the CD-ROM or floppy into the appropriate drive. Your distribution might open the file manager for you, or you might need to open the file manager manually. Regardless, your goal is to run the installation routine, which is typically SETUP.EXE. You can double-click this icon in the File Manager and, when asked what program you want to use to open this file, answer winelauncher.

Figure 15-20:
The Wine-
SetupTk
Wine
configura-
tion tool.

As I write this, I'm trying out the instructions with the set of National Geographic CD-ROMs that I purchased years ago. Because it's difficult to describe a standard Wine session, I thought I'd walk you through how this goes for me.

The installer loads just fine even though there's a brief error message that I have to close along the way. I stick with the defaults (because Wine is still a work-in-progress and it's best not to taunt it with getting fancy) and then wait while the installer adds all of the files to my Mandrake system. After a while, I wonder why nothing is happening, I minimize the installer's background to see what's going on, and oops! Some dialog boxes are stuck behind it! Watch out for that.

Every once in a while, the installation seems over, but it's not. A Computer icon hovers on the lower left of the screen while the installer continues running, with Setup underneath it. That makes viewing things clearer, especially because it goes away after everything is installed. Oops, now there's a big blue screen that reads QuickTime 4 Setup and never, ever goes away. I press Ctrl+Alt+Esc and can get rid of it.

The main program should have installed just fine. To run a Wine program, I first need to know what the path is to that program. I can find it by looking in the `~/.wine` directory. In this case, the program was installed into `/home/dee/.wine/fake_windows/Program Files/The Complete National Geographic`. The file `NGMAG2.exe` looks like the one for launching the program.

Wine sees the `fake_windows` directory as the main Windows hard drive base. This means that I need to type the following to start my program:

```
wine "c:\\Program Files\\The Complete National
          Geographic\\NGMAG2.exe"
```

Believe it or not, it works (see Figure 15-21)! I now have access to the database of the entire history of National Geographic that I bought a number of years ago, back when Windows 98 was the standard.

Pull out those old Windows 95 and 98 CDs and give them a try!

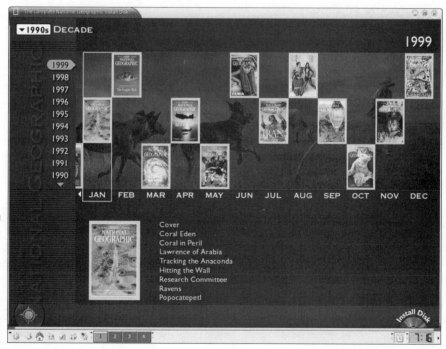

Figure 15-21: National Geographic's CD collection in Mandrake Linux 9.2.

Part IV
Sinking Your Teeth into Linux

The 5th Wave   By Rich Tennant

"I'm not saying I believe in anything. All I know is since it's been there our server is running 50% faster."

In this part . . .

This part is where you reach out with Linux beyond the confines of the operating system in order to dig more deeply into its daily care and feeding. I introduce you to the Linux file system, starting from its low-level layout and partitioning schemes, then adding media and formatting disks, and continuing with the ins and outs of managing a file system and sharing files and printers. Next, you find out how to add software to Linux while dealing with archives, using the Red Hat Package Manager (RPM), and locating and using new software for your system.

Finally, it's time to batten down the Linux hatches as you explore what's involved in securing a system and keeping things secure. Here, you cover everything from picking secure passwords to updating your system and other software to learning the drill necessary to keep your system safe from security threats and compromise.

Chapter 16

Checking Out the Linux File System

I have an existential map. It has "You are here" written all over it.

—Steven Wright

One of the most frustrating things about learning a new operating system can be figuring out where it keeps files. Rather than keep all important system files in a single directory, such as the `C:\Windows` directory in Microsoft Windows, Linux follows the lead of its Unix cousins and spreads things out a bit more. Although the Linux and Windows setups involve different methods, they are both logical. They also both require that you understand where to look.

Another issue you come across is adding new *media* — hard drives, floppy disks, CD-ROMs, DVD-ROMs, zip disks, USB keychain and thumb drives, and more — to the existing file system. In this chapter, I focus on how the file system is organized and other handy topics, such as how to access data on a floppy disk.

Introducing the Linux File System

Linux may be all by itself on your hard drive, or maybe it's sharing your hard drive with another operating system, such as Microsoft Windows. All the hard drive space you allocated for Linux during the installation process is your Linux *file system.* Because you're running your own Linux machine, you must be familiar with how it's put together — especially the sections that are dangerous to mess with!

The Linux file system is deeply layered; it consists of lots of directories and subdirectories. Most of the internal information in an operating system, such as Microsoft Windows, is hidden away in the Windows directory. In Linux, however, this information is scattered around a bit wider and for good reason: Lots of files are involved! After you come to understand Linux, however, you see that it maintains a logical order to where it keeps things.

Meet the root directory

Everything in the Linux file system is relative to the `root` *directory,* which is referred to as / and is the file-system base, a doorway into all your files. The `root` directory contains a mostly predictable set of subdirectories. Each distribution varies slightly, but certain standards exist to which they all conform. The standards keep us all sane.

Rather than flood you with everything at once, I start by talking about just the items that are directly off `root`. Table 16-1 lists the standards and some of the more common extras. An asterisk (*) at the end of a description indicates that you shouldn't mess with this directory unless you have a specific reason because it contains files that are very important to the functioning of your system.

Table 16-1	Standard / Contents in Linux
Directory	**Contains**
/bin	The commands that everyone needs to use at any time*
/boot	The information that boots the machine, including your kernel*
/dev	The device drivers for all the hardware that your system needs to interface with*
/etc	The configuration files that your system and many of its software packages use*
/home	The home directories for each of your users
/lib	The code that many programs (and the kernel) use*

Directory	Contains
/mnt	The spot where you add temporary media, such as floppy disks and CD-ROMs
/opt	The location that many people decide to use for installing new software packages, such as word processors and office suites
/root	The superuser's (root user's) home directory
/sbin	The commands the system administrator needs access to*
/tmp	The place where everyone and everything store temporary files
/usr	The programs that machines can share between them
/var	The data that changes frequently, such as log files and your mail

Some of these directories have some equally important subdirectories, so I dig a bit deeper now.

Meet the /etc subdirectories

Although the exact subdirectories that exist in /etc can change from distribution to distribution, the following two are fairly standard:

- The /etc/X11 directory contains configuration details for the X Window System (X), which runs your Graphical User Interface (GUI). See Chapter 12 for more on the GUI.

- The /etc/opt directory contains configuration files for the programs in the /opt directory, if you decide to use it.

Meet the /mnt subdirectories

You may or may not have any subdirectories in /mnt by default. Typically, however, you at least have the following:

- The /mnt/floppy directory is used for adding a floppy disk to your file system.

- The /mnt/cdrom directory is used for adding a CD-ROM to your file system.

In the "Adding Media to Your File System" section, later in this chapter, I show you how to add these items.

Meet the /usr subdirectories

The /usr directory is often referred to as its own miniature file system hierarchy. This directory has lots of important or interesting subdirectories, as shown in Table 16-2. An asterisk (*) at the end of a description indicates that you need to leave that directory alone unless you have good reason to mess with it — *after* you gain lots of experience with Linux and know exactly what changes you need to make — so that you don't accidentally alter something your system needs in order to function correctly. An important thing to remember about this segment of the file system is that many Linux users often use /usr to store programs that can be shared with other machines.

Table 16-2	Standard /usr Subdirectories
Subdirectory	*Contents*
/usr/X11R6	The files that run the X Window System*
/usr/bin	The commands that aren't essential for users but are useful*
/usr/games	The games that you install on your system, except for those that you can choose to place in /opt
/usr/include	The files that the C programming language needs for the system and its programs*
/usr/lib	The code used by many of the programs in this /usr subhierarchy*
/usr/local	The programs and other items that you want to keep locally, even if you're sharing everything else in /usr
/usr/sbin	The commands that aren't essential for administrators but are useful*
/usr/share	The information that you can use on any Linux machine, even if it's running incredibly different hardware from what this one is running*
/usr/src	The source code that you use to build the programs on your system

Partitions versus Directories

One very important thing you must understand about the Linux file system is that it may not all be on one single hard drive or hard drive partition. If you have dealt with this point during the installation, you probably already know it. But maybe you have sidestepped this issue by using one of the installation methods that does things for you automatically.

What is really liable to confuse people is that partitions and directories tend to blend together. In the Microsoft Windows world, if you use separate hard drives or partitions, you have a specific letter designation for each one. The primary hard drive is C, the next is D, and so on. Under Linux, each of these drives and partitions quietly blends together.

If you partitioned your hard drives on your own, you know that you needed to specify a *mount point* — which is like an empty spot in a puzzle, where the outside partition or media can be plugged into the rest of the file system — for each partition. In the case of a hard drive partition, the mount point isn't in the /mnt part of the file system. It's an item in the root directory — maybe /boot or / or /usr. You literally attach permanent items, such as hard drives and partitions, right into the file system. Linux doesn't want to know or doesn't care about whether the directories or files are all on one drive or are on multiple drives. It just wants to do its thing. Don't worry: You do have reliable designations that are related to where in the scheme of hardware you can find your drive. See Table 16-3 for a breakdown of popular designations.

Table 16-3	Common Drive Designations
Designation	*Description*
/dev/cdrom	CD-ROM drive
/dev/fd0	Floppy drive 1
/dev/fd1	Floppy drive 2
/dev/hda	First IDE hard drive
/dev/hda1	First IDE hard drive, first primary or extended partition
/dev/hda2	First IDE hard drive, second primary or extended partition
/dev/hdb	Second IDE hard drive
/dev/hdb1	Second IDE hard drive, first primary or extended partition
/dev/hdb2	Second IDE hard drive, second primary or extended partition
/dev/sda	First SCSI hard drive
/dev/sda1	First SCSI hard drive, first primary or extended partition

Linux see USB devices as SCSI devices. After you plug in your USB keychain or thumb drive, you can add it to the filesystem with the designation /dev/sda1.

You probably see a pattern by now. A hard drive has a three-letter designation:

✔ An IDE drive's designation starts with /dev/hd; the first drive of this type is a, the second is b, and so on. The third IDE drive looks like this: /dev/hdc.

✔ A SCSI drive's designation starts with /dev/sd; the first drive of this type is also a, the second is b, and so on. The third SCSI drive looks like this: /dev/sdc.

The number that follows the three-letter designation represents your partitions. I cover partitioning your hard drive in Chapter 2.

In Figure 16-1, I break down this concept, hopefully making it a bit more accessible. In this case, the user created three partitions for Linux. The first IDE drive is a single partition, allocated for the root partition. The second IDE drive is broken into two partitions. The first was given /usr; and the second, /var.

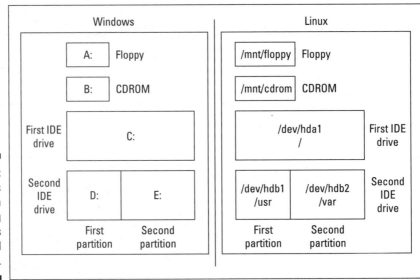

Figure 16-1: Linux versus Windows in handling partitions and hard drives.

If you move around the file system, you can't tell which of these directories is on which drive. The prompt, for example, doesn't change based on which drive each directory is on; the commands used for moving around the file system don't care about the underlying hard drive or drives.

Adding Media to Your File System

The items in /mnt, such as /mnt/floppy and /mnt/cdrom, are *temporary media* — disks you must add to the file system if you want to work with them and then remove them after you're done. Although this task may sometimes be done automatically (some distributions — including Fedora Core 1 — have tools in the GUI that automatically mount a CD-ROM after you close the drive), you often must mount a CD-ROM manually. But you can pretty easily do it as outlined in the following section.

Adding media temporarily

Rarely do you want to keep removable media (floppy disks, CD-ROMs, and even Zip disks) always in the drive. Even if you do, you probably don't always want the same disk, so you need a way to tell Linux that you have inserted removable media and where. You can do so by using the mount command at the command prompt or in a command-prompt window in the GUI by following these steps:

1. **Make note of whether you're trying to access a floppy or a CD-ROM.**

   The newest Linux distributions have a handy feature that automatically mounts a CD-ROM after you place it in the drive — if you're in the GUI. Although not all distributions have this feature, the one I include with this book does. When a CD-ROM, floppy disk, or hard drive is mounted, the contents of the media are then accessible to Linux.

2. **If the media is a floppy, type** ls /mnt/floppy; **if the media is a CD-ROM, type** ls /mnt/cdrom.

   If the directory doesn't exist, you need to create it. If you're not sure about the existence of the directory, navigate to the /mnt directory and use the ls command to display the contents. To create a directory, use the mkdir command as follows: mkdir /mnt/*location* (specifying the location).

3. **If it's a floppy disk, make note of the operating system the disk comes from.**

   Table 16-4 shows which operating system corresponds to which type label.

4. **Put the command together in the following format, and at a command prompt, type the command:**

   ```
   mount -t type /dev/device /mnt/location
   ```

You need to replace italicized words with specific information. To mount a floppy disk that you put together under Windows XP, for example, type this line:

```
mount -t vfat /dev/fd0 /mnt/floppy
```

where `fd0` is the type of device. (USB keychains and thumb drivers also tend to come pre-formatted with `vfat`.) `fd0` is the way Linux refers to the floppy drive — sort of how Windows refers to the floppy drive as A:. `fd0` and A: are part of the operating system definitions.

Table 16-4	**File System Types That Your Floppy Disk Can Contain**
Type	*Description*
ext2	Linux
msdos	Windows 3.11 or earlier
vfat	Windows 95 or later
hfs	Macintosh

If you're mounting a CD-ROM, try using the command as follows:

```
mount -t iso9660 /dev/cdrom /mnt/cdrom
```

You may be able to use just `mount /mnt/cdrom` in some distributions. For a Linux floppy disk, you can skip the type stuff and just try `mount /mnt/floppy` or `mount /dev/fd0 /mnt/floppy`.

To remove the CD-ROM or floppy disk from the file system, type this line:

```
umount /mnt/location
```

Do *not* remove a floppy disk without correctly unmounting it, or else you may wind up with missing data! Although you don't need to worry about losing data with CD-ROMs, you often can't remove the disk until you unmount it. And you can't unmount an item if you're already in it, so make sure that you're not anywhere in its directories before you attempt to unmount the media.

If you have both Windows and Linux set up on your computer and can boot from either operating system (a *dual-boot setup*), you can mount your Windows partition while you're in Linux! This technique is a great way to transfer files back and forth, if you need to. See your distribution's documentation for information about mounting a Windows partition.

Formatting disks

A floppy disk often comes as a blank slate or formatted for Windows or Macintosh use. If the disk is a blank slate, no computer can use it for anything. No computer running any operating system can store data on a blank floppy disk. A disk must have a file system on it to store information within that file system's format. That's what *formatting* a disk is all about: building a file system. You can either format a disk from the command prompt or use a GUI tool to do it. I cover both methods here in case you're not using GNOME, KDE, or the graphical environment.

Formatting at the command prompt

To format a floppy at the command prompt so that Linux can recognize it as a Linux disk, follow these steps:

1. **Place the floppy in the disk drive.**

2. **Type this line:**

```
mke2fs /dev/fd0
```

   Technical information about the information being written to the disk scrolls past. After the light on the floppy drive turns off, you can either eject the disk or mount it onto the file system (as I discuss in the section "Adding media temporarily," earlier in this chapter) and use it.

Formatting in GNOME

To format a floppy in GNOME so that Linux can recognize it as a Linux disk, follow these steps:

1. **On the icon bar, click the Main Menu button.**

   In default GNOME and KDE setups, the Main Menu button in the lower-left corner is a footprint in GNOME or a big K in KDE. If you installed Fedora Core 1, the Main Menu button is the Red Hat fedora icon in both GNOME and KDE.

2. **Choose System Tools➪Floppy Formatter.**

   The Floppy Formatter dialog box opens, as shown in Figure 16-2.

3. **Place the floppy disk in the floppy drive.**

4. **Make sure that the File System Type drop-down list box is set to Linux Native (ext2). (Refer to Figure 16-2.)**

5. **Make sure that the Floppy Density drop-down list box is set to High Density 3.5 (1.44 MB). (Refer to Figure 16-2.)**

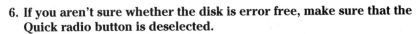

Figure 16-2:
The Floppy
Formatter
tool in
GNOME.

6. **If you aren't sure whether the disk is error free, make sure that the Quick radio button is deselected.**

   Deselecting this option makes the formatting take longer. It may take a minute or so to finish.

7. **Click the Format button to format the disk.**

   The Format Progress dialog box, with a progress bar, opens. After this line fills in, the format is complete. Then the Floppy Formatted Successfully dialog box opens.

8. **Click OK to close the Floppy Formatted Successfully dialog box.**

   Both this dialog box and the Format Progress dialog box close. Now the Format Another Floppy dialog box opens.

9. **Click No if you're done; click Yes if you want to format another floppy disk and start the process all over again beginning with Step 3.**

   If you click No, the Format a Floppy dialog box closes along with the Format Another Floppy dialog box.

Care and Feeding of Your File System

Regardless of which operating system you're using, you need to keep your file system healthy and happy. Everything that you need to operate the machine and do your work (or play) on it exists in that file system. Keep it in good shape, and it's sure to treat you well in return. Fortunately, Linux does some of it automatically for you.

Checking the file system

Whenever you shut down your machine, you can use the `-f` option to skip the file system check after the machine comes back up. Even if you do this step every time, Linux enables you to get away with it only a set number of times before it decides to take over and do a check anyway. However, I recommend *not* always using `-f` because you never know when a failure could occur. Checking the file system costs you an extra minute or so in boot time, although it can save you panicked hours of trying to revive a damaged machine later.

You can also manually check file systems by using the `e2fsck` command:

1. Type df to see whether the item that you want to check is mounted.

The `df` command lists the mounted partitions and media in addition to some statistics about them. You may, for example, see what's shown in Figure 16-3.

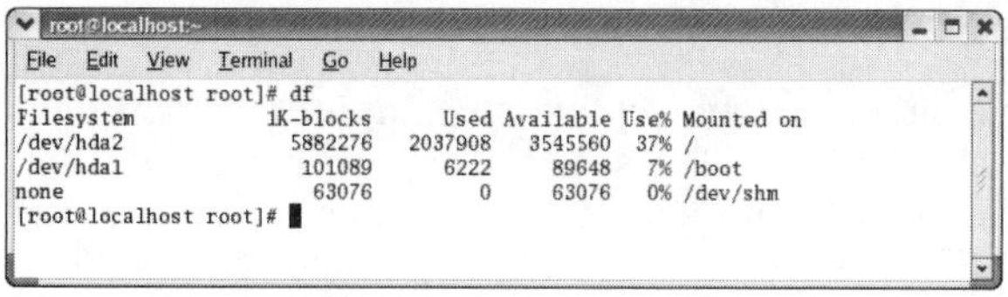

Figure 16-3:
Sample
output from
the `df`
command.

```
root@localhost:~                                                    _ □ ×
File   Edit   View   Terminal   Go   Help
[root@localhost root]# df
Filesystem           1K-blocks      Used Available Use% Mounted on
/dev/hda2             5882276    2037908   3545560  37% /
/dev/hda1             101089        6222     89648   7% /boot
none                   63076          0     63076   0% /dev/shm
[root@localhost root]# ▊
```

2. If the item is mounted and not vital for using the system, such as a CD-ROM full of pictures, type umount *mount point* **(specifying a particular mount point) to remove it from the file system.**

If you want to manually check a portion of the file system that's vital for the running of your Linux machine (`/` and `/bin`, for example), you must boot with rescue disks so that you can unmount these directories to check them. (*Rescue disks* are special boot disks that you use in emergencies, such as when your system isn't booting correctly. Refer to Chapter 5 for more information.) This task is a huge pain! Luckily, Linux checks the directories that are crucial for the system while it's booting so that you don't need to do so manually.

3. Type e2fsck /dev/*device* **(specifying a particular device) to run the check.**

This step can take a while. Table 16-5 shows a few options you may be interested in adding. If you decide to use an option, use the format `e2fsck` *options* `/dev/`*device* (specifying any options and a particular device).

4. **Type** mount /dev/*device mount point* **(specifying a particular device and mount point) to put the partition back in the file system if you want or need to do so.**

Table 16-5	Commonly Used Options for e2fsck
Option	*Purpose*
-f	Convinces e2fsck to check the file system, even if it tells you that the file system has already been checked and declared clean
-n	Answers No to all questions regarding whether things should be fixed
-p	Repairs the file system without asking any questions; subsequently, you can't see what has been done
-y	Answers Yes to all questions regarding whether things should be fixed

Leaving spare room

One of the most insidious problems that all computer users run into from time to time is a lack of disk space. The scope of this problem really depends on a number of things. The primary issue is that, if your root partition becomes 99 or 100 percent full, you need to use emergency rescue techniques (refer to Chapter 5) to boot the machine and clean it out. That's no fun, is it?

In the beginning, you're probably not in danger of filling the drives, unless you barely had enough room to install Linux in the first place. However, over time, you may forget about watching the drives for remaining space. Even experienced administrators run into this problem, so certainly you're forgiven if you do it too! Save yourself the worry and make sure that you know how to get regular updates about how full all your partitions are. To access the drive updates, follow these steps:

1. **Log in to the account you tend to use the most.**

2. **On the icon bar, click the Main Menu button.**

3. **Choose Accessories⇨Text Editor.**

   The text editor displays the contents of your home directory.

4. **Click the Open button. In the Selection field, type** .bash_profile **and press Enter.**

   The contents of the .bash_profile are displayed in the text editor window.

5. **Use the mouse or the arrow keys to place the vertical insertion bar on a blank line at the end of the file.**

6. **Type** df -h.

   You really only need the df command by itself; the -h option refers to *h*uman-readable, making the amount of space used and available easier for you to read. For an example, see Figure 16-4.

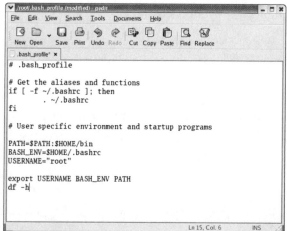

Figure 16-4:
An example
of the
.bash_
profile
file in gedit.

7. **Click the Save button on the application's toolbar.**

8. **To close gedit, click the X in the upper-right corner of the gedit window.**

   The next time you log in to this account, and from then on, you get a list of the space available and used on all mounted media.

Sharing Files by Using NFS

If you install multiple Linux computers on a network, you may want to share a partition or section of the file system between two or more of them. You can accomplish this by using the Network File System (NFS), which comes with almost all Linux distributions by default. Fortunately, Red Hat Linux 10 comes with a GUI tool that helps you to set up this service.

Today, a common home use for NFS is sharing music files from CDs that you purchased across multiple Linux computers. The rest of this section focuses on this use as an illustrative example.

NFS shared directory

You first need to tell NFS to share the directory containing your music archive. You may want to make this its own partition, or even a separate hard drive, depending on how many users you actually have and how much space you expect them to use. I assume that the archive is in /home/bob/Music. Adjust the directory accordingly for your needs.

Red Hat Linux offers a GUI NFS server configuration tool. See Chapter 17 for how to use the software management system to add it.

To set up a shared directory, follow these steps:

1. **Log in to the machine with the music archive as** root.

2. **Open the file** /etc/exports **in your preferred text editor.**

   This is the Network File System (NFS) central configuration file. By default, it's empty.

3. **Type this line:**

   ```
   /home/bob/Music networkaddress(rw,root_squash)
   ```

   This line ensures that the /home/bob/Music directory and all its subdirectories are sharable between all the computers in networkaddress. If the outside computers access this share, they can both read and write to their directories.

   The format of networkaddress is important here. It can be any one of the following:

   - **A single full IP address:** You can have a copy of this line for each individual machine if you want to allow it, rather than merge them into one line.

   - **A single machine's full name and domain information:** This takes the form host.domain.extension.

   - **All the machines in a domain:** This takes the form *.domain.extension.

   - **The entire network IP information:** This takes the form network/netmask.

   Inside the parentheses, you set the rules for access. In this case, rw refers to read-write access so that people can both play the music in this directory and save their own music files to it. The root_squash part means that root can't use this shared directory. Although you can remove this item, you often should leave it alone. The root account has lots of high-level permissions, and you want to limit its capability to move from one machine to another as much as possible.

4. **Save and exit the** /etc/exports **file.**

The exact method of exiting depends on which text editor you're using.

5. Reboot the machine.

You have other ways to apply the changes in the /etc/exports file, but beginners — as do some lazy advanced users — often find rebooting easiest. Doing so loads all the configuration changes you just made.

Permanently mounting a remote NFS directory

In the preceding section, I tell you how to set up one of your Linux machines so that your other Linux machines can access a directory by using NFS. In this section, you tell the secondary machines where to find the shared directory.

Each Linux machine has a central file it uses to tell it what to mount on the file system at boot time. This file also contains any shortcuts that may be on your system for typing things, such as mount /mnt/cdrom rather than mount -t iso9660 /dev/cdrom /mnt/cdrom. Within this file, you can tell your machine to automatically mount the remote /home/bob/Music directory. To accomplish this task, follow these steps on each secondary machine in turn:

1. Log in as root.

2. Open the file /etc/fstab **in your favorite text editor.**

This file may look something like what you see in Figure 16-5. Don't let it intimidate you, but don't change anything unless you really understand what it does.

3. Start a new, blank line at the end of the file.

Figure 16-5:
An example
of an /etc/
fstab
file in vi.

4. **Add the new line in the following format (and adjust for where your music files are stored):**

```
host:/home/bob/Music    /Music    nfs    defaults    0    #
```

This line tells Linux to use NFS to go to the machine *host* (name or IP address) and mount its /home/bob/Music directory as this machine's /Music directory with the same settings all the other drives have. The # represents where in the mount order to mount the drive. Look in the last column (with the padding spaces used in the file, the entries look like they're in columns) for the largest number and use one bigger. In Figure 16-5, for example, the largest number on the right is 2. You would use a 3 for # in this case.

5. **Save and exit the** /etc/fstab **file.**

6. **Type** mount -a **to activate your new** /etc/fstab **entry.**

Handle the boot process as you always do, making sure that you boot into Linux. When you come back up, everyone should be able to change to the /Music directory and enjoy its contents.

Accessing Shared Files on a Windows Computer

If your Linux computer is on a network with Windows machines, you can access files on the Windows computers across the network from your Linux system. The only requirement on the Windows side is that file sharing is turned on and at least one folder is shared. The user or administrator of the Windows system determines which folders are *shared,* which enables their contents to be accessed from another computer on the network.

To access a shared Windows directory from your Red Hat Linux 10 computer, first create a user account on this machine for each person to whom you want to allow access (refer to Chapter 6), and then follow these steps:

1. **Choose Main Menu⇨System Settings⇨Server Settings.**

If you can't find an entry named Samba Server, you need add this program (refer to Chapter 17) before you can proceed with these steps. If you find an entry named Samba Server, continue to Step 2.

2. **Select Samba Server.**

The Samba Server Configuration program appears.

3. **Click the Add button.**

The Create Samba Share dialog box appears (see Figure 16-6).

Figure 16-6:
The Samba
Server
Configu-
ration tool's
Create
Samba
Share dialog
box.

4. **Click the Browse button, browse to the directory you want to share with Windows users, and click OK after you have selected it.**

5. **In the Description text box, enter a brief description of what's in this directory.**

6. **If you want Windows users to be able to make changes to this direc-tory's contents, select the Read/Write option.**

7. **Click OK to close this dialog box.**

8. **Choose Preferences⇨Samba Users to open the Samba Users dialog box.**

9. **Click Add User.**

   The Create New Samba User dialog box appears (see Figure 16-7).

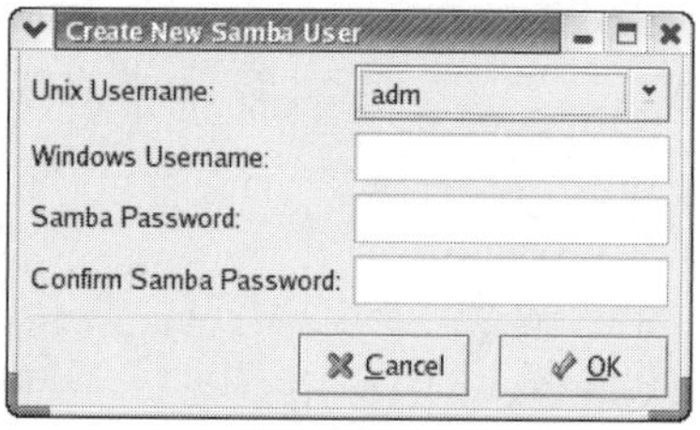

Figure 16-7:
The Create
New Samba
User dialog
box.

10. **In the Unix Username drop-down list box, select the login name for the person you're giving access to.**

11. **In the Windows Username text box, enter the login name the person uses to log in to their Windows box. If they don't have one, leave this text box blank.**

12. **In the Samba Password and Confirm Samba Password text boxes, enter the password you want this person to use when accessing the shared directory.**

13. **Click OK when finished.**

    This person's Linux login is now listed in the user list.

14. **If you want to add another user, return to Step 9. Otherwise, click OK.**

    The Create New Samba User dialog box closes.

15. **If you want to add a new directory to share, return to Step 3. Otherwise, click the small X to in the upper-right corner to close the Samba Server Configuration dialog box.**

That's it! The appropriate Windows users should now be able to access your shared Linux directories. But what if you want your Linux users to view directories on your Windows boxes? Have I got a trick for you!

To browse the shared Windows folders on your network, open the Konqueror Web Browser (see Chapter 9) and type **smb:/** in the Location (URL) field.

The contents of the browser window display any devices found on your network that are running the Windows file-sharing service.

To view the contents of the shared Windows folder, double-click the folder icon in the Konqueror window.

If you want to copy any of the Windows files in the shared directory to your Linux system, right-click the item in the browser window and choose Copy To from the shortcut menu. Navigate through the locations displayed on the menu to locate the destination. To cancel the Copy To selection, drag the mouse off the menu and release the mouse button.

Chapter 17

Adding Software to Linux

• •

In This Chapter

▶ Recognizing tarballs, RPMs, and compressed files

▶ Creating tarballs and archives

▶ Compressing files

▶ Opening tarballs, archives, and compressed files

▶ Installing and removing RPMs

• •

I will make you shorter by the head.

—Queen Elizabeth I

*W*hen you start using a new operating system, one of the most frustrating things is trying to figure out all the goofy file extensions. The Windows world has `.exe` and `.zip`. The Macintosh world has `.bin` and `.hqx`. What about the Linux world? It certainly has its fair share of bizarre extensions; but, really, they make a great deal of sense after you know the programs that make them. In this chapter, you find out all about `.tar`, `.gz`, `.tar.gz`, `.tgz`, `.bz2`, and `.rpm`. Anyone up for a game of Scrabble with alphabet soup?

Getting Tarred and Feathered

The Linux and Unix worlds are full of strange terms. If someone comes up to you out of the blue and starts talking about tarballs, you probably get a mental image of sticky, smelly balls of tar, maybe rolled in feathers. Yet a tarball is something you run into regularly in the Linux world, especially when you're looking for software or you need to save yourself some space. A *tarball* is a bunch of files (and possibly directories) packaged together in a `tar` file and then compressed by using the `gzip` utility.

Thunder and tar-nation

A long time ago, in a galaxy far, far away, most data backups were done on tapes. Large installations still use tapes, but this practice is getting more and more rare among home users because users' needs aren't as complex as in a corporate setting. The tar (Tape ARchive) program's job is to grab a set of directories and files and preserve everything about them, including their permissions, where they were in the file system, and more.

You have many more options these days for backups, but plenty of reasons to use tar are still around. Trying to make a backup of your home directory on CD? Want to have a single compressed file that contains all your word processing documents? You use tar whenever you want to group a bunch of files and directories into a single file.

More often than not, you need the tar command to open a file ending with the .tar extension that you may have downloaded. To open a tar archive, use the command in the format tar -xvf *filename*. For example, perhaps you created the file mydocs.tar months ago and saved it to another drive so that you could clear out space in your home directory. To restore these items to your home directory, you must first type cd ~ (the ~ is a useful shortcut for your home directory) to enter your home directory, and then type tar -xvf mydocs.tar to see output similar to the following:

```
./docs/doc1.txt
./docs/doc2.txt
./docs/doc3
```

Then, when you do a directory listing, you find that you now have a home subdirectory named ~/docs that contains the files doc1.txt, doc2.txt, and doc3. Some useful options to use with tar when dealing with existing tar files are listed in Table 17-1.

Table 17-1	tar Extraction Options
Option	*Purpose*
-f	Operates on a specific archive file.
-k	For a file that already exists in the same location, doesn't replace it with the same filename from the archive.
-t	Lists what is in the archive.
-v	Gives *verbose* output, meaning that you see everything that's going on.
-w	Asks for confirmation before extracting each file.
-x	Extracts files from an archive.

Although you mostly need to open tarballs and `tar` files, from time to time you want to create a tarball or a `tar` file. Usually, the format you use in this case is `tar -cvf filename.tar list_of_items`, where `filename` is the name of the archive you want to create and `list_of_items` is a space-separated list of the files and directories you want to package. For example, if you want to archive only parts of your home directory, you can type `tar -cvf homefiles.tar docs data scripts`, where `docs` (~/docs), `data` (~/data), and `scripts` (~/scripts) are all directory names. Because you include `-v` for verbose, you get a long list of every individual file that's being added. (I'm a bit paranoid and like to make sure that I'm adding what I really want to add!) See Table 17-2 for a list of useful archive-creation options.

Table 17-2	tar Creation Options
Option	**Purpose**
`-f`	Operates on a specific archive file.
`-k`	Doesn't overwrite the old versions of files if you're adding newer ones.
`-P`	Doesn't just store relative path names (for example, ~/docs); stores absolute path names (for example, /home/dee/docs).
`-r`	Adds files to an existing archive file.
`-u`	Adds files to an existing archive file only if they're newer than their previous versions that are already in the archive; erases previous versions.
`-v`	Gives *verbose* output, meaning that you want to see everything that's going on.
`-w`	Asks for confirmation before adding each file.
`-z`	Automatically `gzip`s the archive to create a tarball.

If you want to check out an alternative to `tar`, type `man pax` to see another powerful tool at your disposal.

gzip it up

Hard drives may be getting cheaper, but you always have to worry about running out of space. You're probably used to WinZip and all those `.zip` files out there in the Windows world for compressing files for storage or sending groups of files to other people. In the Linux world, you see lots of files that end in `.gz`, for `gzip`.

The gzip utility isn't as tricky to use as tar. To compress a file, you type gzip *filename*, and you end up with *filename*.gz. When you want to decompress a file, you use gzip's cousin, gunzip, in the same manner. So, if you want to open dogpic.gz, you type gunzip dogpic.gz. The important thing to know is that when you decompress a .gz file, the original file goes away! So, you have no more dogpic.gz; just dogpic — though you also could have named the file dogpic.jpg.gz so you could see which format the image file was in. Be sure to make a copy of the compressed version if you want to keep it around, although you can just make another one at any time.

Rolling the ball

Now that you know all about tar and gzip, what's with all this talk about tar-balls? As you may imagine, a .tar file can get pretty big with all those individual files and directories in it. Typically, after you archive something, you then compress it. You may have even noticed an option in Table 17-2 (the -z option) that allows you to compress your archive automatically after it's created.

Red Hat Linux comes with a program named File Roller that enables you to work with tarballs in a GUI. Click the Main Menu button to open the Main Menu and then choose Accessories⇨File Roller.

In default GNOME and KDE setups, the Main Menu button in the lower-left corner is a footprint in GNOME or a big K in KDE. If you installed Fedora Core 1, the Main Menu button is the Red Hat fedora icon in GNOME.

To create a tarball, you first tar the items you want to archive, and after that action is completed, gzip the resulting archive file. Suppose that you want to save all configuration files in /etc, just in case something bad happens. Make sure that you're logged in as root for this one; you need read permissions for every file in /etc, and not all the files in /etc are accessible to general users. (Aren't you glad?) An alternative is to utilize tar's -z option, as mentioned earlier, in a format such as tar -cvfz etcbackup.tgz /etc. (Yes, that's .tgz — it's shorthand for .tar.gz.)

WinZip can open tarballs with no problem on a Windows box!

When it's time to open a tarball, you first gunzip it and then un-tar it — oops, that can get confusing because there is no untar command. To open etcbackup.tgz, you first type gunzip etcbackup.tgz, which leaves you with the file etcbackup.tar. Then, you type tar -xvf etcbackup.tar. You should be aware of one little issue, though. When you unpack a .tar file, it typically creates all its subdirectories, starting wherever you are. So, if you have `etcbackup.tgz` in your home directory, when you unpack you end up with the directory ~/etc, containing the entire archive's contents.

If you aren't sure about the file's internal structure, you can check by typing `tar tvf` *filename.tar* `| more`.

You can also use the shortcut `tar -xvfz etcbackup.tgz` and skip using `gunzip`.

bzip2, the gzip alternative

There's a new kid on the block when it comes to compressing files in the Linux world. That kid is `bzip2`. You use this program exactly the same way you use `gzip`, except that its files have the extension `.bz2`. To compress `mysong.mp3` using this (usually) more efficient program, you type `bzip2 mysong.mp3` and get the file `mysong.mp3.bz2`. To uncompress it, you use `bunzip2`, so you type `bunzip2 mysong.mp3.bz2`.

You can also use this command in conjunction with `tar` to create files ending in `.tar.bz2`. I haven't seen any "B-Balls" with a `.tbz2` extension yet, but I suppose that it's only a matter of time.

Revving Your RPMs

For a long time, keeping track of what was installed on your Linux machine was a bit of a nightmare. Problems cropped up especially when the time came to install new software. If a program relied on a specific version of another tool to be installed and didn't work because you didn't have that tool, you could spend ages trying to figure out what the problem was.

Red Hat to the rescue! The folks at Red Hat Linux wrote the Red Hat Package Manager (RPM), and a number of other high-profile Linux distributions now include this tool. You can tell a file that's meant for use with the package manager by its `.rpm` extension. What makes RPMs so special? An `.rpm` file contains more than just the package itself: This type of file also holds information about the package it contains, which other packages it depends on, and more.

When you install an RPM (or when the installer adds it during the installation process), the additional package information is added to a central RPM database. Your system knows exactly which software you have, which packages are dependent on which other packages, and other information.

Manually working with RPMs

Working with RPMs on the command line can seem daunting at first, especially if you type `man rpm` and look at the help materials. So many options! Don't worry, though: You need to know only a short selection of the available options. The remaining options are things you can experiment with later — after you feel that you have the basics down.

Installing an RPM by hand

The most common RPM task is installing a new package, which you do by typing `rpm -ivh` *packagename* (where i refers to Install, v means Verbose, and h means Hash, or to show progress with # characters). If your system doesn't have the necessary items for this program to run properly, you see an error message identifying the name of the package you need or the name of the file. The important thing is usually the version number. The file `gnome-linuxconf-0.65-1.i386.rpm` refers to the program `gnome-linuxconf`, version .65-1 or maybe .65.1, for a personal computer.

If you type `rpm -ivh gnome-linuxconf-0.65-1.i386.rpm`, it may go just fine (in which case, you see a line of hash marks (#), and then you return to the command prompt), or you may see the following error message:

```
Error: failed dependencies:
     linuxconf >= 1.17 is needed by gnome-linuxconf-0.65-1
```

This error message tells you the following information:

- The package `gnome-linuxconf` requires the `linuxconf` package to be installed before it can properly be installed.
- The version of `linuxconf` that needs to be installed is `linuxconf-1.17` or newer.

Installing a new version of an RPM you already have? You type `rpm -Uvh` instead. The U stands for *U*pdate, and the vh portion is identical to that of `ivh`.

Checking your RPMs by hand

Sometimes, you need a bit of information. Similar commands exist for getting data about RPMs that are already installed and those that aren't installed yet. The main difference is the option `-p` — yes, p, which stands for *package*. Think of it this way: If you don't have the RPM installed yet, you have to open its packaging first. If you do have it installed, you don't have to deal with any packaging.

To read the informational blurb about an RPM you haven't installed yet, you need to find out about *yet another* RPM option, `-i`. This option enables you to read the "about" information stored in the RPM. If you want to see this information for a package that you haven't installed yet, you type `rpm -qip` *full_package_name* from inside the directory where you have the file. For example, you may type `rpm -qip gnome-linuxconf-0.65-1.i386.rpm`. To get information about a package that's already installed, you don't need the `-p`, as I mention earlier, so you use `rpm -qi` *short_package_name* (for example, `rpm -qi gnome-linuxconf`).

Notice that if you already have the package installed, you don't use the version number, type of machine, or file extension.

You can also see which files a package installs in the same type of format. To see a list of files that a package (that you haven't installed yet) will add, you use `rpm -qlp` *full_package_name*. With an installed package, you type `rpm -ql` *short_package_name*. So, you use `rpm -qlp gnome-linuxconf-0.65-1.i386.rpm` before installation and `rpm -ql gnome-linuxconf` after. The file-listing component is quite handy if you're looking for a configuration file!

You can see a list of every RPM you have installed by typing `rpm -qa`, where the `-a` option stands for *all* (and tends to be used in conjunction with only a few other options, such as `-q` for *q*ueries). A number of packages are out there; type `rpm -qa | more` so that you can look at just one screen at a time. On the other hand, if you're curious about whether you have a particular package installed, type `rpm -q` *short_package_name*.

Removing an RPM by hand

One of the best things about RPM is its ability to remove an application *completely*. When you remove an application RPM, you can be sure that you removed all of the application files, except perhaps for configuration files it may create backups of, just in case you need them later. To delete an RPM from your file system and the RPM database, you type `rpm -e` *short_package_name*.

Package point-and-click

Hate working on the command line? No problem! Red Hat provides a point-and-click package-management tool for Fedora Core 1. Click the Main Menu button, and then choose System Settings⇨Add/Remove Applications to open the program shown in Figure 17-1.

If you're not using Red Hat Linux 8.0 or later (Fedora Core 1 is considered "later"), you don't have this tool. Instead, look for GnoRPM or Kpackage, depending on whether you're using GNOME or KDE or your own distribution's custom package manager.

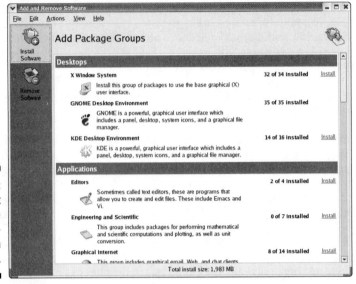

Figure 17-1:
The Red Hat
Package
manage-
ment tool in
GNOME.

The Package Management tool is arranged in themed groups, as you can see in Figure 17-1. Next to each group, you see a total, such as `32 of 34 installed`. This line means that not all options in this particular group have been installed. You can click the Install link to the right to take a look at what's left in this group (see Figure 17-2), and then check the boxes of anything in that group that you want to add to your machine.

Figure 17-2:
The Red Hat
Package
manage-
ment tool's
Install
Server
Configu-
ration Tools
Packages
dialog box.

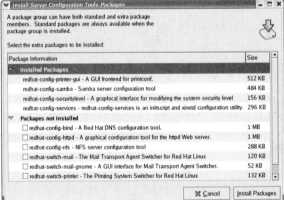

To install or remove a package, follow these steps:

1. **Open the package manager (if you haven't already) by clicking the Main Menu button and then choosing System Settings⇨Add/Remove Packages.**

   In default GNOME and KDE setups, the Main Menu button in the lower-left corner is a footprint in GNOME or a big K in KDE. If you installed Fedora Core 1, the Main Menu button is the Red Hat fedora icon in GNOME.

2. **Select Install Software if you want to add, or select Remove Software if you want to delete.**

3. **Click the Install or Remove link to the right of the package group containing the item you want to work with.**

   The Remove dialog box shows only one list of packages. In the Install dialog box are two sections: Installed Packages and Packages Not Installed. Use the check boxes to pick and choose the packages you want to add or remove, depending on what you're trying to do.

4. **Click Install Packages or Remove Packages to close the dialog box and begin the package installation or removal.**

   The program walks you through the addition or removal process. First, the tool makes sure that either you're not removing something another program depends on, or that you have added anything this new program depends on. Then, you're directed to insert the DVD-ROM into the drive as necessary.

5. **Return to Step 2 if you're not finished removing and installing packages.**

6. **Click Update to proceed to the installations and removals you've requested, and then click the X in the upper-right corner to close the dialog box.**

Updating Your Machine

Red Hat Linux includes a tool called up2date, which allows you to see what new versions of your software might be available, and can then automatically get and install them for you. You can find this tool in you GUI on the right side of the panel, next to the date. The icon is a round button that has three different apppearances, as follows:

✔ Blue with a check mark — nothing new is available.

✔ Red with an exclamation point — there are updates available.

✔ Green with aarows pointing left and right — the ool is in the process of synchronizing with the update servers.

More often than not, the updates include fixes for bugs or security issues. Exploring this tool is highly recommended if you want to keep your Linux system secure.

Finding New Software

One of the fun things about a new setup is hunting down software to add to it. The best place to start is usually right there on your distribution medium (DVDs, usually). You know that everything on there is compatible with your system. From there, you're smart to go to the distribution's Web site, such as www.redhat.com, www.suse.com, or www.mandrake.com. There, you can find updated versions of goodies you already have, security fixes, bug fixes, and more.

Looking for a specific piece of software? Do a quick Web search to see whether it has a home page. It's the safest bet, and you get the latest version.

After you start venturing into the big, bad world, you need to be a bit more careful. Although viruses, worms, and other nasties aren't as prevalent in the Linux world as they are in the Windows world, you still don't want to be sloppy. If you're not careful, you can download a tampered version of a program, and then you may end up in a world of hurt! I have compiled a list of places to start when you're looking for new software:

- www.rpmfind.net
- linux.tucows.com
- www.zdnet.com

This list isn't as short as you think after you get started digging. Also check out Chapter 2 for more options. Enjoy!

Chapter 18

A Secure Linux Box Is a Happy Linux Box

I am Inspector Clouseau, and I am on official police business.

—Inspector Clouseau

Security is a buzzword that you can't escape. Anywhere you read about the Internet, you see reports of break-ins, threats by new viruses, and dire warnings about the security of your systems. In some ways, this hype is necessary to keep people on their toes. The biggest problems you get with security — whether it's in your home, at work, or on a computer somewhere — happen when you get lazy.

You don't leave the front door of your house open when you go to work, do you? How about leaving it shut and locked but with a few nice, big windows open? The problem is that many people do this every day with their computers, and they don't even know it! In this chapter, I take a look at where your open doors and windows are and what you can do to secure them.

Every user's actions affect your overall system security. If your family members or officemates need access to your Linux machine, take the time to sit down and explain the facts of secure life to them. They can then apply this information to the other computers they use, because these issues aren't specific to Linux.

Choosing Secure Passwords

The first line of defense from intruders is the collection of passwords used on your system. For each account you have set up on your system, the passwords must be strong and difficult to figure out. If even one of the accounts has a weak password, you may be in for some trouble. Amazingly enough, in 70 percent of the cases where unauthorized individuals gained access to systems, the password for an account was the word *password* itself! When choosing good passwords, follow these rules:

- ✔ Don't use any part of your name.
- ✔ Don't use the names of friends, loved ones, or pets.
- ✔ Don't use birthdays, anniversaries, or other easily guessed dates.
- ✔ Don't use dictionary words.
- ✔ Don't keep your password written down near your computer, unless it's buried in something else, such as writing it into an address.
- ✔ Don't tell anyone your password. If someone needs to access specific files, give the person an account and set up permissions and groups properly so that they can do so.
- ✔ Do use a mix of lowercase letters, capital letters, and numbers.
- ✔ Do ensure that your password contains a minimum of eight characters.
- ✔ Do use acronyms made from sentences, such as having the password M8yodniT to stand for "My eight year old dog's name is Tabby."

Every person on your system needs to follow these rules, including you! Consider keeping a sheet of paper with these rules on it next to the machine.

I can't stress this advice enough: *Never* give out your password. Make sure that the people using your machine understand this rule. You can always find alternative methods to accomplish a task without giving out your password. If someone wants to use your machine, make an account for that person. Then they can have their own password!

Updating Software

All users can download and install new software. Of course, the programs they install are limited to the user's own permissions. The thing to be careful of here — with any operating system — is that you don't get a version of a program that has been tampered with or is even an all-out fake trying to trick folks into installing it.

Most Linux applications and other Linux software programs are distributed by way of the Internet. In fact, the development cycle of new (and updates to) Linux software revolves around the Internet for file exchange, e-mail, and forum or newsgroup discussions. Make sure that you and other users of your Linux system are comfortable with the Web sites that are used and visited. You need to develop a *list* of trusted sites that provide you with the information you need and are not misleading in their presentation. As a starting point, you can *trust* all the Web sites referenced in this book because I have accessed them all. If either you or a user of your Linux system is unsure whether you can trust a particular Web site, do some research and perhaps ask others for their opinions.

Plugging Security Holes

As the person in charge, your job is to make sure that this computer stays intruder-free. In addition to making sure that you do all the same things a user would do for both your user accounts and the superuser (root) account, no matter which Linux distribution you're running, you must keep up-to-date with security problems.

Every operating system has security issues. You can't escape them. The people who manage to avoid break-in problems are those who stay informed and apply fixes whenever they appear. Almost all Linux distributions offer the ability to find out about and grab fixes. If the instructions aren't in their documentation, they're on the distributors' Web sites.

In the case of Fedora Core, you have the Red Hat Network (RHN) icon in the lower-right corner of your panel as discussed in Chapter 17. One of the major reasons your RHN icon turns red is for security updates. Be sure to install these!

When you get a warning message — or find one on a Web site — about a particular piece of software, keep the following questions in mind:

- **Are you using this program?** You potentially can receive warnings about everything that comes with the distribution. You can determine whether the warning pertains to you in a number of ways, depending on the distribution and the package. A quick way of telling whether you're using a program is to type `man program`, where *program* is the name of the application. If the package is installed, you see the help information for it; the help information isn't installed unless the program is.

- **Are you using the same version of the program you're being warned about?** You may be using an older or newer version. You have to read the warning message carefully to see what range of versions it covers. If it doesn't mention one, you should assume that the warning applies to you too.

✔ **Consider the source.** If your warning came directly from your distribution's security mailing list or from a well-known, trusted security Web site, then this is something to heed. However, if it's just a forward from a friend, take it with a grain of salt.

Although you can't plug some holes until you find them — such as the items pointed out in security notifications — others come prepackaged. The natural thing to wonder when you're reading about a known security hole in the shrink-wrapped version of a Linux distribution is, "Why, if they're known holes, are they not plugged up in the first place?" It's a good question. The answer is that the people building the Linux distributions don't know exactly what you, in particular, want to do. They do their best to meet the security needs of average users, which isn't exactly right for everyone. But rest easy because this issue is much easier to deal with than you may think.

Mandrake and SuSE also offer update e-mail lists and software update tools. Check their Web sites and documentation to find out more!

Network holes

On a Linux server or workstation, you must not have any network services running that you don't intend to use. To understand why, you first need to comprehend a bit about how these services work. Every network service listens to an assigned place leading to the outside world. For example, if you're running a Web server, it's listening to port 80. You can think of a port as an apartment number. Whenever a person wants to look at one of your Web pages, they point their browser toward your Web server, typically named something like `www.mywebserver.org`. This name represents the street you live on. Along with a name, this server also has an IP address, which is something like `172.16.3.9`. This number represents the street address assigned to your apartment building. The apartment building is full of doors leading to various network services. Apartment (port) 80 always leads to the Web server — unless you set yours up differently. (Don't change the port unless you want people to have a hard time getting to it.)

You can see in the `/etc/services` file which port corresponds to which network service.

You can have a certain amount of security protecting each port, just like an apartment door. You may have just a bit of security, like a normal key lock. Or, you may have a deadbolt, a combination lock, and other gizmos protecting the point of entry. This is where the metaphor begins to break down, though. You're not likely to decide that a particular apartment can't have anyone going in or out. With a computer's network services, however, this situation is important to consider. If you don't run an FTP server, for example, having ports 20 and 21 functioning just provides more doors through which potential intruders can attack.

Linux manages incoming connections in two different ways. The first involves individual programs. You can control these by using the tools I describe in the section, "Software holes," later in this chapter. The second method of managing incoming connections, however, involves a central program that watches many ports. This program then answers the door when a network client — maybe an FTP client — comes knocking and starts the program that handles the service.

Red Hat, Mandrake, and SuSE Linux all come with security settings you can adjust both during and after installation. In Red Hat Linux 10, you can access this tool by choosing Main Menu⇨System Settings⇨Security Level to open the tool shown in Figure 18-1.

Figure 18-1:
The Red Hat
Linux
Security
Level tool.

Your options are Enable Firewall and Disable Firewall. If you have your computer directly connected to the Internet — and most computers are — make sure to use Enable Firewall. The only time that you should not have this firewall is place is when your machine(s) are behind a strong firewall already, or you have a critical application that won't work otherwise. For just one application, though, that's one huge risk!

These strategies work for any firewall, including the ones available in Mandrake and SuSE.

To poke holes in the firewall, you need to work with the lower two sections of the dialog. After you have done this, you have access to two different boxes with options. *Do not select as a trusted device the hardware that connects you to the Internet!* If you do, you may as well not bother using a firewall! On the other hand, if you have a modem connecting you to the Internet and an Ethernet card connecting you to other machines in your house, you can select the Ethernet card and mark it as Trusted if you trust the folks in your house.

If those people have sloppy security on their internal machines, however, you may not want to make them trusted either.

A better approach is to use the Allow Incoming check boxes. If you set up a Web server on your machine and want to let people access it, select the check box next to WWW (HTTP). The same advice applies if you have set up an FTP server (in this case, you want to select the FTP check box) or if you're trying to let someone connect securely via SSH (select the SSH check box) to your computer. I talk more about SSH in a moment. If you want to receive e-mail, you definitely need to select the Mail (SMTP) check box to allow it.

When you're done fiddling with your security options, click OK to activate them and close the dialog box.

The Secure Shell game (SSH)

One cool thing about Linux is that you can connect to your account from any-where, as long as you have the right software (and the machine you're connect-ing to isn't behind some kind of corporate firewall). Most people tell you to use the `telnet` program to do this, but I beg you not to. Do not open the Telnet port in the security tool, and do not use the `telnet` program. It sends infor-mation across the Internet in nice, raw text that anyone can snoop through.

Before you can connect either in or out using `ssh`, you have to set up your *keys*. These keys are complex bundles of encrypted stuff built around pass-word phrases. Think of them as the extra deadbolt on the door to each of your accounts, where the normal password is the regular lock. First you install the deadbolt (analogous to creating your SSH keys) and then you use it (analogous to logging in using SSH).

The cool thing is that Fedora Core is set up to do this for you so that you don't have to worry about it. All you have to do in Fedora Core 1 to enable `ssh`-ing into your Linux box is read the section, "Network holes," earlier in this chapter, and select the SSH check box. (Doing this tells the firewall to open up that steel door it has blocking any access to the *network port* that SSH needs to use.) Save the changes and that's it!

In order for someone to SSH into this machine from the outside, you'll need to know its name or IP address. The IP address is pretty quick to get. Open up a command line terminal window and type **/sbin/ifconfig**. Ignore the section labeled with `lo`; this refers back to your own machine and is only used for internal networking purposes. What you're looking for is the part labeled `eth0`. In that section, find the `inet addr` entry. What follows is your machine's IP address, in the format `xxx.xxx.xxx.xxx`; for example, `192.168.1.90`.

Installing a Windows SSH program

If you want to connect to your SSH-enabled Linux box — or, actually, to any computer set up to accept SSH connections, not just a Linux one — from a Windows computer, go to http://www.siliconcircus.com/penguinet/ and get the PenguiNet telnet and SSH client for Windows. A 30-day trial version is available, and if you like it, the full version is only around $25.

To install PenguiNet under Windows after downloading PN2setup.exe, just follow these steps:

1. **Open your file manager (such as Windows Explorer) and double-click the** PN2setup.exe **program.**

   This action opens the PenguiNet Setup Wizard.

2. **Click Next to proceed.**

   The License Agreement dialog box opens.

3. **After you read the agreement (something you should always do), click I Accept This Agreement and then click Next to proceed.**

   The Select Destination Directory dialog box opens. I usually just stick with the defaults.

4. **After you select the directory in which to install PenguiNet, click Next.**

   The Select Start Menu Folder dialog box appears.

5. **After you select the proper folder, click Next.**

   The Select Additional Tasks dialog box appears. If you want to create a desktop icon or Quick Launch button, select the appropriate check boxes.

6. **After you have chosen your additional tasks, click Next.**

   The Ready to Install dialog box appears.

7. **Click Install to begin your PenguiNet installation.**

   An installation progress dialog box appears. When the installation is finished, the final installation screen appears.

8. **Select one or both of the final items.**

   I recommend that you check at least Run PenguiNet. You may also want to select View the PenguiNet Documentation if you like to get familiar with programs by reading their manuals.

9. **Click Finish.**

   The PenguiNet window appears (if you checked Run PenguiNet), as shown in Figure 18-2.

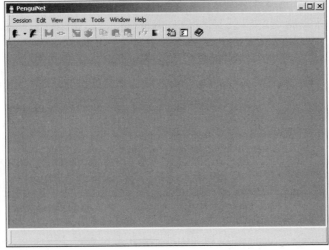

Figure 18-2:
The
PenguiNet
connection
program in
Windows.

Setting up and making your SSH connection in Windows

Either you have PenguiNet open from having installed it, or you need to open it now from your desktop shortcut or the Start menu. After you have done this, follow these steps:

1. **Choose Session⇨Connection Profiles.**

   The Connection Profiles dialog box opens, as shown in Figure 18-3.

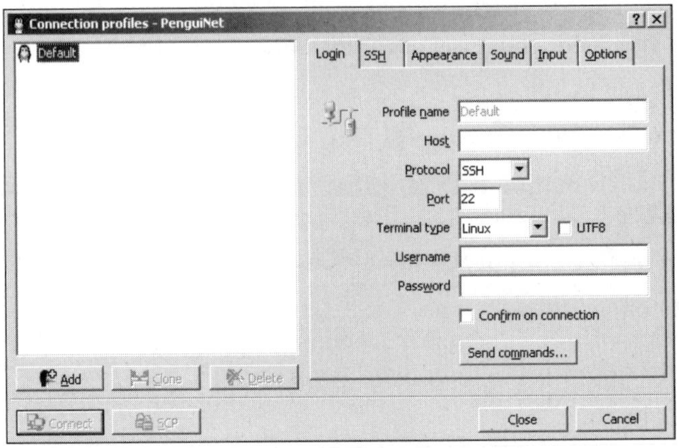

Figure 18-3:
The
PenguiNet
Connection
Profiles
dialog box.

2. **Click Add to open a new profile.**

3. **Enter the name for this profile in the Profile Name text box.**

4. **Enter your Linux box's IP address in the Host text box.**

5. **Enter your Linux login name in the Username text box.**

   You cannot use the root account here. Doing so is terribly bad for security.

6. **Enter your Linux login password in the Password text box.**

7. **Click Connect to make the connection to your Linux machine.**

   The Host Key Not Found dialog box opens the first time you connect this way. Click Connect and save the host key. You don't have to do this step again from this Windows machine. Check out Figure 18-4 to see a Linux command-line interface window on a Windows box!

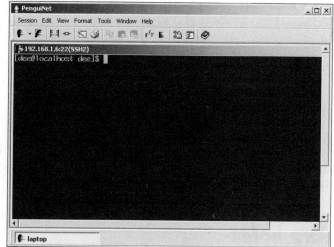

Figure 18-4:
Your Linux command line in Windows!

When you're finished, type **logout** at the command line, and your connection closes.

Connecting to your Linux box from another Linux box with SSH

Yes, you can connect from another Linux box, too. This task is a bit less complicated, unless the ssh program isn't already installed (it's already installed if this is another Red Hat Linux 10 machine). Follow these steps:

1. **Type ssh *ipaddress username* to open the connection.**

   For example, type **ssh 192.168.1.6 dee**. After you do this step, the following text appears:

   ```
   The authenticity of host '192.168.1.6 (192.168.1.6)'
           can't be established.
   RSA key fingerprint is
           ed:68:0f:e3:78:56:c9:b3:d6:6e:25:86:77:52:a7:66.
   Are you sure you want to continue connecting (yes/no)?
   ```

2. **Type** yes **and press Enter.**

You now see these lines:

```
Warning: Permanently added '192.168.1.6' (RSA) to the
         list of known hosts.
dee@192.168.1.6's password:
```

3. **Enter your login password and press Enter. Now you're in!**

Close the connection by logging out of the account (type **logout**).

Connecting to your Linux box from a Macintosh running OS X with SSH

The process from a Macintosh is similar to that under Linux. Go to Applications⇨Utilities⇨Terminal.app, which opens a command line window for you. Then type

```
ssh IPaddress
```

to access the same user account on the remote machine, or type

```
ssh login@IPaddress
```

if you want to access the account *login* instead of the same account you're using on the Mac.

Software holes

When someone is already in your system — whether or not they're allowed to be there — you have additional security concerns to keep in mind. One of these involves what software you have on the machine. Believe it or not, each piece of software is a potential security hole. If someone can get a program to crash in just the right way, they can get greater access to your system than they should. That's a very bad thing!

One way to close software holes is to remove all programs you don't need. You can always add them later, if necessary. How exactly you do this task depends on the package-management scheme your distribution runs. The following steps work at the command prompt in Red Hat and all other distributions that use RPM.

To remove all programs you don't need, follow these steps:

1. **Type** rpm -qa | more **to see every package you have installed, a screen at a time.**

The list that appears is probably a bit daunting! I suggest that you not try to review and delete them all at one time. Do a group of packages, and maybe come back the next day and do another. The beginning of the list may look like this:

```
mailcap-2.1.11-1
basesystem-7.0-5
chkconfig-1.3.6-2
```

You can also use the GUI package manager. (Refer to Chapter 17 for more information.)

2. **In another virtual console, type** rpm -qi *packagename* **for the package you want to investigate, without the version number.**

   Detailed information about this package is displayed. For example, see Figure 18-5 to see the data on glibc-2.1.91-18. I got this information by typing **rpm -qi glibc.**

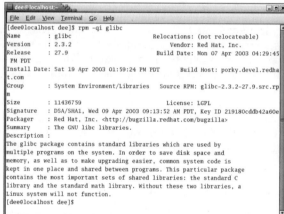

Figure 18-5: Information about the glibc RPM.

3. **Read the package information and determine whether you need this program.**

   I know — sometimes, this is easier said than done. You may want to make several passes through the list. Get rid of the obviously unnecessary programs first. After that, go through again when you understand the system better and get rid of some more. Remember that you can put programs back if it turns out that you need them.

4. **If you don't want or need this package, type** rpm -e *packagename* **to get rid of it, where you designate the package name without the version number.**

Although you probably don't want to get rid of `glibc` (which is required to help some programs run), stick with this example. Type **rpm -e glibc** to get rid of that package.

If you see an error message telling you that this package is required in order to satisfy *dependencies,* it means that other packages use this package to function. You have to decide whether you want to get rid of all the packages that need this package before attempting to delete the original package.

I know that this is an intricate process. You get to know quite a bit about your system along the way, however, and the more you know, the better off you are.

Keeping an Eye on Your Log Files with the System Log Viewer

One other security issue you may want to configure concerns *log files.* Your network programs, kernel, and other programs all run log files, which contain records of what has been happening on your system. You may be amazed at just how much information gets put in them! They're mostly in `/var/log`; take a look sometime.

Fortunately, tools are available that can help us mere mortals sift through the wheat to look for the chaff of bugs and intruders. The one I focus on in this section is System Logs viewer, which is included with Red Hat Linux 10 and installed by default.

To use the System Logs viewer, follow these steps:

1. **Log in as root.**

   This step gives you access to the most log files. You would have less access if you used another login account.

2. **From the main toolbar, click the Main Menu button.**

   The main Red Hat Linux menu opens.

3. **Choose System Tools⇨System Logs.**

   The System Logs viewer opens, as shown in Figure 18-6.

4. **Scroll through the boot log's contents to examine normal system operation, and then select the next item from the list on the left, repeating this technique until you have looked through them all.**

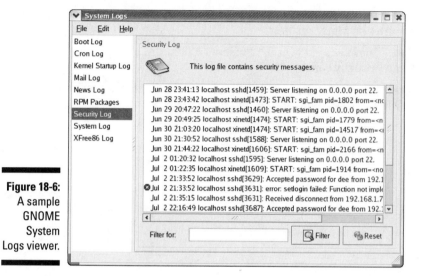

Figure 18-6:
A sample
GNOME
System
Logs viewer.

Give yourself a few weeks to get used to this process. If you look closely at Figure 18-6, you notice an X next to one of the Security Log entries. This program is set up to watch for common problems. Look more closely at anything with a red X to see whether you remember causing that problem. If you don't, and it shows up often, someone may be trying to break into your machine. Double-check with the Red Hat Network (choose Main Menu➪System Tools➪Red Hat Network) to make sure that all your software is up-to-date, and apply any updates, if needed.

Securing Your System

You can find a plethora of information on the Internet about desktop, network, and Linux security. Because of the massive volume of information available, I have listed some Web sites I like for security issues (refer to Chapter 2 for this list too):

✔ www.sans.org: One of the of the major security-related sites on the Internet.

✔ http://grc.com/intro.htm: Provides some interesting tools, such as tools to test which ports are open on a system. Also, this site features many excellent articles dealing with system and network security.

✔ http://seifried.org/lasg/: Contains the *Linux Administrator's Security Guide*.

✔ www.linux-firewall-tools.com/linux/: Offers tips for firewalls and security on Linux systems.

✔ www.linuxsecurity.com/: Presents a plethora of information from Linux Security.com.

✔ www.securityspace.com/sspace: Has lots of information about security issues and tools for different operating systems.

Part V
The Part of Tens

The 5th Wave   By Rich Tennant

"We're much better prepared for this upgrade than
before. We're giving users additional training, better
manuals, and a morphine drip."

In this part . . .

*I*n this part of the book, I cover answers to the questions most frequently asked about Linux. I explain some key Linux installation and setup points, as well as share more routine troubleshooting tips and tricks. One of the many strengths of Linux is its community, all those people out there helping each other, so I also show you where the good Linux stuff lives online and in print so that you can continue to explore this fascinating computing environment. I only hope you enjoy reading this part of the book as much as I enjoyed writing it!

Chapter 19

Eleven Troubleshooting Tips

. . . .

In This Chapter

▶ Dealing with frozen installations

▶ Changing your boot environment

▶ Recovering when you see some black-and-white text screen!

▶ Escaping a hung GUI

▶ Using multiple resolutions

. . . .

Troubleshooting is like reading a mystery novel. You have some facts, symptoms, and details, but you don't know whodunit. You have to take whatever information you have, work with that data, weigh the various possibilities, and then narrow them to a single suspect. Finally, you need to test your theory and prove that your suspect is the guilty party.

Troubleshooting problems in Linux (or any operating system) can encompass many hardware and software issues. Whether the operating system, the hardware, or a service is giving you fits, you can use some basic troubleshooting techniques to start your investigations:

✔ **Document the problem.** Write down any and all symptoms that the system is showing, including actions you can and can't do. Jot down any information you see in error messages.

✔ **Examine the Linux log files.** You can find most of these in the /var/log directory. Look for the word "error."

✔ **Compare your problem system with a working system.** Sometimes, comparing configuration files and settings may uncover the problem or narrow the possibilities.

✔ **Check connections.** Check to make sure that all the hardware is connected properly and powered on. Verify that all cables and connections are attached properly and are set at the correct specifications.

- **Remove new hardware.** Remove any hardware that you have changed or added recently (before the problem started) and see whether the problem disappears. If so, you can probably conclude that the new or changed hardware is the culprit.

- **Reduce the number of active programs.** Stop running unnecessary services and applications that aren't related to the problem at hand. You may more easily figure out what's happening if other services and applications aren't getting in the way.

- **Check to see whether the problem is reproducible.** Does the same sequence of events produce the same problem? Suppose that when you try to print to a color printer, nothing happens. If nothing happens *every* time you attempt to print, the problem is reproducible. If, instead, sometimes your information is printed and at other times it isn't, the problem pattern isn't the same and isn't reproducible — or it's caused by something more complicated than just clicking one button. Unfortunately, problems that are nonreproducible are more difficult to resolve because no set pattern of events re-creates those problems.

After you have come up with a solution, take a few moments to document the situation. Note the symptoms of the problem, its cause, and the solution you implement. The next time you encounter the same problem, you can call on your notes for a solution rather than reinvent the wheel.

If you don't have any problems to troubleshoot (yet), document your environment *before* you do. You may want to print some of this information because a future problem may prevent you from accessing your files. For a list of files to document, see the section "Conquering Configuration Problems," later in this chapter. You should also back up your data files regularly (no matter what!) and back up system files to tape or removable media if you have that option.

In this chapter, I cover some points to ponder and tips to try whenever you encounter problems with Linux.

"The Linux Installer Froze"

When you're installing Linux, the installation may just freeze. If it does, wait a bit and make sure that the installation program really froze. (Sometimes, the software just takes a while to process information.) If the software looks like it has frozen, there's no harm in rebooting your computer and starting over — just as you would do with any operating system installation. Sometimes, you can reboot and never have that problem again. At other times, the problem may happen twice in a row and then be fine the third time. Be sure to try several times before giving up.

If the installation still freezes, go to the distribution's Web site and check through the bugs and *errata pages* (Web pages where the distribution lists a collection of problems and solutions to them) in the technical support area. These pages may talk about some known problems and solutions that can help you. Otherwise, diagnosing the problem can be tricky and may seem more like voodoo than science. Here are some tips:

- ✔ **If this problem happens repeatedly at exactly the same spot, you may have a bad installation disk.** If you're a Fedora Core user, see the following section, "For Fedora Core Users." If you're *not* using Fedora Core or a version of Red Hat Enterprise Linux, try the disk in another machine if possible, and see whether the installation fails in the same place there. If you purchased this disk with a Linux distribution, contact the distribution's technical support team. If you got the disk with a book, contact the publisher's technical support team. If you burned the disk yourself, try burning a new copy at a slower speed.

- ✔ **If this problem happens repeatedly at exactly the same spot and you don't have a bad installation disk, the trouble may be with one of your machine's hardware components.** If you can, try trading hardware between machines. If not, you may need to choose a different machine on which to install Linux or try another distribution.

- ✔ **If the problem seems to happen randomly, your particular Linux distribution may not be compatible with that particular machine.** Again, you can try trading some hardware around, installing Linux on another machine, or using another distribution.

If you're not sure whether your installer has frozen, try pressing various combinations of Alt+F#, where # corresponds to one of the function keys. The installer has not completely frozen if you can see different screens when you try this technique. If nothing changes when you press these keys, the installer has definitely frozen.

For Fedora Core Users

When installing Red Hat Linux 7.3 or later (Fedora Core 1 is considered "later"), a special solution is available to people who run into problems that seem to have absolutely no explanation, such as the installer freezing. If your installation keeps dying while Anaconda (the Red Hat Linux installer program) is placing packages on your hard drive, follow these steps to try to fix it:

1. **Place the DVD-ROM or the first Fedora Core CD-ROM into your drive.**

2. **Reboot the machine.**

3. **Wait until you reach the black-and-white screen where you select which installer to use.**

   This screen has a black background with text in a combination of white and colors. If you reach a graphical installation screen, you missed the screen. You need to reboot and repeat this step, and then proceed.

4. **At the prompt, type** `linux mediacheck` **and then press Enter.**

   Text scrolls by, and then you see a screen with a bright blue background. Then, the CD Found dialog box appears.

5. **Select OK and press Enter to proceed to the media examination.**

   This step opens the Media Check dialog box. If you have changed your mind and just want to start the installation, use the Tab or arrow keys to select Skip, and then press Enter.

6. **If you want to test the first CD-ROM or the DVD-ROM, select Test.**

7. **If you want to test another installation CD-ROM, select Eject CD.**

   Remove the first CD-ROM from the CD-ROM drive and replace it with the CD-ROM you want to test. Close the CD-ROM drive and make sure that Test is selected.

8. **Press Enter to begin the media check.**

   The Media Check status box opens and shows you the name assigned to the DVD-ROM or CD-ROM and how much progress has been made. At the end of the inspection, the Media Check Result dialog box opens.

9. **Look at the text after** `and the result is.`

   If the result is `PASS`, nothing is wrong with the DVD-ROM or CD-ROM itself. Your installation woes are caused by something else. Go to the Fedora Core site (`fedora.redhat.com`), and then to the Errata page, and look for a new boot disk image. The instructions on how to download and make your boot disk are on the page relating to the update.

   If the result is `FAIL`, the DVD-ROM or CD-ROM you just tested is flawed. If you purchased this CD-ROM or DVD-ROM, you need to talk to the company you purchased it from to see whether you can get a replacement. On the other hand, if you burned your own DVD-ROM or CD-ROM, I recommend doing one of the following:

   • Burn the DVD-ROM CD-ROM again, at a speed of 4x or lower.

   • Burn the DVD-ROM CD-ROM again on a newer CD-ROM drive with BurnProof technology (`www.burnproof.com`) or something similar.

If the DVD-ROM that came with this book is defective, contact the technical support address listed in this book, not Red Hat.

"My Graphics Fail the Installer Test"

You need to install the proper server software because the installation program doesn't do it for you. Here are a couple of places to find useful help with this problem online:

- ✔ www.linuxnewbie.org/nhf/
- ✔ www.tldp.org/HOWTO/HOWTO-INDEX/apps.html#GUIXWIN

"The Installer Tested My Graphics Fine, but My GUI Won't Start"

If your Linux installation program showed you a GUI test screen saying that you were ready to proceed with the rest of the installation, you probably expected that the GUI would start with no problem. Unfortunately, that doesn't always happen.

Each distribution has its own set of graphics configuration tools. If you boot your machine for the first time and see error messages when you're trying to enter the GUI automatically or when you type startx to start the GUI manually, use the following tools to fix the problem:

- ✔ For any Linux distribution, you should have a tool named XF86Setup. It may not be installed by default, but it's a good option if you can't find any fancier tools (such as the next four items in this list) to use.
- ✔ In Fedora Core, use Xconfigurator or redhat-config-xfree86.
- ✔ In Mandrake Linux, use XFdrake.
- ✔ In SuSE Linux, use sax2 or sax.
- ✔ Your last resort is xf86config. This fully text-based tool should be available with all distributions. It may be called xf86config4.

You may have to install these tools from your original distribution disks before you can run them from the command line.

"I Think I'm in Linux, but I Don't Know What to Do!"

Two different screens tend to cause panic to folks new to Linux. The first of these screens, shown in Figure 19-1, is in fact a sign that you installed the software and booted the machine successfully! Jump for joy! It's just that you're booting into the command-line environment rather than the GUI environment. If you reach a screen similar to the one shown in Figure 19-1, the computer is asking you to log in with the username for an account and a password that you created during the installation process.

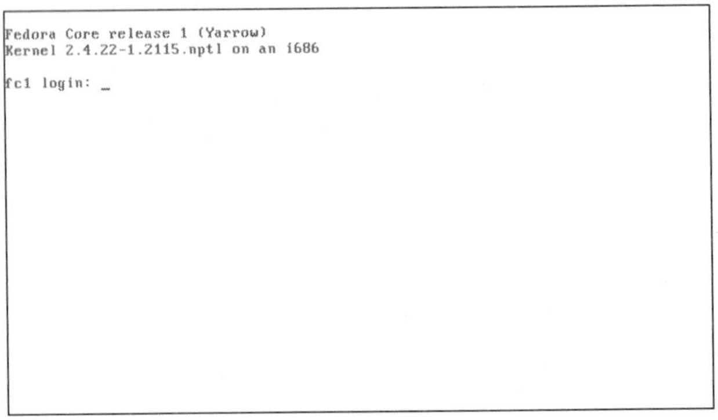

```
Fedora Core release 1 (Yarrow)
Kernel 2.4.22-1.2115.nptl on an i686

fc1 login: _
```

Figure 19-1:
A Linux
command-
line login
prompt.

If you created only the root account, you can log in there as `root`.

After you enter the username and password, you find yourself at the screen shown in Figure 19-2, which just happens to be the second spot where people get worried. If you see this screen, you have not only booted properly into Linux, but you're also logged in and using the machine! Give yourself a good pat on the back.

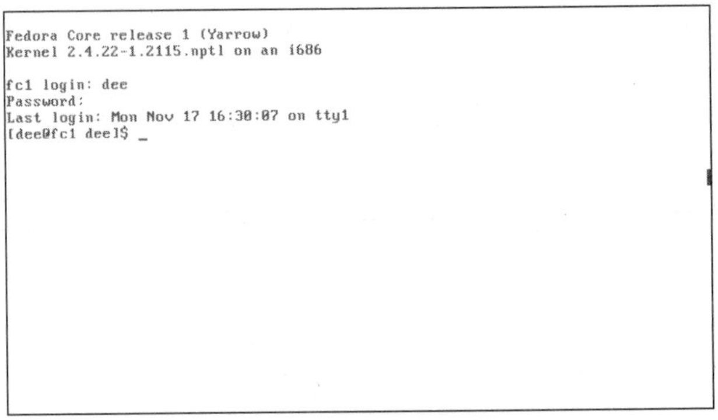

```
Fedora Core release 1 (Yarrow)
Kernel 2.4.22-1.2115.nptl on an i686

fc1 login: dee
Password:
Last login: Mon Nov 17 16:38:87 on tty1
[dee@fc1 dee]$ _
```

Figure 19-2:
Logged in at
the Linux
command
line.

What do you do from here? Anything you want. Surf through this book for commands you want to run. Type `startx` to start up the GUI.

"I Don't Want to Boot into This!"

Are you booting into the command-line environment when you only want to use the GUI? Or, are you finding that you're already booting into the GUI and you would rather boot to that nice, clean, black-and-white command-line screen? You're not stuck with either of these options. You can change them at any time.

Changing your boot environment "permanently"

The word *permanently* is in quotes in the heading because you can, of course, go back and change this setting later, if you want. *Permanently* just refers to the fact that after you have made this change, every time you boot the system, it automatically goes into the preferred environment until you change it.

To make this change, you need to edit what's called a *runlevel*. I can't be certain which Linux distribution you're using, so I cover the most generic method for accomplishing this task:

1. **Log in as the root user.**

2. **If you're in the GUI, open a terminal window.**

   The terminal window is typically offered as an icon on the Panel in both KDE and GNOME. It usually looks like a little computer screen.

3. **Type** ls /etc/inittab **and press Enter.**

   If this file exists, proceed to Step 4. If not, then it may be stored in a different location in your Linux distribution. Type `find / -name inittab` to hunt down where it is in your file system. If you track down `inittab` in a directory other than `/etc`, be sure that you change the directory path appropriately in the rest of this sequence.

4. **Type** cp /etc/inittab /etc/inittab.old **to make a backup.**

   Now, if something happens while you're editing the `inittab` file, you can always restart fresh with the old version.

5. **Open the** inittab **file in your preferred text editor.**

   Some Linux text editors are covered in Chapter 13.

6. **Scroll down until you find a line similar to the following:**

   ```
   id:5:initdefault:
   ```

   This line appears near the top of the file. What you're interested in here is the number. In most mainstream Linux distributions, the number 5 tells Linux to boot into the GUI, and the number 3 tells Linux to boot into the command line. In the preceding example, therefore, I boot into the GUI.

7. **Change the number in this line.**

   If it's a 5, change it to 3, and vice versa. Make sure that all colons and other items are left properly in place, or else your machine will have problems booting later.

8. **Save and exit the file.**

   The changes go into effect the next time you reboot the system.

If you do end up having problems booting the system, in many current Linux distributions (including the one that comes with this book) your installation disk can be used as an emergency boot disk. Check your documentation for information about the distribution you're using if it's not Red Hat 10.

Changing your boot environment just for now

At any time, you can have your Linux box switch between full command-line mode and full GUI mode. The instructions I give here assume that you're using one of the mainstream Linux distributions that use a runlevel of 3 for the command line and 5 for the GUI. Type runlevel on the command line: If you see a 3 or a 5, you're fine, but if you see any other number, see your distribution's documentation to find out which runlevel corresponds to the full command-line session with networking and which is for the full GUI session.

To switch between modes, do the following:

- ✔ To change from the GUI login to the command-line login, open a terminal window and type (as root) init 3.
- ✔ To change from the command line login to the GUI login, type (as root) init 5.

"I Want to Use Multiple Screen Resolutions"

Do you want or need to swap between resolutions in the GUI? Suppose that you want to use 1024 x 768, but you work on Web pages and want to be able to see how they look in a browser at 800 x 600 or even 640 x 480. You can set up your Linux machine to do it, but you need to edit a text file. Type the following line at a command prompt to locate this file on your distribution:

```
find / -name "XF86Config*"
```

You may find multiple versions. For example, you may find XF86Config and XF86Config-4. If you have both, you want to edit XF86Config-4. To change your screen resolution settings now, follow these steps:

1. **Exit the GUI.**

   If you boot into the GUI by default, type init 3 at a command prompt to leave the GUI for now. If you had to type startx to get into the GUI, click the GNOME footprint or KDE K icon and choose Log Out.

2. **Log in as root.**

   If you're not logged in from the root account (and you normally shouldn't be), log in as root to edit this file.

3. **Change to the directory containing the file.**

   You probably type cd /etc/X11 for this step.

4. **Make a backup copy of the file.**

   You type either cp XF86Config XF86Config.old or cp XF86Config-4 XF86Config-4.old to make the backup.

5. **Open the file in your favorite text editor.**

6. **Jump to the end of the file.**

   This file can be a long one, and the text you want is close to the end.

7. **Move up through the file until you see this text:**
   ```
   Section "Screen"
   ```

8. **Look beneath the section header for a line similar to this one:**
   ```
   Subsection "Display"
   ```

9. **Look beneath this section header for a line similar to this one:**
   ```
   Modes       "1024x768"
   ```

10. **Add to the line the other modes you want to use, using the following line as an example:**

```
Modes    "1024x768" "800x600" "640x480"
```

Be sure not to go beyond your monitor's capabilities. Check your monitor's documentation to see what it can handle if you want to raise the resolution.

11. **After you finish making changes, save and close the file.**

Now you can return to the GUI. Log out of root and back into the account you usually use, and then type one of the following commands:

- ✔ startx: If you don't normally boot into the GUI
- ✔ init 5: If you normally boot into the GUI

You can change resolutions after they're set up (as shown in the preceding section) by pressing the key combination Ctrl+Alt+Plus, where Plus is the big plus (+) sign on your number pad — you can't use the plus sign on the main keyboard for this one. If you're using a keyboard without a number pad, you have to edit the file as shown in the preceding section and move your preferred resolution to the beginning of the list. Then, if you're already in the GUI, log out and log back in.

"My GUI Is Hung and I'm Stuck!"

One quick solution to this problem is the key combination Ctrl+Alt+Backspace. If this doesn't do the trick, your system is in really bad shape! Try to switch to a virtual terminal by using Ctrl+Alt+F5. If this key combination also does nothing, you need to reboot the machine.

"Help, my machine hangs during boot!"

When configuring a Linux machine, you may encounter problems with the /etc/grub.conf file. This file indicates the operating system or systems to which your system can boot, and the file also contains Linux startup settings. Linux can boot from any of your hard drives — not just the master IDE drive on the primary IDE channel. Consider this list of potential solutions if the /etc/grub.conf file makes trouble:

- ✔ If you have altered or added hard drives, you may need to change the boot line in the /etc/grub.conf file.
- ✔ If you haven't made hardware changes, check to make sure that your /etc/grub.conf file is referring to the correct location of the Linux

image (the program code that loads and executes at runtime and is located in the /boot directory).

✔ If the location under the /boot directory or the device for the root entry is incorrect, your system can't boot to Linux. In this situation, a rescue or emergency disk is helpful. Refer to Chapter 5 for instructions on using a rescue disk.

✔ If you're working with a multiboot operating system environment, be sure that your /etc/grub.conf file contains entries for each of your operating systems. Each operating system or Linux installation needs to be in separate entries.

✔ If your file contains entries to switch to a higher-resolution display and you have boot problems, try reducing the video setting to simple VGA.

Linux allows you to use spaces and other characters in filenames that you may or may not be able to use in filenames on other operating systems. However, some Linux applications may stumble when they encounter file or directory names containing spaces. Usually, a safe bet is to stick with alphanumeric characters and avoid spaces and odd characters, such as question marks and exclamation points.

"How Do I Stop Scripting Screw-Ups?"

A *script* contains a series of commands designed to perform a task (usually repeatedly) to save you from typing all those commands at a prompt, one line at a time. If you have trouble with a script, follow this advice:

✔ Make sure that spelling or syntax errors aren't causing the problems. Remember that most things in Linux are case sensitive, so a simple slip of the Shift key can make an entire script nonfunctional.

✔ If a script contains several sections to perform different tasks, try commenting out all lines except for one task. If the script works for the specified task, uncomment one line at a time and run the script between each edit. When you encounter your first error, you probably have a good idea of where the error occurred and how to make an appropriate correction.

✔ Start simple when you write any script from scratch. Make sure that the script works before you start doing *fancy* stuff. If a recent addition causes the script to fail, you know where the problem resides.

✔ Verify values for any variables on which your script may depend. Use the echo statement in the script to display the contents of any variables you use. You may need to use echo at several places in your script so that you can watch what happens to the values of those variables. (Refer to Chapter 11 for more information on variables.)

"Aaargh! I Forgot My Root Password! What Do I Do?"

Fear not. You have a way around this problem! First, you need to reboot your machine. While it's rebooting, it reaches a boot loader, whether it's a graphical boot loader or a command-line boot loader. This boot loader is either GRUB or LILO. If you're using the DVD-ROM that came with this book, it's GRUB (unless you went out of your way during installation to specifically choose LILO).

If you're not sure, don't worry. Just try the GRUB option first, and then try the LILO one:

- ✔ **GRUB:** At the GRUB boot screen, press **E**, which takes you to a configuration file. Use the arrow keys to go to the line starting with kernel, and press **E** again to edit that line. At the end of the line, add the word single, press Enter to put the change into place, and then press **B** to boot the machine.

- ✔ **LILO:** At the LILO boot prompt, type linux single.

In both cases, the machine boots to a prompt. If it asks you for a login, type root and press Enter. It doesn't ask you for a password. Now's your chance to change the root password to one you can remember. Type passwd, and then enter the new password twice as directed. When you're done, type reboot and then boot the machine normally.

Chapter 20

Ten Superior Sources of Linux Information

L inux isn't just an online phenomenon (in fact, it's one of the few major-league operating systems you can download from the Internet for free); it's also the stuff of which Internet infrastructure is made. For that reason, it's no surprise that more good information about Linux is available online than you could ever absorb, even with an extra lifetime or two. That's why I had such a hard time coming up with the ten *best* Linux resources for this chapter. That's also why I cheated — the last section is a grab bag that contains more good Internet stuff than I could cover in the first nine entries!

The Best-Ever Linux Resource

I had trouble picking only ten Linux resources, but if I had to pick only *one*, www.linux.com would be it. This site is the ideal general starting place for any Linux-related investigation and includes a great search engine, plus a broad range of useful Linux information, downloads, pointers, and documentation. For example, when I went looking for sources of Linux distributions, I quickly figured out that it was easier to go through www.linux.com (via software. linux.com, part of the same site) to get to all the key sites than to visit each vendor or organization, one at a time!

Keeping the Bad Guys at Bay

Although plenty of security-related sites and information are available on the Web, I was initially hard-pressed to find a site that approached this important topic from a Linux point of view. But Linuxsecurity.com fixes that problem in a hurry. It's a terrific clearinghouse for Linux security news, advisories, documentation, and resources. At www.linuxsecurity.com you can find pointers to security documentation, news sites, archives, mailing lists, discussion groups, and much, much more.

Other good Linux security resources include

- ✔ **System Administration Security Resources:**
  http://security.ucdavis.edu/sysadmin/linux.cfm
- ✔ **The Linux Center:** www.portalux.com/system/security

The Kernel's at Linux Headquarters

Linux headquarters operates a kernel-focused (or should I say kernel-obsessed?) Web site at www.linuxhq.com. In addition to providing pointers to information, downloads, patches, change logs, and more for two versions of the Linux stable kernel (what ordinary mortals use) and one version of the developer's kernel (what hackers and demigods use), this site has pointers to all kinds of additional information. This info includes an extensive list of Linux distributions, helpful information about kernel programming for those who are so inclined, Linux vendors you can turn to, and a whole lot more.

Everything Linux

How can you go astray at a site named Everything Linux? It's easy — you may not exactly go astray, but you can find so much interesting stuff to distract you from your task at hand that you may find yourself looking blearily up at the clock at 3 a.m. and asking yourself "Where did the time go?" Visit www.everythinglinux.org and start losing time.

At this site, you can find news, reviews, and opinions about Linux topics, along with pointers to most of the good Linux stuff on the Web (including, not coincidentally, all the other stuff that appears in this chapter).

Looking for Linux Applications?

The Linuxapps site links to all kinds of Linux software and has more than 30 categories, from Audio/Sound to X Window. Click any category to see anywhere from a handful to more than a hundred Linux-ready applications, ready for you to download. After you have Linux installed and are looking for things to do with your system, you could do worse than go there looking for more software. Visit `www.linuxapps.com` to see what I mean.

Lifelong Learning Includes Linux

A cornucopia of online tutorials and information about Linux is on the Internet, and it's just waiting for you to dig in. Although I haven't yet found a clearinghouse for locating Linux training online, here are some strategies I used to turn up thousands of free online training courses on everything from basic Linux commands and operation to hacking the kernel yourself:

- ✔ Visit your favorite search engine and search for Linux tutorials.

- ✔ Visit a Linux-focused site and search for tutorials within the site. I got great results at `www.linux.com`, where my search turned up nearly 300 responses, many of them extremely interesting.

- ✔ An ultimate directory of information on learning Linux in the classroom is at `www.linux.org/vendors/training.html`.

Peerless Linux Publications Online

As with everything else about Linux, you find no shortage of online newsletters, magazines, and other periodical sources of information. Here's my short list of the best ones, purely for your perusal:

- ✔ *The Linux Gazette* (`www.linuxgazette.com`): This monthly online Linux-focused publication is also part of the Linux Documentation Project (LDP). This magazine includes lots of timely, useful information and a plethora of pointers to other Linux information online.

- ✔ *Linux Journal* (`www.linuxjournal.com`): This monthly Linux publication is available in print as well as online. Published by SSC (Specialized System Consultants, Inc.), this magazine includes information about Linux distributions, product reviews, industry news, and other cool stuff.

- ✔ *LinuxWorld* (`www.linuxworld.com`): Industry news and technical coverage round out this particular publication. I'd say more but I'm biased — I'm one of the editors.

> ✔ *Linux Weekly News* (`www.lwn.net`): This weekly Linux-oriented news and information publication covers a broad range of topics. It's probably the most timely of all the online (and print) journals I mention.
>
> ✔ *LinuxToday* (`www.linuxtoday.com`): LinuxToday has worthwhile content from a number of sister sites, including *LinuxPlanet* (`www.linuxplanet.com`), revolving around many facets of Linux.

Supporting Linux Online

Linuxcare is a professional, for-profit organization devoted to Linux training, technical support, and information sharing. If you need serious professional Linux help, you need Linuxcare. You find, in addition to for-a-fee information and services, plenty of free white papers and other good stuff on this site. Visit this excellent outfit at `www.linuxcare.com`.

You can also visit the AnswerSquad (`www.answersquad.com`), where you can pay a monthly fee to join a discussion mailing list. There, you can ask as many computer questions as you want, and a team of computer book authors — who know how to explain things to normal people — will help you out. The topics here are not limited to Linux, either. You may even recognize a few AnswerSquad member names from the Dummies author roster!

Slashdot: The Crème de la Nerd

The subtitle for this Web site, "News for Nerds," says it all: Slashdot is a Web site for Linux bigots by Linux bigots about deeply technical subjects of all kinds, some more related to Linux than others, but all weirdly fascinating. I had to include this site in my list, but I can't explain why. If you come up with a good, inarguable reason, please tell me what it is. (My e-mail address is listed in the author bio in the front matter of this book!) Visit the Slashdot site at `www.slashdot.org`.

More Tips off the Linux Berg

I have had a tough time closing in on only *ten* top Linux resources online. That's why I cheated and turned this last one into a grab bag of additional Web sites, newsgroups, and even some information about updating Fedora Core (otherwise, I would be neglecting this book's poster child — Fedora Core 1 — after all).

Web sites

The following list describes Web sites that didn't quite fit into any other sections in this chapter, although their rich and useful content merits special attention. Be sure to visit these sites while exploring Linux information online:

- ✔ www.tldp.org: The Linux Documentation Project is a great bookmark for your browser. You may return often when trying to find specific answers or even just to browse for topics of interest. The LDP contains several types of documentation, including full-length books, HOWTO documents, FAQs, and much, much more.

- ✔ www.redhat.com/apps/support/resources/: This site is the Red Hat support resources center, where you find a wealth of Linux support information, albeit with a strong Red Hat flavor. In addition to errata and update information on specific versions of Red Hat, you find tutorials to help you configure services on a Red Hat Linux computer.

- ✔ freshmeat.net: Do you ever feel left out while your cronies yak about the newest Linux software or latest version releases? Now you can keep up with a healthy daily serving of bug fixes, new software releases, announcements, commentary, and a comprehensive index of all known Linux software. Freshmeat is a staple for the *release early, release often* hackers so prevalent in the open source community.

- ✔ fedora.redhat.com: The Fedora Core distribution site.

Newsgroups

Newsgroups are online discussion groups in which people read and post messages to one another on specific topics. The Internet now hosts more than 80,000 newsgroups, with more being introduced daily.

Google Groups (groups.google.com) provides access to Usenet postings and archives and is the largest discussion archive on the Internet. You can search and browse Usenet (newsgroup) discussions and other public online forums with a single simple search. This site is a great place to look for technical support or information or to locate online groups that reflect your interests.

From the following list, see whether you can pick out the newsgroup that appeals broadly to Linux lovers everywhere but has nothing to do with Linux *per se.* (**Hint:** "Thank ya. Thank ya vurry much!")

- ✔ comp.os.linux.advocacy: Updates you on what kinds of products and services are new and interesting

- ✔ comp.os.linux.hardware: Keeps you informed on what's going on with Linux hardware and computers

- `comp.os.linux.misc`: Lets you know what's happening with all kinds of miscellaneous Linux topics

- `comp.os.linux.networking`: Tells you what's going on in the wonderful world of Linux networking

- `alt.elvis.sighting`: Keeps you up-to-date on the current and past activities of that hunka hunka burnin' love

Keeping your Fedora Core system up-to-date

The Fedora Core 1 utility named Red Hat Update Agent enables you to install new packages as they become available, directly from the Red Hat Web site. It also enables you to refresh installed software with the latest enhancements and bug fixes. To run the Red Hat Update Agent, click the main menu and choose System Tools⇨Red Hat Network. You must be connected to the Internet to successfully run the Update Agent.

When you register your Red Hat installation at `http://rhn.redhat.com/`, you're issued a username and password that you must use to configure the Red Hat Update Agent.

Part VI
Appendixes

The 5th Wave   By Rich Tennant

"OH YEAH, AND TRY NOT TO ENTER THE WRONG PASSWORD."

In this part . . .

This part adds some extra material to support the rest of this book. Starting with the ever-popular and useful Appendix A, you'll find a reasonably comprehensive and friendly compendium of common Linux commands, ready for use as a desktop reference. Appendix B provides an overview and information about the DVD included with this book (and how to get a set of CDs if you don't have a DVD-ROM drive), including basic booting instructions when installing Red Hat Linux and a list of what's on the DVD.

Appendix A

Common Linux Commands

Computing novices often marvel at the keyboard dance Linux experts typically perform. Sure, these experts know about modern advances, such as the mouse and graphical interface, but these keyboard musicians prefer the home keys and find that they can work faster with the keyboard. It takes some time to reach this level of proficiency, but every expert was a novice at one time, and any novice can become an expert by delving into the various commands available and getting plenty of practice.

In this appendix, you will find the commands listed by themes, according to what they can actually do for you.

So, read on — and dazzle your friends with your command-prompt finesse. When they ask you how and where you figured out all those commands, just smile and mumble something about the voices in your head — and of course, keep this section dog-eared and within reach of your computer.

Linux Commands by Function

Because every command serves a specific purpose, organizing these tools into groups according to their individual functions isn't difficult. If you know what you need to do but don't know which command does the job, flip through this section to start your search. From here, you can dig further by referencing man pages and other help information (online sites and reference books, for example) or by looking in this book's index for further coverage.

To access a man page, type **man *command*** at a command prompt. For example, man ls shows you the help information for the file listing command.

Archiving and compressing

Although disk space isn't as much of a premium as it once was, bandwidth and backup media still are. Subsequently, this group provides a potpourri of tools for compacting and organizing data for storage:

```
ar, bzip2, compress, cpio, dump, gunzip, gzexe, gzip,
restore, tar, uncompress, unzip, zcat, zcmp, zip
```

Built-in bash commands

Some commands don't even seem to exist if you try to look up their help information in the man pages, and the commands don't show up as files on your system. Remember, as you type commands at the prompt, that you're communicating with a type of program called a *shell.* (In my case, it's bash, the default Linux shell.) The shell has a set of commands, included in the following list, that you can use to communicate with it:

```
alias, bg, cd, export, fg, history, jobs, logout, set,
source, test, umask, unalias, unset
```

If you try to view the man page entry for some of these commands, you'll find instead that the help information for BASH BUILTINS loads. To search through this massive manual, press the forward slash (/) key to open the man search interface, and then type the name of the command you want to search for. Press Enter to start the search. The interface stops in the first spot where the term is found. If you want to try again, press the N key to proceed to the next occurrence of the word.

When you're digging around for help on a command, you can call on an interesting range of shell commands for assistance:

```
apropos, info, man, manpath, type, whatis, whereis, which
```

Locating details about the command-prompt options of a command is a never-ending pursuit. The man page system provides some helpful guides at your fingertips for rapidly finding this detailed information.

Communication

As a system administrator, you find these utilities useful for providing information about your users and communicating with them:

```
finger, wall, write, who
```

Files and file system

No matter which operating system you're using, it's hard to do anything without being able to find your way through and work with the file system. The following utilities help you find your way:

File organization

Boxing, packing, sorting, shipping — I'm always shuffling files around on my system. File organization commands provide tools for moving files and file system units around:

```
cp, dir, ln, mkdir, mv, pwd, rename, rm, rmdir, shred
```

File attributes

Files are much like candy bars. The wrappers provide information about the ingredients, size, and package date — all descriptive of the tasty nugget inside. (Perhaps the wrapper is even childproof.) Files keep all this wrapper information in an *inode*. Along with the capability to change file inode information, these commands can return data about the content of the file:

```
chage, chattr, chgrp, chmod, chown, file, stat, sum,
touch, wc
```

File filters

A *file filter* enables you to take the contents of one file and process them for a new result. To sort the contents of the password file alphabetically, for example, you can type the command `sort /etc/passwd`. Listed here are a few of the tools available for mulching data into something meaningful:

```
cmp, colrm, column, comm, csplit, cut, iff, diff3, expand,
fmt, fold, join, look, merge, paste, rev, sort, split,
strings, tac, tr, unexpand, uniq, uuencode, uudecode
```

File locators

Where, oh, where can my file be? These commands help you locate files in Linux's monster tree-structure file system:

```
find, locate, which
```

File utilities that deserve their own category

Although some may argue that these utilities are *just commands*, others can argue that the ceiling of the Sistine Chapel is *just a painting*. These commands sport short names, even though nothing about them is simple or powerless.

These commands are industrial-strength data-manipulation tools. You need just a few minutes to get the basics, and a lifetime to master the tools. If you manage the ability to wrangle these beauties, you achieve respected geek status:

```
convert, gawk, grep, sed
```

File viewers

File browsing is a favorite pastime of many a system user. These tools provide a variety of utilities for viewing the contents of readable files of all sizes. Unlike using a full-screen editor, you cannot damage the contents of a file with these commands because they're read-only tools:

```
cat, head, less, more, tail
```

Miscellaneous file commands

These file commands don't seem to fit into any other category:

```
basename, dircolors, hexdump, newer, nl, od, patch, test, xxd
```

Wholesale file system commands

These commands provide information or perform actions on the entire file system, from creation and tuning to repair and recovery. Some of these commands return data only, whereas others also provide you with surgical instruments for serious file-system hacking:

```
badblocks, debugfs, dumpe2fs, e2fsck, e2label, fdformat,
fsck, mkfs, df, du, ls, lsattr, mount, quota, quotacheck,
quotaon, resize2fs, sync, tune2fs, umount
```

Miscellaneous

The leftovers are in this group — I can't classify these commands anywhere else:

```
bc, cal, clear, date, dc, echo, eject, expr, oclock, openvt,
resize, script, tee, toe, unbuffer
```

mtools

The mtools suite of utilities provides a nice way to transfer information to your Microsoft friends. Although Linux has native support for Microsoft Windows and DOS file systems, your Microsoft cohorts don't have access to Linux (ext2 and ext3) file systems. To keep everyone happy, you can buy preformatted MS-DOS disks and use them with the mtools commands so that you can swap them back and forth with your friends who are using Windows:

```
mcat, mcd, mcopy, mdel, mdeltree, mdir, mdu, mformat, mlabel,
mmd, mmount, mmove
```

Printing

The printing system is the combination of programs that handles the routing of data from you to the printer. These commands enable you to add, verify, and remove print jobs from the queue:

```
cancel, lp, lpq, lpr, lprm, lpstat, lptest, pr
```

System control

These commands provide system-wide information and control. Normal users can run many commands to obtain system information; however, commands that actively change the configuration of the system need to run while you're logged in as root — or have utilized the su command to temporarily become the superuser.

Kernel module handling

You may sometimes need to add kernel support for an additional device (software or hardware). If this need arises, you have a limited number of choices: You can either rebuild the kernel or install a loadable kernel module. Although rebuilding a kernel doesn't exactly require a Ph.D. in nuclear science, consider it a time-consuming nuisance that's best to avoid. The following commands enable you to include the kernel support you need while the system is running, without having to rebuild the entire thing from scratch:

```
depmod, insmod, lsmod, modprobe, rmmod
```

Processes

Most of your system activity requires processes. Even when your system appears idle, a dozen or so processes are running in the background. These commands enable you to check under the hood to make sure that everything that needs to be running is running and that you're not overheating or overtaxing resources:

```
at, atq, batch, crontab, env, fuser, kill, killall, nice,
pidof, pkill, ps, pstree, renice, sleep, top, usleep, watch
```

System action commands

System action commands provide tools for controlling your host. Rather than get or set information your host may need, these commands incite your system to action:

```
dhcpcp, halt, kbdrate, logger, mesg, mkbootdisk, poweroff,
reboot, sash, setleds, setterm, shutdown, stty, tset,
tzselect
```

System information

System information command tools are for setting and checking your host configuration. These few *doctor* tools are for probing and prodding your system for vital statistics (the command uptime, for example, tells you how long your system has been running since the last time you booted it):

```
arch, date, ddate, fgconsole, free, hostid, hostname, hdparm,
hwclock, ifconfig, kernelversion, netstat printenv, route,
runlevel, top, tty, uname, uptime, vmstat
```

Users and groups

Who are the people in your neighborhood, and what are they doing? These commands enable you to change user profiles and provide specific information about your system users:

```
checkalias, chfn, chsh, faillog, gpasswd, groups, id, last,
lastlog, listalias, mkpasswd, mktemp, newalias, newaliases,
newgrp, passwd, su, users, uuidgen, w, who, whoami
```

Appendix B

About the DVD-ROM

. . . .

*T*he DVD-ROM included with this book contains everything you need to install and run Fedora Core 1. This is the equivalent of the six CD-ROMs you would have to download from Red Hat's Fedora Project Web site (http://fedora.redhat.com), and includes the following:

- ✔ **Fedora Core 1:** A complete copy of the latest and greatest version of the consumer-level Red Hat Linux, for your computing pleasure.

- ✔ **RPM (Red Hat Package Manager):** The Red Hat software distribution and installation management environment, wherein Linux updates and new facilities are packaged for easy installation on your Linux machine.

- ✔ **KDE (the K Desktop Environment) and GNOME (GNU Network Object Model Environment):** The two leading graphical user interfaces for Linux. You can pick the one you like best!

- ✔ **Mozilla:** The best-of-breed Web browser for your Linux machine, just waiting for your surfing pleasure.

- ✔ **Samba:** The best way to integrate Linux servers with Windows users. Samba lets your Linux machine masquerade as a Windows server so that Windows users can grab files and print documents hassle-free.

- ✔ **Apache Web Server:** The world's most popular (or at least, most frequently used) Web server software.

- ✔ **Games!:** Tons of games; enough to help you procrastinate for weeks!

- ✔ **OpenOffice.org:** A full-featured and popular office suite.

If you don't have a DVD-ROM drive, send the coupon in the back of this book to us to receive the CD set. (See coupon for details.)

System Requirements

Make sure that your computer meets the following minimum system requirements. If your computer doesn't match up to most of these requirements, you may have problems using the contents of the DVD-ROMs:

✔ **A PC with an Intel-compatible Pentium-class processor:** I recommend a 400MHz Pentium II or better for using Graphical mode, and a 133MHz Pentium or better for Text mode.

✔ **MS-DOS 6.02 or Microsoft Windows 3.1 or later:** These systems conveniently help you set up your system, but you can install from a Linux bootable floppy disk without needing DOS or Windows, if you prefer.

✔ **At least 64MB of total RAM installed on your computer for text mode:** You need at least 64MB of RAM for Text mode, and at least 128MB is recommended for Graphical mode. (Linux can handle as much RAM as you can fit into a typical PC, and more is almost always better than less.)

✔ **At least 650MB (the barest minimum) of hard drive space:** I recommend 2.5GB and as much as 5GB if you want to install all the software from the DVD-ROM. You need less space if you don't install every program, but you should go ahead and make 5GB of space available, to give yourself more options.

✔ **A DVD-ROM drive — double-speed (2x) or faster:** The faster the DVD-ROM drive, the faster your installation experience.

✔ **Just about any VGA monitor:** Just about any monitor does the trick, but you want one that's capable of displaying at least 256 colors or grayscale.

✔ **A keyboard and a mouse:** You need both items so that you have a way to communicate with your Linux system and tell it what to do!

✔ **A 3½-inch floppy drive:** You have to create an emergency boot disk for your Linux system. (And although I hope that you never need one, you may thank your lucky stars that you have one, if you ever do need one.) With this tool in your PC, you can also use it to boot from a floppy disk, if you ever need to do that.

✔ **A modem with a speed of at least 56,000 bps (optional):** Again, the faster your Internet connection, the less time it takes to update your installation to the most recent versions. I use a cable modem for my Internet connection, and I like the increased speed when it comes to dealing with the many and varied sources of Linux software and updates online.

If you need more information on PC basics, check out *PCs For Dummies,* 9th Edition, by Dan Gookin (published by Wiley Publishing, Inc.).

Using the DVD-ROM

You can take either of two basic approaches to using the Fedora Core installation DVD-ROM. I cover each one in separate step-by-step lists. I tell you in this section how to pick which set of instructions to follow. The two ways to use this DVD-ROM are shown in this list:

✔ If you can boot from your DVD-ROM drive (which probably means that you have a newer PC), follow the instructions in the following section.

✔ If you can't boot from your DVD-ROM drive, for whatever reason, follow the instructions in the section "Booting from a Linux floppy disk," a little later in this chapter. Choosing this option means that you boot from a Linux boot floppy disk, with the DVD that came with this book already inserted into your DVD-ROM drive. (To create a Linux boot floppy disk to enable this approach, please check out the instructions in Chapter 2.) The floppy disk handles the beginning of the process and then turns the rest of the installation over to the DVD-ROM.

Booting from the DVD-ROM

To install items from the DVD-ROM to your hard drive, follow these steps:

1. **Insert the DVD-ROM into your computer's DVD-ROM drive.**

2. **Reboot your PC.**

   As long as your PC is configured to boot from the DVD-ROM, this step starts the Linux installation process for you automatically.

Congratulations! The Linux installation process is now under way. For the rest of the gory details on this fascinating task, please consult Chapter 3. If you had to order the CD-ROMs, then boot with the first CD for the same effect as booting with the DVD.

Booting from a Linux floppy disk

To install the items from the DVD-ROM to your hard drive with a boot disk (I show you how to make one in Chapter 2), follow these steps:

1. **Insert the DVD-ROM into your computer's DVD-ROM drive and insert a bootable Linux floppy disk into your computer's floppy drive. See the instructions in Chapter 2 for creating a bootable Linux floppy disk.**

2. **Reboot your PC.**

   This step starts the Linux installation process for you automatically.

Congratulations! The Linux installation process is now under way. For the rest of the gory details on this fascinating task, please consult Chapter 3.

And some people say that installing Linux is hard! What could be easier than this? On the other hand, if all you want to do is investigate the contents of the Linux installation DVD-ROM, simply insert it into your machine's CD-ROM drive. After that, you can browse through the DVD-ROM's contents right there in Windows. The contents are described in the following section.

What You Find in Fedora Core 1

Here's a summary of the software on the DVD-ROM, arranged by directory organization. If you use Windows, the DVD-ROM interface helps you navigate the DVD-ROM easily; you can use most of its contents only if you already have Linux installed.

The contents of the DVD consist of all six CD-ROMs' worth of material for Fedora Core 1. Not all of the software is installed automatically. You find out in Chapter 3 how to customize what's added. Aside from that, the DVD has useful install utilities and a handy-dandy README file that explains precisely what you find. The directory structure may look similar to the following (except for lacking my handy annotations, of course):

```
/mnt/redhat
   |----> RedHat
   |          |----> RPMS        -- binary packages, incl:
   |          |                       OS, GUIs, Apache, etc.
   |          |----> base        -- info on release 10
   |          |                       used by install process
   |          |                  -- source code for the packages
   |          |                       in RPMS
   |----> images                 -- boot & ramdisk images
   |----> dosutils               -- DOS install utilities
   |----> isolinux               -- boot files
   |----> README                 -- general read me file
   |----> RELEASE-NOTES          -- current info about release 10
   |----> RPM-GPG-KEY            -- GPG sigs for Red Hat pkgs
```

Both CDs include *GPG signatures,* allowing the installer to check the contents of the files against the stored security data to make sure that the files haven't been changed. (The assumption is that all changes would be for the worse, such as Trojan horses or viruses.) Thus, signatures provide a way to make sure that everything is safe and wholesome for your computer!

If You've Got Problems (Of the DVD-ROM Kind)

I tried my best to locate programs that work on most computers with the minimum system requirements, as Red Hat did for its operating system. Alas, your computer may differ, and some programs may not work properly for some reason.

The two likeliest problems are that you don't have enough memory (RAM) for the programs you want to use or that you have other programs running that are affecting the installation or running of a program. If you see error messages like `Not enough memory` or `Setup cannot continue`, try one or more of the following methods and then try using the software again:

- ✔ **Close all running programs.** The more programs you're running, the less memory is available to other programs. Installers also typically update files and programs; if you keep other programs running, the installation may not work properly.

- ✔ **In Linux, close your GUI environment and run demos or installations directly from a shell.** The interface itself can tie up system memory or even conflict with certain kinds of interactive demos. Use the command prompt to browse files on the DVD-ROM and launch installers or demos.

- ✔ **Have your local computer store add more RAM to your computer.** This step is, admittedly, a drastic and potentially expensive one, depending on the price of RAM at the time. If you have a modern PC with less than 64MB of RAM, however, adding more memory can really help the speed of your computer and enable more programs to run at the same time.

If you still have trouble with the DVD-ROM, please call the Wiley Product Technical Support phone number: (800) 762-2974. Outside the United States, call 1(317) 572-3994. You can also contact Wiley Product Technical Support through the Internet at: `http://www.wiley.com/techsupport`. Wiley Publishing provides technical support only for installation and other general quality control items; for technical support on the applications themselves, consult the program's vendor or author.

To place additional orders or to request information about other Wiley products, please call (800) 225-5945.

Index

• *H* •

• *J* •

• *K* •

• *L* •

• Q •

• R •

GNU GENERAL PUBLIC LICENSE

Version 2, June 1991
Copyright (C) 1989, 1991 Free Software Foundation, Inc.
59 Temple Place - Suite 330, Boston, MA 02111-1307, USA

Preamble

The licenses for most software are designed to take away your freedom to share and change it. By contrast, the GNU General Public License is intended to guarantee your freedom to share and change free software—to make sure the software is free for all its users. This General Public License applies to most of the Free Software Foundation's software and to any other program whose authors commit to using it. (Some other Free Software Foundation software is covered by the GNU Library General Public License instead.) You can apply it to your programs, too.

When we speak of free software, we are referring to freedom, not price. Our General Public Licenses are designed to make sure that you have the freedom to distribute copies of free software (and charge for this service if you wish), that you receive source code or can get it if you want it, that you can change the software or use pieces of it in new free programs; and that you know you can do these things.

To protect your rights, we need to make restrictions that forbid anyone to deny you these rights or to ask you to surrender the rights. These restrictions translate to certain responsibilities for you if you distribute copies of the software, or if you modify it.

For example, if you distribute copies of such a program, whether gratis or for a fee, you must give the recipients all the rights that you have. You must make sure that they, too, receive or can get the source code. And you must show them these terms so they know their rights.

We protect your rights with two steps: (1) copyright the software, and (2) offer you this license which gives you legal permission to copy, distribute and/or modify the software.

Also, for each author's protection and ours, we want to make certain that everyone understands that there is no warranty for this free software. If the software is modified by someone else and passed on, we want its recipients to know that what they have is not the original, so that any problems introduced by others will not reflect on the original authors' reputations.

Finally, any free program is threatened constantly by software patents. We wish to avoid the danger that redistributors of a free program will individually obtain patent licenses, in effect making the program proprietary. To prevent this, we have made it clear that any patent must be licensed for everyone's free use or not licensed at all.

The precise terms and conditions for copying, distribution and modification follow.

TERMS AND CONDITIONS FOR COPYING, DISTRIBUTION, AND MODIFICATION

0. This License applies to any program or other work which contains a notice placed by the copyright holder saying it may be distributed under the terms of this General Public License. The "Program", below, refers to any such program or work, and a "work based on the Program" means either the Program or any derivative work under copyright law: that is to say, a work containing the Program or a portion of it, either verbatim or with modifications and/or translated into another language. (Hereinafter, translation is included without limitation in the term "modification".) Each licensee is addressed as "you".

    Activities other than copying, distribution and modification are not covered by this License; they are outside its scope. The act of running the Program is not restricted, and the output from the Program is covered only if its contents constitute a work based on the Program (independent of having been made by running the Program). Whether that is true depends on what the Program does.

1. You may copy and distribute verbatim copies of the Program's source code as you receive it, in any medium, provided that you conspicuously and appropriately publish on each copy an appropriate copyright notice and disclaimer of warranty; keep intact all the notices that refer to this License and to the absence of any warranty; and give any other recipients of the Program a copy of this License along with the Program.

    You may charge a fee for the physical act of transferring a copy, and you may at your option offer warranty protection in exchange for a fee.

2. You may modify your copy or copies of the Program or any portion of it, thus forming a work based on the Program, and copy and distribute such modifications or work under the terms of Section 1 above, provided that you also meet all of these conditions:

    a) You must cause the modified files to carry prominent notices stating that you changed the files and the date of any change.

    b) You must cause any work that you distribute or publish, that in whole or in part contains or is derived from the Program or any part thereof, to be licensed as a whole at no charge to all third parties under the terms of this License.

    c) If the modified program normally reads commands interactively when run, you must cause it, when started running for such interactive use in the most ordinary way, to print or display an announcement including an appropriate copyright notice and a notice that there is no warranty (or else, saying that you provide a warranty) and that users may redistribute the program under these conditions, and telling the user how to view a copy of this License. (Exception: if the Program itself is interactive but does not normally print such an announcement, your work based on the Program is not required to print an announcement.)

    These requirements apply to the modified work as a whole. If identifiable sections of that work are not derived from the Program, and can be reasonably considered independent and separate works in themselves, then this License, and its terms, do not apply to those sections when you distribute them as separate works. But when you distribute the same sections as part of a whole which is a work based on the Program, the distribution of the whole must be on the terms of this License, whose permissions for other licensees extend to the entire whole, and thus to each and every part regardless of who wrote it.

Thus, it is not the intent of this section to claim rights or contest your rights to work written entirely by you; rather, the intent is to exercise the right to control the distribution of derivative or collective works based on the Program.

In addition, mere aggregation of another work not based on the Program with the Program (or with a work based on the Program) on a volume of a storage or distribution medium does not bring the other work under the scope of this License.

3. You may copy and distribute the Program (or a work based on it, under Section 2) in object code or executable form under the terms of Sections 1 and 2 above provided that you also do one of the following:

    a) Accompany it with the complete corresponding machine-readable source code, which must be distributed under the terms of Sections 1 and 2 above on a medium customarily used for software interchange; or,

    b) Accompany it with a written offer, valid for at least three years, to give any third party, for a charge no more than your cost of physically performing source distribution, a complete machine-readable copy of the corresponding source code, to be distributed under the terms of Sections 1 and 2 above on a medium customarily used for software interchange; or,

    c) Accompany it with the information you received as to the offer to distribute corresponding source code. (This alternative is allowed only for noncommercial distribution and only if you received the program in object code or executable form with such an offer, in accord with Subsection b above.)

    The source code for a work means the preferred form of the work for making modifications to it. For an executable work, complete source code means all the source code for all modules it contains, plus any associated interface definition files, plus the scripts used to control compilation and installation of the executable. However, as a special exception, the source code distributed need not include anything that is normally distributed (in either source or binary form) with the major components (compiler, kernel, and so on) of the operating system on which the executable runs, unless that component itself accompanies the executable.

    If distribution of executable or object code is made by offering access to copy from a designated place, then offering equivalent access to copy the source code from the same place counts as distribution of the source code, even though third parties are not compelled to copy the source along with the object code.

4. You may not copy, modify, sublicense, or distribute the Program except as expressly provided under this License. Any attempt otherwise to copy, modify, sublicense or distribute the Program is void, and will automatically terminate your rights under this License. However, parties who have received copies, or rights, from you under this License will not have their licenses terminated so long as such parties remain in full compliance.

5. You are not required to accept this License, since you have not signed it. However, nothing else grants you permission to modify or distribute the Program or its derivative works. These actions are prohibited by law if you do not accept this License. Therefore, by modifying or distributing the Program (or any work based on the Program), you indicate your acceptance of this License to do so, and all its terms and conditions for copying, distributing or modifying the Program or works based on it.

6. Each time you redistribute the Program (or any work based on the Program), the recipient automatically receives a license from the original licensor to copy, distribute or modify the Program subject to these terms and conditions. You may not impose any further restrictions on the recipients' exercise of the rights granted herein. You are not responsible for enforcing compliance by third parties to this License.

7. If, as a consequence of a court judgment or allegation of patent infringement or for any other reason (not limited to patent issues), conditions are imposed on you (whether by court order, agreement or otherwise) that contradict the conditions of this License, they do not excuse you from the conditions of this License. If you cannot distribute so as to satisfy simultaneously your obligations under this License and any other pertinent obligations, then as a consequence you may not distribute the Program at all. For example, if a patent license would not permit royalty-free redistribution of the Program by all those who receive copies directly or indirectly through you, then the only way you could satisfy both it and this License would be to refrain entirely from distribution of the Program.

   If any portion of this section is held invalid or unenforceable under any particular circumstance, the balance of the section is intended to apply and the section as a whole is intended to apply in other circumstances.

   It is not the purpose of this section to induce you to infringe any patents or other property right claims or to contest validity of any such claims; this section has the sole purpose of protecting the integrity of the free software distribution system, which is implemented by public license practices. Many people have made generous contributions to the wide range of software distributed through that system in reliance on consistent application of that system; it is up to the author/donor to decide if he or she is willing to distribute software through any other system and a licensee cannot impose that choice.

   This section is intended to make thoroughly clear what is believed to be a consequence of the rest of this License.

8. If the distribution and/or use of the Program is restricted in certain countries either by patents or by copyrighted interfaces, the original copyright holder who places the Program under this License may add an explicit geographical distribution limitation excluding those countries, so that distribution is permitted only in or among countries not thus excluded. In such case, this License incorporates the limitation as if written in the body of this License.

9. The Free Software Foundation may publish revised and/or new versions of the General Public License from time to time. Such new versions will be similar in spirit to the present version, but may differ in detail to address new problems or concerns.

   Each version is given a distinguishing version number. If the Program specifies a version number of this License which applies to it and "any later version", you have the option of following the terms and conditions either of that version or of any later version published by the Free Software Foundation. If the Program does not specify a version number of this License, you may choose any version ever published by the Free Software Foundation.

10. If you wish to incorporate parts of the Program into other free programs whose distribution conditions are different, write to the author to ask for permission. For software which is copyrighted by the Free Software Foundation, write to the Free Software Foundation; we sometimes make exceptions for this. Our decision will be guided by the two goals of preserving the free status of all derivatives of our free software and of promoting the sharing and reuse of software generally.